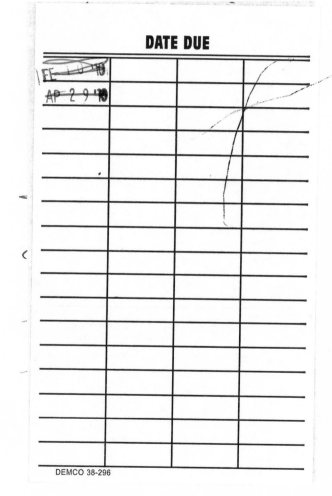

DATE DUE

FE 1 0 '05			
AP 2 9 '05			

The Fall of
Che Guevara

❧ The Fall of
Che Guevara

*A Story of Soldiers, Spies,
and Diplomats*

HENRY BUTTERFIELD RYAN

New York   Oxford
Oxford University Press
1998

Oxford University Press

Oxford   New York

Athens   Auckland   Bangkok   Bogota   Bombay   Buenos Aires
Calcutta   Cape Town   Dar es Salaam   Delhi   Florence   Hong Kong
Istanbul   Karachi   Kuala Lumpur   Madras   Madrid   Melbourne
Mexico City   Nairobi   Paris   Singapore   Taipei   Tokyo   Toronto   Warsaw

and associated companies in
Berlin   Ibadan

Copyright © 1998 by Oxford University Press, Inc.

Published by Oxford University Press, Inc.
198 Madison Avenue, New York, New York 10016

Oxford is a registered trademark of Oxford University Press

Library of Congress Cataloging-in-Publication Data
Ryan, Henry Butterfield.
The fall of Che Guevara : a story of soldiers, spies, and
diplomats / Henry Butterfield Ryan.
    p.   cm.
Includes bibliographical references and index.
ISBN 0-19-511879-0
1. Guevara, Ernesto, 1928–1967.   2. Guerrillas—Bolivia—
History—20th century.   3. Insurgency—Bolivia—History—20th
century.   4. United States—Foreign relations—Bolivia.   5. Bolivia—
Foreign relations—United States.   I. Title.
F3326.G84R93   1997
327.73084—dc21   97-11627

9 8 7 6 5 4 3 2 1

Printed in the United States of America
on acid-free paper

For my brother, Webster,
and my granddaughter, Katie

Preface

The purpose of this book is to tell the story of the U.S. government's response to Che Guevara during his insurgency in Bolivia in 1966–67. This story serves as a case history of U.S. counterinsurgency practices as they developed following World War II and were honed to a fine point during the tense Cold War years of the 1960s. Many people who remember how disastrously wrong the attempt at counterinsurgency went in Southeast Asia tend to forget that it succeeded in Latin America.

Guevara hoped not just to start a guerrilla war in Bolivia but to ignite a rebellion against the established order in all of South America, while at the same time delivering a major blow to U.S. influence there—to "Yankee imperialism," he would say. Readers must determine for themselves whether the defeat of Cuban aspirations should be regretted or applauded, but unquestionably it had an important effect on politics in the Western Hemisphere. Guevara's failure not only diminished Cuban revolutionary hopes but also reduced the value of Cuba's hand in its bitter struggle within international communist circles over the proper way to create revolution. Consequently, the case had greater significance for both sides than indicated by the limited dimensions of the actual fighting, and therefore it merits close attention.

In studying the U.S. response to the insurgency, I will closely examine the controversial involvement of U.S. officials in Guevara's death. I will also present biographic sketches of the main actors in the drama and occasionally focus on disputes among officials and on personal tensions between allies, in the belief that individual histories and interpersonal struggles, sometimes even petty ones, have more to do with diplomacy than students of the subject are often given to believe.

According to an old adage, history is written by victors, but if so, the story of Guevara's insurgency in Bolivia is a notable exception. His defeat there has been told again and again by writers professing and demonstrating their admiration for both him and his cause, and he was indeed an admirable man. But only a few—Leo Sauvage and Daniel James, for example—write critically, and even they criticize his performance more than his purpose. A different version, as told by Bolivian military leaders, remains mostly untranslated and consequently enjoys comparatively limited circulation, an important exception being the account of Captain Gary Prado Salmón, whose company captured Guevara.

Even today, nearly thirty years after Guevara's death, it is difficult to write dispassionately about the events in his life. Feelings still run strong among people who recall his career, and a historian trying for impartiality continually fears the danger of belittling or caricaturing one side or the other. Nevertheless, I have tried in this book to tell without bias the story of two groups of human beings, each with powerful and conflicting convictions, resolving their differences in the unfortunately primitive way that is still humanity's habit.

In much of the literature, the Americans involved in countering Guevara in Bolivia are depicted as murky figures, hovering ominously in the wings and manipulating Bolivian puppets—a portrayal resulting partially from an automatic aversion many writers of this story have to names such as Green Berets, Central Intelligence Agency (CIA), or U.S. Military Advisory Group (MILGP). Furthermore, the necessarily secret nature of those groups has kept them far out of focus, even though everyone who has written about these events knows they played prominent roles.

By far the greater reason for the continuing obscurity of the Americans, however, lies in the fact that the U.S. government did not release any documents concerning its role until I, perhaps rashly, decided to spend what became the equivalent of three years (actually spread out over five) in the tedious process of prying these documents out of their secret files through various procedures established for that purpose. Should any young scholar or writer be tempted to try this route to gain quick publication, let me cite two letters. One is from the State Department saying my appeal of June 3, 1992, for release of certain documents had been granted; this letter is dated November 18, 1996. Another was a letter from the National Archives that brought me part of the material I requested on September 5, 1991—dated June 21, 1994. Two requests, one to the House of Representatives and one to the Kennedy Library, though many years old and after frequent reminders, have still been neither granted nor denied. Nevertheless, despite the ponderousness of the process, a huge number of secret documents have come to light; and as they have, the U.S. officials involved in the capture of Che Guevara have stepped out of the shadows.

Within our story of the struggle with Guevara in Bolivia lies a sub-theme about the role of diplomatic establishments, notably embassies and consulates. It has particular relevance at the end of the century, when their functions, all but unknown in much of the United States, have nevertheless become the subject of intense scrutiny in the smaller world of foreign affairs. Furthermore, with the end of the Cold War, the foreign-affairs community—Congress, the executive branch, the press, universities, and think tanks, among others—has also begun to question seriously the role of intelligence in U.S. foreign relations, especially the part played by the CIA. The U.S. government's interaction with revolutionary Cuba, including its response to Guevara in Bolivia, provides some useful, if far from conclusive, data for this debate also. I will return to that subject at the end of the narrative.

Many people and a number of institutions have given me invaluable help in writing this book, although none bear responsibility for its content.

I am especially thankful to Clare Hall, Cambridge, where, as a Life Member, I can return at will. Consequently, I spent two summers there writing much of the text. I also am grateful to the Institute for the Study of Diplomacy at Georgetown University, where I spent approximately 18 months working on several projects, including this book.

The Foreign Affairs Oral History Program, a service of the Association for Diplomatic Studies and Training, also aided me greatly. That program provides an ever-growing and invaluable collection of interviews based on the careers of U.S. officials who have served abroad.

I am very much indebted to Senator David L. Boren and Congressman Dave McCurdy, then chairmen of the Senate and House Select Committees on Intelligence, respectively, and to Senator Sam Nunn and the late Congressman Les Aspin, then chairmen of the Senate and House Armed Services Committees, respectively. They proved to be very effective advocates on my behalf when the CIA and the Army apparently got the notion that the Freedom of Information Act no longer applied to them.

I want also to thank those persons who have reviewed parts of the text, while exonerating them from any responsibility for what has ultimately been published. They are Wayne S. Smith of the Center for International Policy and Johns Hopkins University; Dolores Moyano Martin of the Library of Congress, a friend of the young Guevara in Argentina; Douglas Henderson, U.S. ambassador to Bolivia, 1963–68; Charles Grover, chief political officer at the U.S. embassy in La Paz, 1966–70; Major Ralph Shelton (ret.), leader of the Green Beret detachment sent to Bolivia in 1967 and an anonymous former CIA official. All have also provided me with interviews and information about materials and sources.

It is traditional for authors to thank families, especially spouses, for their patience. In addition to tolerating a husband engaged in what others consider a thoroughly boring pursuit, my wife, Patricia, has done many of the chores of daily life, not only keeping us fed but keeping us insured, our bills paid, our car tuned up, and so on, all while I wrote. She also assisted me with some of my interviews. Indeed, my entire family helped. My son, William, aided me with some of my research, and both he and his wife, Kristina, rescued me many times when my computer and I marched to different drummers.

It is impossible to thank all of the people who have assisted me, but I must mention a few more. Georgie Anne Geyer permitted me to review the notes and interviews she used in writing her book, *Guerrilla Prince: The Untold Story of Fidel Castro*. Dan Buck and Anne Meadows, who have great knowledge of South America and especially Bolivia, have given me many useful materials and much information. Marc Pachter and his circle of biographers in Washington, D.C., have given me help and encouragement, and a number of former military officers have provided me with documentation. The latter are William Tope, Lawrence Horras, Edward Fox, Ernest Nance, and Ralph Shelton. Senate Historian Richard Baker and his deputy, Donald Ritchie, provided me with bibliographic information, a number of useful oral histories, and access to the Senate library. Andrew Hewson, literary agent of London, has very kindly provided me with a great deal of criticism and advice in preparing this manuscript, and my friend and indefatigable agent, Margery Boichel Thompson, has not only brought enormous energy and editorial skill to my aid but provided tea and literary conversation in her garden with her husband, Gordon, thus periodically revitalizing my faith in the writing life-style.

Marjorie Weisskohl and Margaret Roman, both of the State Department, were extremely helpful, Weisskohl in arranging an important interview and Roman in striving to have documents declassified in a timely manner. John D. Wilson and Regina Greenwell of the Johnson Library and David C. Humphrey, formerly with that library and now with the State Department Historian's Office, all helped far beyond the requirements of their jobs.

Finally, I want to thank all of the people who consented to give me interviews and whose names are listed in the sources.

The documents declassified especially for this book should be available to anyone wishing to consult them at the organizations that created them, which are indicated in the endnotes. An easier route, however, may be to consult them at the National Security Archive, a private research institute in Washington, D.C., which helped me through the arduous process of obtaining them and where I now have deposited them.

In addition to these, I have used many unclassified or already declassified government documents. I have also conducted extensive interviews with persons involved in the events this book discusses, some of whom have sent me their files from that time. Furthermore, I have relied heavily on oral histories done by participants at or near the time of those events. These can be consulted in the archives indicated in the bibliography and the endnotes.

Washington, D.C.   H. B. R.
February 1997

Contents

Abbreviations   xv

Introduction   3

1   The Road to Revolution   10

2   Contact and Alarm   40

3   The Obstacles Accumulate   61

4   The Green Berets   82

5   Guerrilla Triumph and Trouble   103

6   The Kill—and After   126

7   Memories and Legacies   155

Appendix: Chronology   167

Notes   171

Bibliography   201

Index   217

A section of illustrations appears after p. 60.

Abbreviations

The following abbreviations are used throughout the book.

AID   U.S. Agency for International Development
CIA   Central Intelligence Agency
DIA   Defense Intelligence Agency
INR   U.S. State Department Bureau of Intelligence and Research
LASO   Latin American Solidarity Organization
MAP   U.S. Military Assistance Plan
MILGP   U.S. Military Advisory Group
MTT   Mobile Training Team
OAS   Organization of American States

The Fall of Che Guevara

Introduction

During his short lifetime, Ernesto "Che" Guevara fought battles on three continents, but he always considered the U.S. government and the economic oligarchy he believed supported it to be his principal enemy. Still, in the considerable number of works and reports that have been written and broadcast about him, Washington's role has always been outlined in vague and general terms, with the U.S. government viewed as a shadowy antagonist, sometimes simply as "the CIA." Indeed, the notions exist throughout the world that the Central Intelligence Agency (CIA) was Guevara's main American opponent, especially in his final battle in Bolivia, and that the CIA was responsible for his death. Neither is true. The facts, which cast much light on the way America's military, diplomatic, and espionage establishments operate abroad, are far more interesting than these simplistic assumptions suggest.

This study may surprise readers who assume, not altogether unreasonably, that whenever secret files are opened, they reveal official chicanery even beyond their suspicions—that new details will only darken the picture. In the Guevara case, however, these details brighten the picture slightly. For example, contrary to widespread assumptions, the U.S. government exerted a moderating influence on its Bolivian allies in dealing with Guevara and his insurgency in their country. It refused to give them weapons that would have been far more destructive than necessary, and it constantly urged them to spare prisoners' lives. It intervened powerfully to save French intellectual Régis Debray, at some cost

3

to its relations with the Bolivian government. And although it was deeply involved in eliminating Guevara's guerrilla band, it neither killed him nor ordered him to be killed.

Unfortunately for Guevara, U.S. officials remained silent after his capture, and Bolivians took matters into their own hands. The embassy in La Paz made no effective move to save him. Indeed, why should it have? The repercussions would have been worse than with Debray. Meanwhile, most of official Washington, including the White House, lacked a clear picture of what had happened to him, despite the presence of a CIA agent at his execution.

The Need to Reassess Guevara's Life

In the light of documents declassified for this study, a very different Guevara emerges than we have seen heretofore. In the decades following his death, he has continually been portrayed in books and prominent news media—the BBC, Great Britain's Channel 4, the *New York Times*, and the Discovery Channel, for example—as a freelance, roving revolutionary who broke with Fidel Castro in Cuba and then, of his own volition, went to the Congo and later to Bolivia to try his hand at fomenting rebellion.[1] Alternatively, he is seen as an unmanageable iconoclast who was dispatched to these remote places as a kind of punishment.[2]

One cannot write a nuanced account of Guevara's life, public or private, based on research in U.S. materials alone. Nevertheless, U.S. diplomatic documents and a degree of common sense make it clear that the old and continuing interpretations of Guevara's career cannot be accurate. We need not accept the analyses of U.S. diplomats or intelligence officers but need only view where he went and with whom, what he said, and what Cuba was doing in the world at the time to know that we must reevaluate Guevara's life. I will outline here some aspects of Guevara's life that require reassessment. I have no doubt that biographers working in Cuban, Argentine, and other Spanish-language materials will reinforce these findings.

1. *Che Guevara owed his career as a revolutionary to Fidel Castro, who in effect provided the framework for Guevara's adult life, not only in Cuba but also until his death in Bolivia.* The relationship that began in Mexico in the mid-1950s ended forever the young Guevara's poignant search for an acceptable direction for his energies and his con-

science. The importance of that partnership for Guevara never diminished.

2. *Other than Castro himself, Guevara for many years served as Cuba's principal diplomat.* Although his official posts were economic ones, in which his performance often has been criticized, Guevara constantly traveled on diplomatic missions. Some of these missions reaped enormous economic benefits for Cuba at a time when its economy was in desperate condition, its links with the United States having been strained and eventually breaking. In this, he performed a signal service for the new regime, for which he rarely receives credit.

3. *Guevara played a key role in establishing Cuba's presence in Africa.* In his diplomatic capacity, he made a major trip in the winter of 1964–65, first to the United Nations, then throughout much of Africa. This was far from a purely ceremonial exercise or a thinly disguised exile, as is sometimes suggested.[3] Guevara was playing a principal role in a projected major thrust of Cuban diplomacy; namely, to increase Cuba's influence in Africa and thereby raise its stature in the communist world, especially as Cuban efforts to create revolutions in Latin America remained ineffective.

Havana determined to focus its African efforts on the Congo, where it sought to breathe life into a foundering rebellion. After returning from his African diplomatic tour, Guevara spent approximately a month in Cuba making preparations, then headed for the Congo to direct Cuban operations there.

It was during that month in Cuba that Guevara was rumored to have fallen out with Castro; the wildest stories even said that Castro had him shot. Other works will have to provide the details of Guevara's relationships during that time, not only with Castro but also with Cuba's governing council, which may well have been problematic, perhaps concerning issues involving the Soviet Union, as suggested by Llovio-Menéndez, for example.[4] Nevertheless, because we know that Guevara spent a great amount of time arranging for Cuba to assert itself in Africa and then proceeded to head that effort, it becomes nearly impossible to view his mission as some kind of punishment or exile or to believe that he left Cuba in anger or despair to begin an adventure of his own devising.

4. *The attempt at revolution in Bolivia was an important element of Cuban policy and far from a crazy caper of Guevara's in which Castro simply acquiesced, as some still suggest.*[5] Whether or not it was

Guevara's idea, the Bolivian scheme represented a major foreign-policy undertaking for the Cuban regime, which still wanted to spark a large-scale uprising in its own hemisphere. Besides believing in the social and economic necessity of such a rebellion, it sought the prominence among communist countries that a revolutionary success would provide. In addition, Cuba was determined to prove that its views of revolution, seriously at odds with the Kremlin's, had a validity that the mainline communist world had thus far refused to recognize. Guevara was not simply indulging a proclivity for violent revolution—although indeed he deeply believed in it—but carrying out an important mission for Cuba. That is why Castro did not simply send arms, money, and a few cadres, as in many of his other revolutionary attempts in Latin America (with the major exception of the Dominican Republic). Instead, he sent Guevara with a band of some 16 stalwarts from Cuba's own revolution and ample resources to foment a major uprising.[6]

Some writers state that Castro abandoned Guevara in Bolivia when Guevara ran into trouble there. But such commentators do not suggest how Castro could have rescued Guevara, who was isolated in the center of a continent of hostile governments with an underground network that failed him almost immediately after hostilities began, as we shall see.

5. *Finally, Guevara spent his entire career after he met Castro in the service of Cuba.* That he acted for the good of humanity as he interpreted that cause seems certain. Nevertheless, he was a Cuban operative. Whether or not he had disagreements with Castro in the course of his career, he was always a prominent figure in Cuban affairs. Furthermore, his efforts at revolution abroad were carried out not only with Cuban men and resources, as is well known, but also in the service of Cuban foreign policy, a point often overlooked. Undoubtedly, that policy for the most part suited Guevara's revolutionary aspirations; if it had not, he might well have abandoned it. But that should not obscure the fact that from the time of Castro's victory in Cuba until Guevara's death, Guevara remained an agent of Cuban foreign affairs and was never a freelance agent provocateur.

An Epoch in Hemispheric Affairs

A major chapter in American foreign relations opened with the 1961 attempt at the Bay of Pigs to overthrow the Cuban revolutionary regime, in which Guevara by then figured prominently. It closed with Guevara's defeat and death in Bolivia in 1967. During that six-year period, the U.S. government so improved its counterinsurgency capability in Latin America that it effectively ended Havana's prolonged effort to spark a revolutionary conflagration in the Western Hemisphere.

Near the end of the century, under very different geopolitical circumstances, the United States still ponders the dilemma of armed intervention overseas, something it is now more reluctant to undertake than in the 1960s, when U.S. interests seemed more clearly at stake. Still, as policymakers look at today's military options, the Latin American experience of the 1960s provides important lessons and examples, as we shall see. It also demonstrates the ways the U.S. government operates abroad, even today, and the sometimes conflicting roles of its soldiers, spies, and diplomats.

In the 1960s, Guevara was one of the most renowned of guerrilla leaders in an age when they loomed like giants on the world political stage. His ongoing war with Washington pitted U.S. theories of counterinsurgency against Cuba's unique theories of revolution. It also represented a clash of fundamental beliefs. Cuba's efforts to "export revolution," as U.S. officials put it, threatened U.S. interests and influence, especially in Latin America, and largely accounted for Washington's energetic response. It would be a mistake, however, to assume, as is often done when his story is told, that ideological motivation existed only on Guevara's side.

Unquestionably, few, if any, historical figures have displayed more loyal adherence to an ideology than Guevara, whose dedication to principal is inspirational, regardless of what one feels about his beliefs. He brings to mind early reformers of the Christian church, with his extensive learning, his disregard of worldly rewards, his devotion to an ideal, his despair over the imperfect commitment of colleagues, and his certainty that he would someday become a martyr for the faith, as indeed he did.

On the other side, most representatives of the U.S. government overseas have always displayed a powerful ideological commitment, and never more so than during the Cold War years of the 1960s. They are often criticized, in fact, for taking a messianic approach to diplomacy. Their ideology encompasses individualism, personal rights, equal opportunity, popular democracy, and free-enterprise economics, despite whatever gaps may exist at home between ideals and reality. The two

American officials who had the most to do with checking Guevara in Bolivia had especially good reason to espouse those ideals. One, Douglas Henderson, the U.S. ambassador in La Paz, was a carpenter's son who had won scholarships to prestigious eastern schools and subsequently gained admission to the career foreign service. When this book was written, he was living in retirement in a comfortable house, partially built by his father, in a rural suburb of Boston.

The other official, Ralph "Pappy" Shelton, headed the Green Beret detachment sent to train the Bolivian army in methods of countering guerrillas. The son of a Tennessee dirt farmer, Shelton joined the army as a private, learned Spanish, and developed an easy rapport with the Bolivian peasants (campesinos), something Guevara was never able to do. He rose to become a commissioned officer and retired with the rank of major, serving, when this was written, as a federal government executive in Memphis.

But the difficulties of hardscrabble farming in rural Tennessee could never compare with the misery in much of Latin America that Guevara encountered in extensive travels through the region as a boy and a young man. He wanted desperately to alleviate the suffering he witnessed, searching for ways to do so, first through medicine and then through violent revolution. An armed confrontation with the democratic, capitalist powers was, he came to believe, the only way to solve the problems of the hemisphere and much of the rest of the world, especially Africa, where he also focused his efforts. Out of that great conflict, he believed, would emerge Marxist states dedicated to improving the material well-being of the masses.

Both in theory and in actuality, such societies were anathema to Americans, who for many years dedicated their diplomacy to preventing them from spreading. A Green Beret sergeant in Bolivia put it as well as anyone, if inelegantly, when he said of Guevara, "He believed in his way, and we believe in our way. We ain't buyin' communism. In the United States and these other countries, it ain't movin' in . . . not if I can help it."[7]

The story of Washington's response to Guevara's Bolivian insurgency begins at the end of World War II, when the United States started creating systems of economic aid, military advice, and intelligence gathering in the Western Hemisphere designed to forestall exactly what Guevara attempted. Some of the structure was left over from the war, some from even earlier. But the Cuban Revolution led by Castro, Guevara, and others electrified Washington, and in the shock that resulted, it saw Latin America in a strong new light. The consequent renewal of U.S. involvement in the Western Hemisphere, begun late in the administration of President Dwight D. Eisenhower, was intensified by President John F. Kennedy and continued by President Lyndon B. Johnson.

Effective counterinsurgency techniques ranked high among Washington's new approaches to Latin America, beginning in Kennedy's administration. Fortunately for the U.S. government, when it became aware of Guevara's rebellion in Bolivia in 1967, it stuck to carefully designed tenets for combating guerrilla warfare. Despite Bolivian fears and pressure, Washington did not panic, nor did it Americanize the conflict. It avoided repeating the mistakes it had made and continued to make in Southeast Asia, and did so to a great extent because of Ambassador Henderson's calming influence. As a result, Guevara's announced intention to create another Vietnam quickly became a hopeless cause.

CHAPTER ONE

The Road to Revolution

Che Guevara's body, strapped to the landing skid of a Bolivian helicopter, was on its way to the town of Vallegrande from the tiny backwa-
ter settlement of La Higuera, where he had been executed. Beside the
pilot rode CIA agent Félix Rodríguez, an intelligence adviser to the Bolivian Army, especially its Second Ranger Battalion. He had helped
shape that unit into an effective antiguerrilla force during its special
training by American Green Berets and had continued to assist it during
its two weeks in the field, culminating in Guevara's capture.[1]

Rodríguez was one of a team of Cuban exiles brought by the CIA to
work with the Bolivian Army, two with the troops in the field and at
least several others behind the lines.[2] He had been on the scene when a
Bolivian soldier killed the famous guerrilla leader and may even have
been in the chain of command that ordered the execution, though that
remains uncertain.[3]

Indeed, much that concerns Guevara's last day of life remains uncertain, subject to conflicting stories representing conflicting interests,
egos, and political positions. After sifting contrary claims and evidence,
however, a few things emerge. Contrary to widespread opinion, the CIA
did not kill Guevara, but neither did it or any other branch of the U.S.
government try to save him, despite subsequent claims by some officials
that Washington wanted him alive.

The Bolivian Army officers whose soldiers caught Guevara had no
desire to spare him. They intended to interrogate him quickly and exe-

cute him summarily. Their interrogation, however, was hopelessly hostile and accusatory. According to some reports, Guevara spit in the face of the questioning officer. Then Rodríguez took over, apparently getting no information either, but his technique was to go slowly, building friendship and confidence with a prisoner. It is hard to imagine that method working with Guevara either, but, in fact, the Bolivians gave him no time to try it.

One person in Bolivia might have saved Guevara, and he says that he would have tried had he been given the chance. That was American ambassador Douglas Henderson, who, unlike anyone else in the country, could speak officially for the U.S. government. Consequently, he had enormous influence, especially as Bolivia was then greatly dependent on the United States in many ways. Henderson, however, claims that he did not learn that Guevara had been caught until after he was killed.[4] Others on Henderson's staff, however, although maintaining traditional Foreign Service loyalty and politesse, provide evidence that Henderson's memory may be faulty.

Rodríguez claims that the CIA instructed him to keep Guevara alive at all costs, but it is hard to imagine how the agency thought he would do that. Rodríguez played an important role in the effort to check the insurgency, but he was not an influential American official. In fact, a key CIA officer connected with the insurgency denies that any orders went out from Washington to save Guevara, even though officials in Washington and in the embassy in La Paz knew the night before his death that he had been captured.

If Rodríguez had instructions to save Guevara, he seems not to have pleaded the prisoner's case very vigorously. By his own account, he suggested to the Bolivian commander present that the famous guerrilla be spared. But in reply, he says, the commander simply asked him to put Guevara's dead body on a helicopter at 2:00 P.M., then departed for divisional headquarters. Rodríguez agreed, remembering that Guevara not only had helped smash the old Cuba that he loved but also had put friends of his to the wall.

The Bolivians might have been expected to inform Henderson, but, undoubtedly suspecting he would interfere, they said nothing. The president and top army officers were still irritated with him for pressuring them to save the life of French intellectual Régis Debray. Debray, who had taken part in Guevara's conspiracy, fell into the hands of the Bolivians as he was trying to leave the band, having had his fill of guerrilla life. Top Bolivian officials wanted to eliminate him at once, but Henderson, along with many others, urged them to spare him. A long, politically embarrassing trial followed, something they did not intend to repeat in Guevara's case.[5]

By midday on October 9, 1967, with no effort on his behalf from the one person who might have saved him, Guevara was doomed. At 1:10 P.M.—Rodríguez noted the time carefully—the execution order went down to a Bolivian sergeant, who stepped into the room where Guevara was interned and shot him to death.

Sometime within the next few hours, according to Rodríguez's account, he sent a short coded message to CIA headquarters near Washington, D.C., reporting the execution. Peculiarly, that information took two days to reach the White House.

Small Battle with Large Implications

In terms of warfare, the fight in Bolivia had been tiny. Guevara never had even sixty soldiers, and his "battles" with the Bolivian Army were hardly more than skirmishes. But in political terms, the encounter had much larger significance. It was, of course, a chapter in the Cold War, one of many cases in which that confrontation turned violent. Its particular form, however, stemmed in large measure from Washington's determination, reached during the Kennedy years, to develop an effective means of containing guerrilla wars that threatened the stability of U.S. allies. Six years earlier, the Bay of Pigs invasion, intended to topple Fidel Castro's regime in Cuba, had resulted in a humiliating disaster not only for the invading force of Cuban exiles but also for President Kennedy and his administration. It caused Kennedy to insist on finding new means to fight limited wars.

By 1967, those efforts may have gone horribly wrong in Vietnam, but they had not in Bolivia, where the precepts outlined earlier in the decade by Kennedy's staff were remembered. That the conflict there remained insignificant in terms of arms is a testimony in part to the soundness of the "limited warfare" concepts developed after the Bay of Pigs debacle and a tribute to the individuals who carried them out. The insurrection in Bolivia never became another Vietnam, as Guevara hoped it would, partly because the Americans, despite Bolivian panic, did not lose their nerve, did not pour in massive amounts of equipment, and did not permit U.S. personnel to be involved in the actual fighting. The only exceptions, if indeed they are exceptions, were the two Cuban-exile intelligence officers working for CIA and serving with the Bolivian forces.

In Bolivia in 1967, American determination to control brushfire wars confronted Guevara's determination to create a continental revolution, and in this Guevara represented a distinctly Cuban point of view, one that caused enormous concern not just in Washington but also in Moscow. At a time when the Kremlin looked to "peaceful coexistence" as the best and certainly the safest means of spreading Marxism, Havana insisted that violent revolution was the only means of breaking the influence of the "neoimperialist" powers, especially the United States. Guevara, a principal theoretician for the Havana viewpoint, propounded ideas that essentially reflected the actual Cuban revolutionary experience of 1956–59. He believed that a successful revolution must begin in the countryside—the mountains if possible—not in the cities. Any number, no matter how small, could begin it, keeping a low profile while they accumulated recruits, then increasing their daring and their numbers as the movement gained notoriety through its exploits. Along with Castro and all of the leading Cuban revolutionaries, Guevara believed that even after victory the guerrilla army must dominate the revolution and control the political party, not vice versa.

Cuban revolutionary theories represented a significant revision of standard communist doctrine, creating a constant strain in Havana's relations with Moscow. Further, the Cubans, led by Guevara in the field, tried out their theories in the Congo. Although that endeavor failed totally, it did so for reasons that did not necessarily invalidate their concepts of revolution, except in one way: Guevara and the entire Cuban leadership maintained a monumental disregard of local conditions, politics, and sensitivities in both the Congo and Bolivia. They believed the imperatives of Marxist revolution to be so strong and so obvious that populations living in difficult circumstances would flock readily to the banner of rebellion. They failed in both places for very different reasons, but in both cases they were blinded to local conditions by their own faith and dogma.

In Bolivia, the American theory of counterinsurgency and the Cuban theory of revolution met head-on. That, in addition to the presence and death of one of the world's major guerrilla leaders, constitutes the real historical significance of the confrontation. We will look more closely at all of these issues, but first let us consider the main personality in the conflict.

Guevara: The Early Years

Guevara had a profound antipathy toward the United States that began in his youth and antedated even his Marxism. He considered that country a principal source of the misery he saw in his extensive travels as a young man throughout much of Latin America.[6] He believed, and not without reason, that the United States and its business interests backed rightist dictatorships and political and economic oligarchies and that these, in turn, kept masses of the hemisphere's population in ignorance and poverty. By the time he first came to the attention of U.S. authorities, during the U.S.-backed overthrow of the Arbenz regime in Guatemala in 1954, Guevara had reached the conclusion that the only solution to the problems he saw around him lay in violent revolution, overthrowing existing regimes throughout Latin America.[7]

How to do that, of course, was quite another question. Guevara certainly did not have the answer when he left Argentina in 1953 as a young physician, just graduated from the University of Buenos Aires, on a trip of adventure and self-discovery around the hemisphere. In Guatemala, he tried vainly to stimulate popular resistance to the invaders, but as a young, newly arrived immigrant, he found himself too far from levers of power to create any significant effect. He managed only to come to the attention of the police, by then controlled by the victorious invaders and their U.S. backers. He found protection in the Argentine embassy and then fled to Mexico.

In Guatemala, he had met Hilda Gadea, a refugee from Peru's right-wing autocratic government, who not only helped him find work but also honed his revolutionary frame of mind and became his mistress. In Mexico, where she too had fled, they married and had a child. There, Guevara held various jobs, working as a street photographer, a door-to-door book salesman, and eventually a physician. He published at least one medical paper, on the topic of allergies, and meanwhile focused his radical views on the conduct of the profession, which he felt in Mexico as elsewhere catered to the wealthy and gave short shrift to the poor. He did not, however, find means to reform it.

In Mexico, Guevara also met Fidel Castro, and his life took a new course almost at once. Until then, he had been an unsettled young man, a left-wing political radical with no direction to his revolutionary energies. Castro changed that immediately. The two men, both widely read and intellectual, became friends instantly, and Castro pulled the very willing

Guevara into his band of revolutionary Cubans. They had already tried to overthrow the Cuban dictatorship of Fulgencio Batista on July 26, 1953, with an attack on the Moncada Barracks in Santiago de Cuba. ("July 26" henceforth became the name of their organization.) Routed on the battlefield but not in the spirit, they went to Mexico to resuscitate their movement and then go once more into the breach.

After the Moncada Barracks attack failed, Castro was sentenced to a 15-year jail term but released within a year, surely Batista's greatest error.[8] With the enormous revolutionary energy that had characterized him since his student days, Castro upon his release began at once to rebuild his force, raising money wherever he could and training his growing band in Mexico City and its environs. The Mexican government, prodded by Batista, made generally ineffectual efforts to quash its activities, including jailing many of its members for a short period. Indecisive as it was, the government still hastened somewhat the band's departure for Cuba, but not until 16 months after Castro had arrived in Mexico.

Castro with 82 men sailed on November 25, 1956, jammed into one small yacht, the *Granma*, with Guevara as their medic.[9] Guevara had broken with his wife, who returned to Peru, and now, energized and guided by Castro, he was at the beginning of a revolutionary career in the service, as he saw it, of both Cuba and humanity.[10] It should be noted, however, since frequently it is not, that from that time on, even after the victory over Batista, his revolutionary efforts, including those in the Congo and Bolivia, were linked tightly to Castro's policies.

Guevara came to the attention of the world in general and of U.S. officials at about the same time. Castro's expedition, trying for a degree of strategic sophistication beyond its reach, got off to a disastrous start. It was still at sea while an armed rising by confederates in Santiago de Cuba, timed to distract Batista's forces from resisting the invaders, was thoroughly thrashed since Batista had no invaders to worry about. Next, Castro's band landed in the wrong place, lost many of its supplies, and missed a rendezvous with yet another group of supporters.[11]

Nor did Guevara's own revolutionary career get off to a very auspicious start. Three days after landing, Castro's force was nearly liquidated in a firefight at Alegría de Pío. Guevara received a slight wound and believed he was dying until he was ordered to keep moving by one of the band's leaders.[12] Several days later, he and others were scolded by Castro for leaving their rifles behind when they fled into the mountains to join

the fewer than 20 men who survived the first battle.[13] He subsequently
became lost several times in the Sierra Maestra of eastern Cuba, where
the rebel band operated, a harbinger of much worse problems awaiting
him in the jungles on the edge of the Bolivian Andes.

Still, Guevara improved steadily. In 1957, he became a commandante, or major, the highest rebel rank, and began to enjoy a growing
reputation in Cuba. One man, then a student activist, recalls that most
young people he knew in Havana who thought of joining Castro's guerrillas wanted to serve with Guevara, whose popularity, he believed, even
outranked the well-liked and effective commandante Camilo Cienfuegos. Huber Matos, himself one of the main rebel commanders, enjoyed
Guevara's company, although militarily ranking him below the top, saying he was a good guerrilla leader but not a great one. Nevertheless,
Guevara was renowned for his courage and his egalitarian attitude toward his troops; Matos once found him sprawled asleep on a large bed
with three of his men, while another slept on the floor.[14]

One campaign more than any other created Guevara's guerrilla fame
and also helped enormously to bring victory to the rebels. Guevara and
Cienfuegos, with about 230 men divided into two columns, marched out
of the Sierra Maestra and, vastly outnumbered, fought their way up approximately half the length of Cuba to the Escambray Mountains.[15]
There, Guevara consolidated several other rebel bands, bringing them
under the overall command of Castro's July 26 Movement, while also,
with Cienfeugos, engaging in a series of fights with Batista's forces.[16]
In the course of one of his last and perhaps most publicized battles, that
at Santa Clara, his force overcame an armored troop train whose commander, not realizing the rebels had removed the tracks, ran the train
aground while trying to escape. Within hours of that battle, in the early
morning of New Year's Day 1959, Batista fled Cuba.

Guevara and Cienfuegos rushed to Havana and an uproarious heroes'
welcome. Guevara had become a national figure in Cuba and a guerrilla
captain of international reputation at a time when guerrilla chiefs enjoyed almost unparalleled notoriety.[17]

Characteristics of the Cuban Revolution

Guevara had taken part in a revolution notable in many ways. First, a
mere handful of dedicated insurgents had been able not only to start it

but also to keep it going and growing against enormously superior numbers. It was fought against an unpopular dictator, who, as the battle raged, became ever more brutal and therefore ever more despised.[18] In both the cities and the countryside, the rebels enjoyed widespread support that increased as the war continued. Indeed, by the time Guevara began his march up-country, arms, men, and money were pouring into the rebel command from inside and outside Cuba. Although he faced thousands of soldiers and police in his march, they by then had become highly demoralized.[19] Furthermore, although the mountain rebels often scorned and suspected their colleagues in the far-off cities, the urban allies not only harassed Batista's forces themselves, providing important diversions, but also formed a crucial part of the chain that kept the mountain guerrillas supplied.[20] Meanwhile, the communists stood aloof until victory was in sight, constantly urging caution and believing the conditions not right for successful revolution. They had counseled prudence even before the rebel force sailed from Mexico, and therein lay a continuing irritant in the relationship between Castro and orthodox communists around the world. The duty of revolutionaries was to make revolution, said the Cubans, not to stand and wait. The communists' calls for careful preparation before attempting armed action seemed to the Cubans to be little more than a mask for timidity. On the other hand, the communists, especially the Kremlin, considered the Cubans impetuous and naive. They thought that Castro and his aides constantly failed to understand the degree of groundwork successful revolution requires and were consequently a danger to the cause—loose cannons, in short.[21] The defeat of Batista seemed clearly to validate the Cuban position. The experience that awaited Guevara in Bolivia, however, would give the Kremlin the last word.

The Cuban rebels had another serious disagreement with orthodox communists both in Cuba and abroad. It became dogma among the mountain rebels that the guerrilla army should lead the revolution both during the war and after the victory. Here, they directly contradicted communist theory that held that the army was the tool of the party, not its boss. Castro forced the communists at home to relent on this issue, but neither he nor Guevara could force the major communist party in Bolivia to do so, thus creating a grave impediment to Guevara's insurgency there.

With the victory won in Cuba, Guevara wrote a guerrilla manual, *La guerra de guerrillas*, published in July 1960 with an English version,

Guerrilla Warfare, appearing the following year. A discussion of guerrilla tactics and objectives, the book clearly reflected the views and methods of the Sierra Maestra leadership, putting its thoughts about revolution into a theoretical package.[22] It quickly became prominent in a burgeoning contemporary literature on the subject of guerrilla war that included works by Mao Tse-Tung and Vo Nguyên Giap plus scores of volumes on the techniques of counterinsurgency. Unfortunately, Guevara's generalizations later proved ruinous in Bolivia.

One element remained constant, however, in every insurgency in which Guevara partook: The United States supplied and trained his enemies. In Guatemala, it created the force that overthrew the Arbenz government, which Guevara greatly admired. In the case of Cuba, it impeded funds and seized arms headed from the United States to Castro. At the same time, it provided the Cuban government with military training and supplies, even including tanks, until the collapse of Batista's regime; even though it declared an end to military aid in March 1958, supplies continued to flow through alternate channels.[23] Batista's air force, for example, fueled and armed its aircraft at the U.S. naval base at Guantánamo in Cuba until June 1958 when Castro's brother Raúl kidnapped a busload of base personnel plus U.S. and Canadian employees of nearby U.S. businesses. With some 48 hostages, he negotiated an end to the Guantánamo supply operation plus the continuing delivery to Batista of T-28 aircraft, training planes that could be armed.[24]

In the Congo, not only did the United States supply the government forces fighting against the insurgents, but also Cuban exiles contracted by the CIA fought on the government side.[25] Finally, in Bolivia the United States provided arms, training, and intelligence services to the Bolivian government. Guevara had very good reason to believe that in every insurgency in which he was involved, the real enemy behind the screen was the United States, hidden but visible, like a character in an Asian shadow play.

Creating a Guevara Dossier

The U.S. government had been concerned at least since early 1957 with the potential threat Castro's rebellion presented to Batista's regime. Still, in mid-1958, when middle-level officers in the State Department's Bureau of Intelligence and Research (INR) and at the Cuba Desk wanted to know more about Castro and his associates, they could find almost no information on them. Two years earlier, when the Mexican police arrested Castro and his colleagues, they found he had a list of 70 contacts, which they gave to the CIA. Nevertheless, in 1958, the State Department officers found that the CIA had never investigated them.[26]

On Guevara specifically, the agency had only a few sketchy and often inaccurate reports, despite the fact that as early as 1954 Guatemalan authorities had identified him as a troublemaker. But now, given Washington's new interest, reports began filtering in, many obviously second-hand reworkings of conversations with Guevara of one kind or another (the CIA will not reveal their origins), one of the best stemming apparently from a journalist's lengthy interview.

In 1958 a combination of accurate, plausible, and nonsensical information began building up. One report stated that Guevara was educated in France, not Argentina, and another that his father was a doctor rather than a self-proclaimed architect. One described him almost as an oriental potentate from *A Thousand and One Nights,* a pettifogging hedonist insisting upon the very best of everything, including brandy and cigars, someone who was waited upon hand and foot and who made others stand while he sat and dined alone. This last description is especially ironic because Guevara's egalitarian manner, among other things, caused his men to "worship him," as one of the more reliable of these profiles points out.

The better reports stressed Guevara's antipathy for the U.S. government and U.S. businesses. They also highlighted his anger at U.S. intervention in Guatemala and his denial that he was a communist. The communists, he said, according to one account, tried to capture the revolution but seeing the strong popular support for Castro "fell into line, which was the prudent thing for them to do."[27]

Guevara's popularity with his men stemmed in part from his bravery verging on recklessness, which caused Castro to caution him more than once against taking too many risks. "Che seemed to be a man who sought death," Castro told a journalist years later.[28] Indeed, some of the reports to the CIA remarked upon Guevara's courage and also noted his poise and high degree of education, one stating that "'Che' is fairly intellectual for a 'Latino.'" Many spoke of his omnipresent inhaler to combat asthma, and one described him as physically filthy, "even by the rather low standard of cleanliness prevailing among the Castro forces in the Sierra Maestra." This report pointed out, for example, that he would take his men to a stream, where they washed, but he would sit on the bank. It failed to note that cold water in mountain streams could bring on violent asthma attacks.[29]

Exporting Revolution

When Castro won his war in Cuba, U.S. officials feared not only that Cuba would become an outpost of international communism but that it would try to stimulate revolutions in neighboring countries. It soon became very clear that this was indeed high on Castro's agenda and that Guevara assumed more responsibility than anyone else in the new government, except possibly Raúl Castro, for encouraging rebellion throughout Latin America.[30] Venues for Havana's revolutionary efforts included Nicaragua, the Dominican Republic, Guatemala, El Salvador, Venezuela, Colombia, Panama, Honduras, Haiti, Argentina, and, of course, Bolivia. In certain cases, fully armed expeditionary forces relying upon Cuban assistance of various kinds charged into some of these countries, most notably Nicaragua and the Dominican Republic, although none successfully. In the case of the Dominican Republic, the force was unusual in that it consisted mainly of 200 Cuban soldiers who met a quick and thorough defeat.[31]

Money, supplies, and advisers flowed constantly from Cuba to neighboring leftist revolutionary groups, while trainees in insurgency from Third World countries around the globe streamed onto the island to learn from the masters. (Their compatriots in the police and armed forces, meanwhile, streamed into the United States to study counterinsurgency strategies.)[32] In the midst of this intense activity, Washington identified Guevara as a key figure in Cuba's campaign of international subversion. A State Department memorandum noted, for example, that "certain elements in the Castro Government—especially the Argentine Communist-liner Major 'Che' Guevara—are contemplating and planning active support to revolutionary activities against Nicaragua, Haiti, the Dominican Republic and Paraguay. Exiles from all over the Caribbean have flocked into Habana in hope of help."[33]

Not only did appeals for help from aspiring revolutionaries around the world flood Havana, but also many groups sent unbidden representatives, pinning their hopes for assistance on personal contact. Castro's private secretary, Juan Orta Cordova, had instructions to send these suppliants either to Raúl Castro or Guevara, who investigated their political orientation and reportedly helped only the communists. Guevara played such a prominent role in this process that "clear it with Che" became an axiom among the would-be rebels.[34]

Reports of Cuba's efforts to begin insurgencies in neighboring countries sound like reworkings of Ernest Hemingway plots. Defectors told American members of Congress tales of planes landing at night on jungle clearings and fishing boats bobbing across the Caribbean searching for secret ports at which to land shipments of arms or pick up conspirators. They met Soviet freighters on the high seas to transfer cargo, collected arms, including some coming from U.S. ports, and even dropped off passengers in the United States and Puerto Rico.

Meanwhile, the Cuban Department of Fisheries, which operated the boats, deflected attention from their activities by periodically sending one or two into U.S. territorial waters to interfere with American fishing vessels. When caught by the U.S. Navy or Coast Guard, the captains claimed to have been in international waters, and Cuba played the role of a small country oppressed yet again by U.S. imperialism.

"In other words, this was done to embarrass and provoke the U.S. Government, is that correct?" asked an American senator during a 1971 congressional investigation, referring to one of the more spectacular of these episodes. The chief of the Department of Fisheries, by then a defector, replied, "Naturally, because anything like that would automatically make Cuba the victim."[35] U.S. officials suspected that Cuban aircraft and the national tanker and cargo fleet, some 30 ships, also transported arms, but they could not be sure.[36]

The issue leapt into prominence in Washington in early November 1963 when Venezuelan authorities discovered a three-ton cache of arms, many bearing the Cuban shield and markings.[37] Suddenly analyses of Cuban arms supply and revolutionary support became a key preoccupation of Washington's official Cuba watchers, and in 1964, after considering many alternatives, U.S. officials prompted the Organization of American States (OAS) to tighten its restrictions against Cuba, among other actions passing a resolution that members should break off relations with the Castro regime.[38]

The Bay of Pigs Debacle

In April 1962, the United States tried its hand at exporting not revolution but counterrevolution, organizing and supporting an attempt by

Cuban exiles to invade their homeland. The result was a disaster for the invaders, a victory for Castro that helped solidify his rule at home, and a humiliating defeat for the Kennedy administration. The details of the invasion have been chronicled far too extensively to need repetition here, but the aftermath bears directly upon the conflict between Washington and Guevara in Bolivia.[39]

Stunned by the fiasco, the U.S. government began studying it intensely almost before the last shot was fired, and as a result, it had learned from its mistakes by the time it countered Guevara in South America. In fact, the blunders that it made in the Bay of Pigs expedition and that Guevara made in Bolivia were in some ways very similar. Both leapt into complicated military operations with ridiculous optimism, expecting popular support but all the time knowing far too little about the feelings of the people they intended to "free." In addition, neither country had an embassy in the invaded nation that might have given up-to-date assessments of popular attitudes and military capabilities.

Kennedy had little experience with personal defeat. Even the loss of his PT boat in World War II gave him an opportunity for personal heroism. Furthermore, the event was later transformed by political image-making almost into a victory with the lost PT boat becoming his emblem during his presidential campaign. But no gloss could be put on the Bay of Pigs. Kennedy was determined to know what went wrong and not to repeat it.

Washington's inability first to prevent the Cuban rebels from taking power and then to overthrow them highlighted a frustration with guerrilla movements that bedeviled many capitals around the world. Soldiers, politicians, and pundits often portrayed guerrillas as nearly indomitable, requiring prodigious numbers of troops and resources to stop them; 10–20 soldiers to every guerrilla was a commonly quoted estimate.[40] Guevara himself added to this impression. In a widely quoted essay on guerrilla warfare, he wrote that regular armies, the sustaining force of "the exploiting classes, . . . are absolutely powerless when they have to face the unconventional warfare of the peasants on their territory. They lose ten men for every revolutionary fighter who falls."[41]

In fact the picture was not completely bleak by any means for established governments; since World War II, large-scale insurgencies had been defeated in Greece, Malaya, and the Philippines. Nevertheless, guerrilla movements had achieved spectacular successes in China, French Indochina, and now Cuba. Meanwhile, a sizable literature was building up on both sides of the issue, including Guevara's highly publicized contributions, especially *Guerrilla Warfare*.[42]

The burgeoning corpus of counterinsurgency literature included a book entitled *The Uncertain Trumpet* by retired American general Maxwell D. Taylor, who had fought with great distinction in World War II, commanded the U.S. Eighth Army in the Korean War, and served as Army chief of staff from 1955 to 1959. Published in 1959, his book impressed then-Senator Kennedy with its thesis that the government should give up the notion of massive retaliation, prevalent in the Eisenhower years, and develop a greater willingness and capability to fight limited wars. On April 22, almost before the smoke had cleared at the Bay of Pigs, Kennedy asked Taylor to conduct a study of that hapless undertaking. Shortly thereafter, he asked Taylor to head the CIA. Taylor declined the CIA appointment, but, determined to have him in his government, Kennedy retained him in the White House with the title military representative to the president.[43]

Taylor felt strongly that the Joint Chiefs of Staff, who reviewed the Bay of Pigs plan, had served Kennedy especially badly. Any professional military leader, he said, should have known at a glance that the scheme was doomed and told the president so in the most forceful way. The CIA, he said, had neither the expertise nor the capability to carry out an operation as ambitious and as militarily sophisticated as this one was, or at least as it should have been. The more one looked at the arrangements, including the small number of soldiers (1,200), the more its "fragility" and "high probability of failure" leapt out. But at no time, said Taylor, did the president's advisers look him "in the eye and tell him these obvious facts."[44]

Upon entering office, Kennedy thought that Eisenhower had let the National Security Council staff become far too complex and pared it accordingly, but Taylor believed that those reductions had hindered the invasion. He maintained that the parts of the staff the president eliminated could have helped coordinate the Bay of Pigs operation, which would have been especially useful since at that early point in his administration Kennedy scarcely knew his secretaries of state and defense or the top people at the CIA, a common circumstance in the American government.[45]

Needless to say, neither the CIA nor the Pentagon accepted Taylor's critique fully by any means. The CIA's historian, in fact, wrote an 195-page refutation for internal use.[46] But Taylor's views, and those of others who thought like him, prevailed in the area of counterinsurgency, with great effect upon Guevara in Bolivia in 1967.

Taylor believed that the government needed to understand that guerrilla warfare constituted more than a military problem. It called for social, economic, and political action, as well as a military response. Furthermore, he recommended, and Kennedy agreed, that any large paramilitary operation should ultimately be the responsibility of the Pentagon, not the CIA, and that the Joint Chiefs of Staff should offer their views on any issue with military implications, whether or not the Pentagon had primary responsibility in the matter.[47]

At Taylor's recommendation, the Special Group for Counterinsurgency came into being, consisting of very high level military and foreign-affairs officials, plus the president's brother, Attorney General Robert Kennedy, who would act as the president's alter ego. Taylor originally chaired the committee, soon known simply as the Special Group, but surrendered the leadership to Robert Kennedy when the president appointed him chairman of the Joint Chiefs of Staff in 1962.[48]

Under the Special Group's instigation, a school for counterinsurgency was established at Fort Bragg, North Carolina, and later named after President Kennedy. One of the first texts studied by officers there was a rapidly translated version of Guevara's book on guerrilla warfare.[49] The State Department's Foreign Service Institute required U.S. diplomats to take courses on counterinsurgency, and the Pentagon expanded its Special Forces, now called the Green Berets, created to fight low-intensity warfare and to train other countries' armed forces to do the same. The Special Group required U.S. embassies to report regularly on communist activity in their countries and monitored State Department, CIA, and military communications from around the world with a watchful eye for insurgencies, new or ongoing. It maintained a list, which it continually updated, of present or potential problem countries.

Officers from armed forces around the globe came to Washington for training, while military missions abroad were augmented. Police forces received training both in the United States and in their own countries, where special teams sent by the Agency for International Development (AID) instructed them in methods of controlling subversive activities. (This program soon became highly controversial because it caused the United States to be identified with some very brutal police organizations.) Ministers in Central America who held internal-security responsibilities met periodically with U.S. officials to perfect their operations.

U.S. mapping efforts in Latin America were intensified, while teams from AID built and improved roads stretching into the hinterlands, increasing both economic and military infrastructures in remote areas. Intelligence networks, run both by the CIA and the military, were strengthened, and air surveillance, especially of Cuba, was routinely undertaken.[50]

This was the web that Guevara flew into when he began his rebellion in Bolivia. Some of it had been in place during World War II, and some reflected the concern of U.S. administrations with guerrilla movements since the end of that war. Still, there can be no doubt that Washington spun it much larger and finer in response to the Bay of Pigs disaster.[51]

Guevara: Unsung Diplomat

Guevara came to international attention as a leftist guerrilla leader at a time when left-wing ideas and forces were nearing their apogee in the post–World War II era and when guerrilla chieftains inspired both great admiration and great fear. Consequently, his work as a diplomat tends often to be obscured. Yet a case can be made that it is in this role that he best served the Cuban Revolution following the fall of Batista. From almost the moment the rebels won power, Guevara became the principal diplomat of the new regime, making his first of many long diplomatic voyages, this one three months long, in the summer of 1959.[52]

Guevara undertook his missions sometimes to increase Cuba's prestige and tighten its relations with Third World nations, sometimes to stabilize its alliances among Soviet-bloc countries, and once to improve strained relations with China. Frequently, however, his purpose was to make economic deals, especially with the more advanced communist countries, as relations with the United States, previously Cuba's main customer and supplier, deteriorated and finally collapsed in 1961. His diplomatic efforts secured new markets for Cuban sugar, arranged capital and other assistance for new and existing Cuban industries, and established more liberal credit terms with the Soviet bloc than were granted to any other country in the "socialist world."[53]

The revolutionary government's economic record, far from a solid success story, has as one of its most controversial chapters the effort to diversify Cuban industry, advocated strongly by Guevara as minister of industries in the early years of the new regime. Indeed, he acknowledged that much of the responsibility for its failure lay at his doorstep. Nevertheless, following Cuba's estrangement from the United States, Guevara's economic diplomacy, mostly among communist nations, played a significant role in preventing the Cuban economy from collapsing.[54]

It is the political purposes of Guevara's diplomacy, however, that are principally interesting here, especially his trip in 1964–65 to Africa. There, he played a signal role in expanding Cuba's influence, which, although smaller than in Castro's dreams, became a reality for a number of years despite the audacity of the idea. The African connection especially appealed to Cuban leaders in the mid-1960s because they believed that communism could expand there relatively quickly and easily if only they and their African allies could outmaneuver the United States and its "neocolonialist" allies. Furthermore, the enormous efforts that Guevara, along with Fidel and Raúl Castro, had made to export revolution within their own continent had proved singularly unsuccessful, and although they did not give up on Latin America, Africa seemed to offer a chance to revitalize Cuba's position as a revolutionary force.[55]

In December 1964, Guevara set off for Africa, the last of his long diplomatic voyages and a major step in Cuba's effort to play an important role on that continent. It has significance for our story because when that policy failed in the Congo, Cuba refocused its insurgency efforts on Latin America, especially Bolivia. Furthermore, during the trip, Guevara was highly critical, in public and private, of the established communist powers' policies toward the Third World. They paid him back in Bolivia.

Guevara's trip began with a week in New York, followed by a three-month sojourn in Africa, where he visited Algeria, Mali, Congo (Brazzaville), Guinea, Ghana, Dahomey, Tanzania, and Egypt. He also made a side trip to China.[56] In New York, giving vitriolic speeches in the United Nations General Assembly and a tendentious interview on network television, he broadcast a striking image of a firebrand representative from a relentlessly revolutionary regime. Blasting nearly all governments in the Western Hemisphere, wooing newly independent African nations, and applauding the rebels then active in the Congo, he was clearly out to bolster Cuban influence among leftist governments and factions in Africa.[57]

Throughout the trip, Guevara needed to exercise extremely adroit diplomacy because his position was fraught with contradictions. His purpose was to help establish Cuba as a revolutionary leader in the Third

World, especially in Africa, and to do that he needed to arrange Cuban assistance to African revolutionary movements, even though Cuba itself depended on massive assistance from the Soviet Union. He also needed to convince Africans that Cuba not only could help them but also could act independently of the Kremlin, and he needed to do so in a way that never became so offensive to the USSR that it would endanger Cuba's Soviet backing. While hoping to compete with the Chinese and the Soviets as a radical-left force in Africa, he nevertheless did not want to jeopardize Cuba's place at the table of communist nations.

Still, Guevara became strident at times. He lashed out at Eastern European countries, calling them "sharks," not communists, according to a report that came into the CIA. It quoted him as saying that Hungary, for example, offered to sell Cuba items at prices even higher than the French asked. This was part of a theme he would highlight prominently before the trip ended: Communist countries should support each other to the extent required and without considering market factors. Furthermore, he criticized the Soviet Union and China both privately and publicly. A CIA informant, apparently in Algiers, quoted him as saying that Cuban officials were unhappy about the depth of Soviet and Chinese interference in Cuban affairs and that he had come to Africa in part to warn Cuba's "friends" not to get too deeply involved with those countries, especially China. The report leaves unanswered why he felt the Chinese were especially onerous.[58]

Near the end of his trip, Guevara admitted to a newspaper in Cairo that revolutionary Cuba had made "grave mistakes" in developing its economy, but he attributed them to bad advice from the Soviets and their allies.[59] His remarks confirmed indications Washington had already received of discontent among Cuba's ruling circles with the degree that the Soviet Union had become involved in their affairs. The State Department maintained, for example, that the Soviets, dismayed at the drain Cuba represented to their resources, insisted upon taking an active part in managing its finances and trade, even placing their own officials in the relevant Cuban agencies.[60]

In Algeria as an observer at an Afro-Asian Solidarity Organization economic conference, Guevara made another criticism, one that would reverberate throughout the communist world, and indeed it was meant to be heard clearly in Moscow and Peking. Weapons, he said, should be provided free of charge by "socialist countries" to "nations requesting them to fire at the common enemy." But beyond that, socialism required a change of heart about humanity, "a new fraternal attitude. . . . There should be no more talk of mutually beneficial trade," for example. Socialist countries that purchased Third World raw materials at relatively low prices and sold back manufactured items at relatively high prices, he said, were, in fact, "accomplices in imperialist exploitation." "Foreign trade," he added, "should not fix policy. On the contrary, foreign trade should be subordinated to a fraternal policy toward the people."

He then challenged the communist nations to aid developing countries with subsidized trade, technical help, long-term credits, and investments over which the recipient state had complete control with no commitment of monetary payments or credits whatsoever. The beneficiary country, however, would be obliged to supply certain quantities of products to the investing country for a certain number of years and at a certain price. While in effect calling on China and the Soviet Union to make vast new commitments, he acknowledged in both his speech and a subsequent interview their generosity toward Cuba and the rest of the Third World. Still, despite these kind words, he had thrown them an enormous challenge.[61]

Wherever possible in sub-Saharan Africa, Guevara made or confirmed military links with leftist regimes and guerrilla groups, planting military advisers and training missions, for example, in Portuguese Guinea, Congo (Brazzaville), Guinea-Bissau, and the Congo.[62] In Algiers, the visits of Congolese rebel leader Christopher Gbenye and Guevara overlapped briefly, and it is logical to assume that they discussed help from both Cuba and Algeria to the rebels. In any event, Algerian and Cuban assistance became a fact.[63]

Guevara's last substantive stop was in Cairo, where he helped persuade President Gamal Abdel Nasser to support Cuban revolutionary schemes in Africa, something the Egyptian leader did reluctantly and only to a limited degree.

Throughout his trip, Guevara stressed the unlikely proposition that Cuba had relevance for Africa; "a case of the fly and the elephant," scoffed a Ghanaian official. State Department analysts agreed, saying that the mission must have appeared "audacious to the point of absurdity" to sophisticated observers. Nevertheless they judged it "a modest success" for Cuba by the time it was over.[64]

While admitting that "Cuba is a country and Africa is a continent," Guevara emphasized that Cuba had experienced a victorious violent revolution. "From this viewpoint," he said, "there exists an extraordinary similarity between the Cuban Revolution and the African Revolution."[65] Above all, Guevara hoped that tiny Cuba could lead a crusade to blunt an incipient thrust by the American giant into the African continent, which was starting, Havana believed, in the Congo. "Although the North Americans have not completely plunged into Africa," he told students in Accra, "they are doing so now, and they must be stopped," a theme he sounded incessantly during his trip.[66] "For all Africa," he said, "socialism or neocolonialism is the stake in the game being played in the Congo."[67]

Once, in a departure from his African theme, Guevara seemed to preview his future insurgency in Bolivia. Whether or not he or anyone else in Cuba had yet thought specifically about such an expedition, in Algeria Guevara projected an undertaking with many of the Bolivia operation's characteristics, including the same enormously ambitious designs. In an interview, Guevara unveiled a dream of an international revolutionary structure in Latin America "of the proletariat and the peasants" to combat the international repression led by the United States. He forecast a "continent-wide front" that would "fight against imperialism and against its domestic allies." Creation of the organization would require hard work, he admitted, but once it was formed it would "deal a severe blow to imperialism."[68] Besides the resemblance of this scheme to Havana's hopes for the Bolivian campaign, one cannot help noting in these remarks Guevara's complete dismissal of Latin America's communist parties, which must have believed, or at least pretended, that they constituted exactly this kind of an organization.

The View from Washington

Some observers believe that Guevara's speech in Algiers, with its potential to bruise relations with Cuba's patrons, did not represent the policy of the regime in Havana and caused a riff between Castro and Guevara. In Washington, Cuba watchers saw it quite differently. They viewed it as "further impetus to the independent leadership role" Cuba wanted to develop. State Department analysts, who never seemed to assume that it contradicted thinking in Havana, said that Guevara, while acknowledging Cuba's place in the socialist world, still dared to criticize and exhort the major socialist powers. Thus, Cuba through "the example of its revolution and its intellectual leadership hopes to cast a far larger shadow in the 'national liberation' struggle than its small size would otherwise permit."[69]

The CIA's intelligence directorate, while noting Guevara's "implication" that "the logical center of African inspiration should be Havana, not Moscow or Peking," underestimated Cuban efforts to support rebellion in the Congo.[70] "There is no evidence," it stated in February 1965, " . . . to indicate that Cuba has taken a hand in drawing up specific plans or organizing actions for the overthrow of any African government." Nor did evidence exist, its analysts concluded, that Guevara had "offered Cuban arms or personnel to the rebels."[71]

The State Department, more suspicious than the CIA, feared from the start of Guevara's trip that he planned to boost Cuba's commitment to the Congolese insurgency. It asked its posts to report on his activities, especially any that indicated "increasing Cuban involvement in Congo situation." This view came closer to the truth. As Cuban writer and former diplomat Juan Benemelis, who was involved in African affairs in that era, points out, Cuba's efforts to aid Congolese revolutionaries were already under way in 1963.[72]

Guevara Vanishes

Guevara arrived home from Africa on March 14, 1965. He was seen in Havana during the following week, but never again in public, not alive at any rate.[73] The "disappearance" of Che Guevara surely ranks as one of the most spectacular political shadow plays in recent history. The episode, characterized by Delphic pronouncements from Castro, bizarre hypotheses about Guevara's fate, and an infinite number of preposterous "sightings," came to define him more than many of the things he had done in real life. Furthermore, while it had a distinctly humorous side, the disappearance also had significant political ramifications, as we shall see, some relating directly to his eventual insurgency in Bolivia. For one thing, it heightened the nervousness of Latin American governments about his possible activities, fueling their determination to stop him, while conversely it led some high-ranking U.S. officials, especially in the CIA, to believe that he had died.

By mid-April, observers in Havana began to notice that they had not seen Guevara for weeks. Yet no word came from the government about where he was. Reporters, diplomats, and fellow officials, among others, could scarcely fail to notice that he had left his post as minister of industries, now assumed by his deputy, Arturo Guzmán, but the only acknowledgment of the change came in a Radio Havana broadcast.[74]

Needless to say, rumors raced through the city and very quickly flew around the world, explaining in myriad ways why Guevara was missing. In the absence of any facts or even hints from the authorities, speculation ran wild and theories abounded. Behind many, if not most, of them lurked the assumption that some sort of trouble with Castro accounted for Guevara's disappearance. According to most of the theories, which persist to this day, the two disagreed seriously, some say violently, over industrialization, the Soviet Union, or China. One of the most popular theories, however, casts the matter in more personal terms, maintaining that Castro felt threatened by Guevara's popularity and got rid of him. How? By putting him under house arrest, after which the Soviets took him to Algiers, said one of many variations, or by chasing him into asylum in the Mexican embassy after a wild shoot-out, said another.[75]

Because these stories almost invariably criticized him, Castro tried to put them to rest but only exacerbated matters when he said in a radio broadcast on April 18, 1965, that Guevara would always be where he could be most useful to the revolution. At the same time, he emphasized that Guevara was one of Cuba's top leaders and that his African trip had been highly productive. Castro later said that his relations with Guevara were "unimprovable." That, however, was far from enough to end the speculation, nor was the fact that the journal of the armed forces, *Verde Olivo*, twice that month published Guevara's essay, "Man and Socialism in Cuba."[76]

Before long, however, Castro apparently realized that he could turn the tables, changing Guevara's disappearance from a political liability into useful political theater, building a myth of Guevara, knight of the revolution, pursuing a secret quest in far-off lands. He taunted "the imperialists" for their interest and ignorance. "They say that Comrade Ernesto Guevara does not appear in public"; they wonder if there is "contention" or "some problem," he said. "Well, we are going to answer them: 'What business is it of yours?' [Applause] . . . When will the people know about Major Guevara? When Major Guevara wants them to." Castro then added that "Major Guevara has always done and will always do revolutionary things."[77] The famous guerrilla chief was absent performing his duty, Castro told graduating schoolteachers in December 1965, adding, "and I say absent, I do not say dead, for our enemies rejoice at the idea that Comrade Ernesto Guevara is dead. . . . He is alive and in good health. [Applause] However, evidently the imperialists have not been able to ascertain this with their U-2s."[78]

Castro also seems to have enjoyed contributing to the confusion. When, for example, Guevara had gone to aid the insurgency in the Congo, Castro told a West German reporter that "[Guevara] has been in Latin America for a long time. He organized the underground movement. He was last in Venezuela. But they failed to apprehend him. And the number of his followers increases by the hundreds of thousands."[79]

On October 3, 1966, when Guevara had been missing for nearly nine months, Castro read the most mysterious document Guevara ever wrote, though some commentators doubt his authorship. It was a letter to Castro in which Guevara resigned the offices, army rank, and Cuban citizenship that had been bestowed on him and said that he had to go on to other revolutionary chores. He praised Castro extravagantly as a "leader and a revolutionary" and added, "I have always been identified with the foreign policy of our revolution, and I still am."[80]

Guevara's second wife, Aleida March (he had divorced Gadea in 1959), compounded the mystery by attending the speech in which Castro read this letter apparently dressed in mourning. She could, however, have been mourning a relative, perhaps Guevara's mother, who had recently died, and one observer even claims the dress was not black but dark blue.[81] Nevertheless, in a stunning farewell to his family of unquestionable finality and exemplary Marxism, he wrote, "I do not leave my wife nor my children anything material, and I am not ashamed. I am glad it is thus. I do not require anything for them for the state will give them enough with which to live and be educated."

The event added enormously to Guevara's ever-growing mystique and vastly fueled speculation about him. Those who believed Castro had done him harm became more convinced than ever. Castro said the letter "was delivered" on April 1. Why had he waited until October to make it public? Was it a fake? Why was Guevara's wife dressed in "strict mourning," as one source put it, if indeed she was? Was he dead? Killed in the Dominican Republic? Banished? Liquidated, and the letter concocted as a cover-up? Some suggest that the letter was to provide Castro and his regime with "deniability" in case they wanted to distance themselves from Guevara's expedition in the Congo.[82] Considering, however, that Guevara led an expeditionary force of at least 100 Cuban soldiers, to call such a ploy naive would be charitable.[83]

Bolstering the notion that Guevara was politically on the skids in Havana, the CIA noted that Castro's talk followed by two days the creation of a 100-man Communist Party central committee and observed that "three Guevara protégés—currently holding portfolios in the Castro government—are conspicuously absent. The three were the only cabinet ministers not named to the central committee."[84]

On January 2, 1967, Castro, with his flair for drama, tied Guevara's disappearance into one of the oldest of human myths—the return of the warrior hero—and came close to linking it to another—the resurrection. "The imperialists," he said, "have killed Che many times and in many places"; "what we hope is that someday, where imperialism least expects . . . Guevara will rise from his ashes, a warrior and a guerrilla—in good health. Someday we will again have some very concrete news about Che." Later that month, a Chilean writer reported Castro as saying, "In November, you will have news of Che." At that time, Castro may have thought that by November Guevara, who was then in Bolivia, would have achieved enough success for Havana to reveal his location. By November he would, in fact, be dead.[85]

No Break with Castro

Those who believe that Guevara fell from favor maintain that his reception upon arriving home from Africa seemed cool, despite the fact that not only Fidel Castro but also President Osvaldo Dorticós, two ministers of state, and a top-level delegation of the ruling United Party of the Socialist Revolution turned out to greet him.[86] Yes, but he looked grim and depressed, say those who believe the partnership was in trouble.[87] But Guevara, who suffered severe respiratory problems, had been traveling and working solidly for more than three months and had just completed an air journey through seven time zones that had been extended by a day because of engine trouble. That could explain his appearance and also why Castro whisked him past the awaiting press, which some commentators found suspicious. He may have been doing an exhausted Guevara a favor. Or, indeed, perhaps Castro really did want Guevara to avoid public statements for whatever reason until they could confer; nevertheless, subsequent events make it clear that, whether or not he had problems within the ruling circles in Havana, Guevara continued to play a major role in Cuban affairs.

All arguments advanced for Guevara's presumed fall from grace have problems. The most common maintain that he disagreed with Castro over the economy, but they had generally come together on the major points. Guevara had accepted the need to concentrate on sugar production, and Castro in turn had accepted the controversial notion, espoused by Guevara, of moral incentives for work, fearing that material incentives could lead to "neocapitalism." Meanwhile, Guevara, completing the circle, had admitted reluctantly that other incentives had to be provided.[88] Regarding views on the proper relationship with the Soviets and Chinese, both favored violent uprisings closer to the Chinese line than the Soviet, and while neither underestimated the value of the Soviet alliance, both rejected the nonviolent position they believed the Kremlin had adopted.[89]

If we dispense with the notion of a disappearance, however, we see that only about a month after his return from Africa, Guevara led a major undertaking in Cuban foreign affairs, one in which he long had been intimately involved, especially on his final diplomatic trip: the attempt to foster revolution and increase Cuban influence in Africa.

Although it is pure speculation, let us assume that at some time in late 1964 or early 1965 Guevara and Castro discussed new assignments that better suited Guevara. Let us imagine even that for any number of reasons it seemed best for Guevara to leave Havana. Let us add that Castro expressed disappointment with Guevara's economic policies. Finally, let's assume that the discussion or discussions were rough and contentious. Nevertheless, it remains impossible to review the chronology of Guevara's activities in the mid-1960s and continue to regard him as disgraced. To know this, we do not need to consult secret Cuban documents; materials in the public domain suffice. If we know that a bird has flown from point A to point C, it becomes hard to believe he was shot and eaten at point B.

Former CIA director Richard Helms, although not always right about Guevara, supports these views about Guevara's career and relations with Castro. Looking back, Helms said that if Castro and Guevara had any sort of a split, it must have been temporary; at least the agency had no indication that serious enmity existed between the two. He emphasized that the CIA regarded Guevara as the internationalist of the Fidelista movement, which would make his Congo assignment a logical one.[90]

The Cuba desk at the State Department, on the other hand, believed that Guevara left under pressure from the Soviets. Desk staffers assumed that many of his statements criticizing the Kremlin—private as well as public—had reached Moscow, where officials considered them "over the line" and "insisted that he leave the Cuban leadership," as Wayne S. Smith, who was then on the desk, put it. (Smith and his colleagues felt sure, however, that other Cuban leaders agreed with Guevara's remarks, which were also published by the Cuban press.)[91]

If the desk was right in believing that the Soviets wanted Guevara to go, the Cubans may have had a perfect solution, as Smith points out: He was leaving anyway. Much less likely is the hypothesis that Castro or the collective Havana leadership decided during Guevara's diplomatic trip to Africa, or in March after his return, to pack him off to the Congo simply to get him out of town. This assumption apparently stems from an inadequate understanding of the thrust of the African trip and an underestimation of its importance to Cuban policy. The BBC, for example, once presented the trip as a voyage of empty ceremony designed mostly to get an already controversial Guevara out of Cuba.[92] Trivializing the trip obscures both its link to the Congo mission and the significance of both the trip and the mission.

Finally, if sending Guevara to the Congo was Castro's way of getting him out of the Kremlin's hair, it was an odd, or at least an ironic, way of doing it. By aiding the insurgency there, Guevara intended, among other things, to impinge upon the very Soviet influence in Africa he had been warning Africans about during his first trip, warnings that presumably were part of what had riled the Kremlin.

Furthermore, during the period of Guevara's so-called disappearance, Castro built him into one of the greatest Cuban heros since José Martí. Some say that because of Guevara's great prestige, Castro felt the need for delicacy—in effect camouflage—while pushing him aside, but surely there was no requirement for the degree of public adulation accorded Guevara. Castro, like other leaders, praised him constantly, calling him "one of our best fighters" and "my best friend, with whom I stood side by side when we liberated Cuba."[93] Meanwhile, the official media also praised him, quoted him, and carried articles written by him. The 1965 celebrations of the anniversary of the Moncada Barracks raid were held in Santa Clara, honoring Guevara's battle there, rather than in Havana or Oriente Province, where they were normally held. Huge posters of him were displayed there and elsewhere in Cuba, one in Havana replacing a picture of Castro that had hung there for several years, and an exhibit with some 350 photos illustrated his march with Cienfuegos from Oriente to the Escambray Mountains. The Ministry of Education ordered that Guevara's by-then famous resignation letter be read in schools throughout Cuba. Primary-school children were encouraged to compose letters to him, and a group of several hundred young people called "the followers of Camilo and Che" spent a month on a highly publicized hike, retracing the Guevara-Cienfuegos route from Oriente to Las Villas during the war. The homage not only continued in the months and years immediately following his disappearance but also has continued until today. Workers' groups are named after him, his picture appears in public places, and schoolchildren are still urged to remember Guevara, sing songs about him, and make him their model.[94] This is not the way dictatorships usually treat fallen idols.

Guevara "Sightings"

While rumors full of gloom and foreboding about the fate of the vanished Guevara continued to fly, pouring into Washington and other capitals, a fascinating new type arose. Essentially, these were Guevara "sightings," and for the better part of two years, they occurred around the globe, causing Martin Guevara to observe aptly, "Now, my brother is like the white horse of Zapata: He is everywhere."[95]

Besides a persistent suggestion that he was in the Dominican Republic, dead or alive, Guevara was "seen" around the world. For example, he was spotted in Peru, speaking Quechuan to Indian guerrillas; in Colombia, where he arrived via a Russian submarine; in Vietnam, where Castro shipped him to keep him from causing trouble in Latin America; in the Congo, where he died fighting alongside insurgents; in a Mexican sanatorium, where he was being treated for a "nervous disorder"; in southern Brazil, wearing a false beard and accompanied by a young nurse, where a number of "high-class" women invited him to tea; and in Argentina, in priestly garments with blond hair and face makeup.[96]

Silly as many of these stories seem, they received prominent media play, and Latin American governments often took them very seriously. Colombian security forces, for example, searched extensively for Guevara, while the Peruvian government tightened border security and its army's intelligence service tried to determine whether or not he had, in fact, already gotten in. Upon hearing that he was training guerrillas in their country, Uruguayan police patrols scoured the countryside.

Nearly the entire Brazilian Third Army was once reported searching for him along the Uruguayan border, and meanwhile Brazilian police hunted for him in the south near Curitiba. The militia of the state of Minas Gerais in central Brazil carried out intensive antiguerrilla surveillance, searching for Guevara and concurrently arresting suspected communists. (In 1969 some of those detained were released in exchange for the kidnapped U.S. ambassador, C. Burke Elbrick.) Furthermore, since by now he had a formidable reputation as a guerrilla leader, authorities felt compelled to deny strenuously innumerable false reports of Guevara's presence in their areas.[97]

Variations on one particular theme recurred continually: that Guevara had gone to the Dominican Republic in April 1965, during the revolt that President Johnson helped quell with American troops, and had been killed. Helms today, looking back, says that there is no evidence that the CIA's leaders believed Guevara had died, but Ambassador Henderson recalls that Desmond Fitzgerald, the CIA deputy director for operations, told him in July 1967 that Guevara had been killed in the Dominican Republic.[98] In addition, Helms's former agents, with attitudes ranging from amusement to anger, say that in 1965 the CIA's top management not only believed that Guevara was dead but also so advised official Washington. Thereafter, the agency's field officers in the Congo and Bolivia found it impossible to convince headquarters that Guevara was in those countries. Eventually, they found it impolitic even to say so, although they were certain that he was—and, of course, they were right.

One State Department political officer in La Paz in September 1967 told the prominent *New York Times* columnist Cyrus L. Sulzberger during a briefing that Guevara was suspected of being in the country. Sulzberger told him flatly that he was mistaken—Helms had told Sulzberger that Guevara was not there. In fact, Guevara's disappearance gave Sulzberger and the *New York Times* as much trouble as it gave most other observers. Although the columnist believed correctly that Guevara was alive, he was wrong not only about his location but also about his activities. In July, Sulzberger had written that small guerrilla movements in Guatemala, Colombia, Venezuela, and Bolivia were "coordinated, if loosely, by a single command under Ernesto Che Guevara."[99] At that time, Guevara was struggling to survive in the Bolivian jungle, scarcely able to communicate with the outside world.

Guevara himself added spectacularly to the drama and to his own image as a mythic warrior on a secret quest. In April 1967, an article arrived in the offices of *Tricontinental*, a new magazine edited by Osmany Cienfuegos, Camilo's brother—an article on revolution recently written by none other than Che Guevara. Surely much of this had been stage-managed by the Cuban leadership, but to the world it seemed almost miraculous. The article's principal message, regardless of its text, was "Guevara lives!"

Instead of waiting for the magazine's first edition, which was not scheduled to appear until June, Cienfuegos published the article as a pamphlet, including a picture of Guevara being shaved and another without his beard or mustache, just as some of the rumors had described him. The effect was stunning; media around the globe trumpeted the story. Guevara was alive "somewhere in the world," as he himself said in his letter accompanying the article, but he gave no hint of where.[100] Nevertheless, some observers remained skeptical, considering the article an official hoax designed to perpetuate the myth that Guevara was alive. The director of the CIA, for example, according to his agents, did not change his mind.

Although the article's text was almost beside the point under the circumstances, in it Guevara made the statement, famous in its day, that "the battle cry [for revolutionaries] is to create two, three . . . many Vietnams." Some leftists, however—the editors of Mexico's magazine *Siempre*, for example—berated him for calling for more of a kind of war that had caused so much suffering. Raúl Castro felt obliged to refute publicly Czechoslovakian commentators who took the same line.[101] But most leftists around the world and certainly in Latin America simply thrilled at Guevara's reappearance, "arising from the ashes like the Phoenix, a veteran guerrilla," as *Bohemia* put it.[102]

Castro, always ready to swell the scene, said that Guevara's "appearance" must have been traumatic for imperialists, who wondered desperately whether he was "organizing liberation movements or fighting on one of the liberation fronts." He claimed that guerrilla groups in Guatemala, Colombia, Venezuela, and Bolivia (where Guevara was by then) were growing so "vigorously and swiftly" that the United States had deployed increasing numbers of Special Forces in those places, 1,000 having already arrived in Bolivia. This was, of course, a wild exaggeration; the total number sent to Bolivia during the insurgency was 17.[103]

Guevara's Chronology

When Guevara seemed to have disappeared, he actually took a circuitous route through the Netherlands, Algeria, Ghana, Egypt, and the Congo (Brazzaville) before arriving in the Congo in May 1965.[104] He spent approximately six months there until, in a agreement with the Congolese rebels, who had begun moving toward reconciliation with the government, Castro withdrew him and his force.[105] Guevara then spent more than three months in Tanzania, "marking time," as Castro said later, and putting his diary notes from the Congo expedition into a more coherent form.[106] He next went to Prague, where he stayed secretly in a safe house maintained by Cuba's intelligence service, and then returned to Cuba in July 1966. There, he began the preparations for the Bolivian insurgency, including several months of training in a remote mountainous region of Pinar del Rio with the men he had selected to accompany him.[107]

In November 1966, a balding, clean-shaven, middle-aged man wearing impeccable, conservative business clothes and horn-rimmed glasses stepped off of an airplane from São Paulo, and customs officials in La Paz welcomed him into their country. Che Guevara had arrived in Bolivia.[108]

CHAPTER TWO

Contact and Alarm

A day of warlike events," said Guevara of March 23, 1967, a day when small-weapons fire crackled through the jungle on the Bolivian slopes where the mountains drop abruptly to the plains of central South America. While tracking down reports of strange, possibly subversive, activities, a 40-man Bolivian Army patrol fell into a five-man guerrilla ambush, and the struggle Guevara hoped would light the flames of rebellion across the continent had begun. This, the guerrillas' first planned engagement, was short, ending even before word of it could reach Guevara. By then, his band had killed seven soldiers, wounded four, and scooped up their arms and ammunition; disappointingly, they captured no food. In addition, they took 14 prisoners, including the major in command, questioned them (they "talked like parrots," Guevara said), then released them. The guerrillas also seized their plan of operations, convincing Guevara to redeploy his men and keep them at their posts through the night "to see if the famous rangers" would come that night or the next day. But neither rangers nor anyone else returned, not for a while.[1]

Guevara had every reason to scorn the Bolivian Army, one of the world's least effective fighting organizations. As the head of the U.S. embassy political section pointed out later, the army "was made up mostly of one-year conscripts." In the area of the insurgency, they were mostly "transplanted Altiplano *campesinos*"—in other words, peasants from Bolivia's Andean plateau, one of the world's highest inhabited regions, very different from the dry jungle hillsides bordering the plains. A large percentage of recruits could neither read nor write; one of the major missions of the armed forces, in fact, was to teach literacy. They carried German Mauser rifles left over from the Chaco War of 1932–35 with Paraguay, many of which no longer fired. In that first ambush, Guevara's men captured 16 of these, which must have disappointed them when they tried to use them.[2]

The U.S. Southern Command, based in the Panama Canal Zone, said in May 1967, "The recent outbreak of guerrilla activity . . . has pointed up the serious deficiencies in the [Bolivian] armed forces organization, logistics, leadership and intelligence capabilities and has raised the question of whether the military has the capability to counter even a small guerrilla movement."[3] And yet that was precisely what the U.S. government hoped the Bolivian military, like all Latin American armed forces, could learn to do. The top objective of the U.S. Military Assistance Plan (MAP) for Bolivia for fiscal years 1967–72 was to "improve the capability of the Armed Forces to maintain internal security against Communist and other threats of violence and subversion in conjunction with civil police forces when reconstituted." (The police forces had been all but dismantled by the military regime that seized power in 1964 because it doubted their loyalty.)[4]

Cuba's leaders knew the condition of the Bolivian Army; that was one of the reasons they selected the country as the principal *foco* for a South American revolution. On the other hand, they undoubtedly knew also that the Americans had a large Military Advisory Group (MILGP) in Bolivia that was focusing its assistance on certain military units, among them three ranger battalions. The second of these, however, existed only on paper when Guevara's guerrillas fired their first shots in anger. Subsequently stationed in the province of Santa Cruz, that battalion had orders to operate in southern Bolivia, where Guevara began his rebellion; despite Guevara's scorn for the rangers, this unit, with considerable help from the Americans, including Green Beret trainers and CIA agents, eventually brought him down.[5]

Guevara's guerrilla band itself was hardly a formidable military force. For one thing it was small, never many more than 50 men, consisting principally of Cubans and Bolivians but also including a few Peruvians and one or two other nationalities. Some of the Bolivians were trained in Cuba, others recruited by a splinter, Chinese-oriented communist faction in La Paz. Many proved to be unreliable, prone to desertion, and happy to betray the band to the police or the army. Guevara himself described one group of Bolivian recruits as "two deserters, one prisoner 'who talked,' three quitters and two weaklings."[6]

Not the Sierra Maestra

Guevara tried to re-create the campaign of the Sierra Maestra, following his theories of revolution based upon that struggle. Unfortunately for him, while he encountered many of the same conditions as in Cuba, an extremely important one was missing: a sympathetic population. Unlike the Sierra Maestra, campesinos did not flock to the rebel colors. Guevara himself could see as early as mid-April that much of the rural population was more than apathetic in regard to the guerrillas; rather, it was frightened and hostile—"terrorized," as he put it—by the band's presence, an observation that occurs again and again in his diary.[7] The Indians of southeastern Bolivia found the bearded guerrillas outlandish, as many of them literally were, and in what must have been a bitter irony for Guevara, sometimes called them "Gringos" because of their peculiar speech. Although many campesinos spoke Spanish in addition to their native Indian languages, they did not speak it with Cuban or Argentinean accents.[8]

The population was thin in the area in which Guevara operated. Living in rugged, difficult terrain that was unable to support many inhabitants at the best of times, it had been decimated by plague, endemic in the area, a few years before he arrived. Consequently, few recruits were available. Further complicating the situation for Guevara, the region's campesinos, less sophisticated and politicized than their counterparts on the Altiplano and in the Cochabamba Valley, had little understanding of the central government and little feeling for or against it. President Barrientos once told a visiting U.S. general that his greatest political problem was to persuade his countrymen that such a nation as Bolivia existed with a capital called La Paz. Nowhere did national identity have less impact than among the Indians of the southeast. They considered government representatives to be foreigners and regarded them with the same deep suspicion with which they viewed any other strangers. Although they collaborated with the army constantly throughout the guerrilla episode, informed observers, including Charles Grover, the chief political officer at the U.S. embassy, believe that they may have done so occasionally from coercion but principally as a means of freeing them-selves of both soldiers and guerrillas. Furthermore, given the two sets of interlopers, the soldiers seemed less foreign and less threatening.[9]

Had Guevara tried to appeal to the miners, among whom disaffection was rampant and who continued to have bloody clashes with the government, he might have found greater support. Had he headquartered his band near the mines, however, it would have faced much greater danger, especially without the protection of mountains and jungles. As one CIA official pointed out, the government could and often did mass troops in the high, arid mining areas, and it would surely have liquidated his small guerrilla force very quickly had he placed it there.[10]

Once, stopping just outside Muyupampa, a small town in southern Bolivia, Guevara and part of his band met with the village leaders—the subprefect, the doctor, and the priest. The guerrillas pointed out that they were fighting for a "total change in the present structure" and asked for food and medicine. The civic leaders, fearful for the town's safety, agreed to deliver the supplies that afternoon at an agreed-upon time and place. When the time came, the air force bombed the delivery site instead. Some accounts of this event maintain that the civilian leaders did not willingly betray the guerrillas but that military units in the town forced them to change their strategy. Nevertheless, according to Bolivian news reports, the city had organized a volunteer force of some 100 men to stand guard at night, and a similar force was organized at nearby Monteagudo, which suggests that the local populations did indeed fear the intruders.[11]

These units seem to have been something a joke militarily. Guevara, who encountered one near Muyupampa on April 19, said, "One of these, with two M-3s and two revolvers, surprised our outposts but the patrol surrendered without presenting combat." Furthermore, if the guerrillas were unpopular, so, too, were some of the "home guard" groups. A campesino unit formed in Cochabamba, which proceeded to Camiri, so worried the local populace that the citizens complained to the army about its presence. Moreover, the Bolivian Army found them of little military value, but General Alfredo Ovando Candia, armed forces chief of staff, said it tolerated them for political reasons. He did not elaborate, but Grover believes he may have meant to avoid offending the campesinos, especially from Cochabamba, who formed an important element in Barrientos's political coalition.[12] But whatever their drawbacks, these groups were another indication that Guevara's message of the need for revolution was not convincing its audience, if, in fact, most of that audience ever even heard the message.

Rumblings in the Backlands

Vague rumors of an incipient guerrilla uprising in the southeast had been floating around Bolivia since at least late 1966. They filtered into the U.S. embassy through the military attachés and the CIA station, according to Ambassador Henderson. The embassy received reports of people in the hinterlands speaking a peculiar brand of Spanish and heard names that were the same as Castro's confederates, including "Guevara." "Well, there are lots of Guevara's in Bolivia," Henderson added, "and a number of them are known revolutionaries of one kind or another." One of these was Moisés Guevara, head of a radical communist faction, who cooperated closely with Che Guevara, provided recruits, took part in his jungle operations, and died in action.[13]

Early in March, well before the first ambush, rumors reaching the Bolivian government became somewhat more specific: Something very peculiar was going on in southeastern Bolivia, near the Ñancahuazú River. A guerrilla named Marcos, returning from a training march, stopped at a government oil-pumping station and, making the unlikely claim that he was a Mexican engineer, tried to buy food, meanwhile letting his weapon be seen. Thereupon, a suspicious employee followed him much of the way back to the guerrillas' camp. Several days later, Marcos and his group were spotted again, this time from the air. Furthermore, according to Barrientos at least, on March 12 and 13 Indians in the south of the country reported seeing a strange group of bearded men. Barrientos said they reported this to him personally. Although American officials tended to be skeptical of the entire story, it seems very likely that Indian campesino informants brought in some of the earliest reports of Guevara's group to various Bolivian authorities. At first Barrientos and his military commanders doubted that there was much to these stories, expecting at most to find smugglers, probably of narcotics. In fact, on January 19, police arrived at a part of Guevara's encampment looking for the "cocaine factory." They searched a house there, took the pistol of one of the guerrillas, and warned him that "they knew everything."[14]

A day or so before Guevara returned from a long march on which he reconnoitered the area, Bolivian armed forces reached a house at the edge of his encampment. Reminiscent of his headquarters in the Sierra Maestra, the encampment by then had become an enormous settlement of interconnected hubs, complete with a field kitchen, bakery, butchery, infirmary, dormitories, and defensive entrenchments.[15] Searching the area around the house, the soldiers discovered man-made caves that contained suitcases and satchels filled with personal belongings— mostly clothes, some of which, they noted, were made in Cuba and Mexico. In addition, they found a few folders with notes concerning Quechua, apparently part of the group's effort to learn that language, though the predominant Indian language in that region was Guaraní.[16] The soldiers made off with what they found, and the guerrillas, when they returned from their march, failed to understand what had happened. The disappearance of the stashed items immediately became a source of bickering and confusion. One of the guerrillas, Harry Villegas Tamayo (code-named Pombo), recorded on March 21: "We are having a problem with the things we were keeping in reserve. Nato does not know where the things in the caves have been put and accuses Antoio [*sic*] and Marcos of having taken them out. They in turn accuse him."[17]

The find led the Bolivians to conclude correctly that they had an international cabal of some kind on their hands but also to conclude incorrectly that it consisted of various groups spread out over a wide area in southern Bolivia, more than 100 miles in length.[18] Within a few weeks, the guerrillas abandoned the encampment, and the Bolivian Army, discovering the site's entire scope, became surer than ever that it faced many hundreds of insurgents.[19]

On March 15, Bolivian authorities' suspicions that they had a political insurrection on their hands were confirmed. That day, they arrested two men who they noticed were making "unduly generous offers" for food supplies and, according to a U.S. embassy report, attempting to sell a .22-caliber rifle. Under interrogation the following day, the two, who were Bolivian deserters from Guevara's force, described the band—very accurately, as we now know from Guevara's Bolivian diary. Among other things, the men stated that the band had ample but unspecified arms and plenty of funds and that Guevara led it, although oddly they said that they had never seen him. Corroborating the captives' remarks, Bolivian Army sources felt certain they could hear coded radio transmissions from the presumed guerrilla area. Considering all of the available evidence, the Bolivians believed the prisoners' testimony to be accurate, with one important exception: Barrientos did not believe that

Guevara was involved. The Americans doubted the entire story.[20] On March 17, the army captured a Bolivian guerrilla sentry near the camp. He also provided information and completed the undistinguished trio— "two deserters, one prisoner"—mentioned scornfully in Guevara's diary.[21]

Guevara, still on maneuvers with part of his band, knew nothing of the arrests for four days. When he heard of them, he learned also that a six-man unit had attacked "the farm," as he called a part of his camp. Also at about this time, according to Bolivian reports, one guerrilla was killed and two captured. If these reports are accurate, the actions must have occurred in the raid on the farm. In addition, Guevara states that on March 20 one of his men killed a soldier somewhere in the area, possibly in the same attack.

Obviously, the two sides by now were coming into contact and beginning to take casualties. As they did, Guevara encouraged his men to be bold and seek combat, angry that the rear guard he had left at the farm pulled out in the face of a very light Bolivian assault. At the same time, army units began probing cautiously to ascertain guerrilla positions, while small surveillance aircraft buzzed over Guevara's camp and the surrounding areas.[22]

In La Paz, Panic and Opportunism

From the moment it heard about the captured guerrillas, even before the March 23 ambush, the Bolivian government began a relentless campaign for greater U.S. assistance to its armed forces. On their side, the Americans, especially Ambassador Henderson, remained openly skeptical throughout the insurgency that the Bolivians needed anything like the armament they requested, including high-performance aircraft and napalm. Furthermore, it quickly seemed clear to them that Barrientos's top military commanders were putting him under enormous pressure to use the emergency to upgrade their equipment. As the weeks rolled by and the rebellion persisted, however, the Bolivian president and his high command really seem to have doubted their ability to control the problem without significant help.

The first appeal to the Americans was limited, but that approach lasted for less than a day. With the defection of the two guerrillas on March 15, Barrientos called Henderson at once, who went to the presidential residence with his deputy and military attaché. There, the president and his aides relayed the prisoners' description of the guerrilla band, which Barrientos assumed was engaged mainly in a feint to embroil his armed forces in a debilitating struggle in remote, difficult terrain, while urban guerrillas struck in the cities and the mines. While this was certainly a reasonable assumption, it nevertheless was quite wrong.[23] Guevara had nothing close to the resources to carry out such a plan, and the orthodox Communist Party, whose cooperation might have made a scheme like that feasible, had broken with him several months earlier.

Barrientos first made relatively modest requests. He asked Henderson to warn the governments of Paraguay and Argentina of the danger, to provide communications gear for his armed forces, and to supply equipment capable of locating guerrilla radio transmitters. Meanwhile, despite a crippling inability to communicate, the army nevertheless continued cautious probing in the jungle, reporting that two of its squads were trailing a half day behind elements of the guerrilla band. Henderson took the whole story "with some reserve," as he told Washington, but still he agreed to Barrientos's requests. Regarding the radio-locator equipment, he decided to search locally before "calling for further USG [U.S. government] help," undoubtedly looking among the resources of the U.S. MILGP and the CIA station.[24]

But before that day ended, Barrientos's modest requests proved to be the beginning of an avalanche. That evening, he told Henderson that Bolivia needed financial support. Although the embassy still called the group in the wilderness "alleged guerrillas," Bolivian officials expressed no doubts about them, putting their number at 150 to 200 men. But despite the Bolivians' concern, Henderson remained the skeptic. The Bolivians had produced no evidence that a threat existed, he said, and even if it did, Bolivian armed forces as then constituted should have been able to handle it. He relented only to the degree of saying rather bureaucratically that if the Bolivians would "specify and justify their requirements in writing" the U.S. government would give them "further consideration."[25] Cold comfort, but it did not cool Barrientos's determination to get U.S. aid.

The next evening, Barrientos called Henderson to his residence twice. During the course of these sessions, he revealed with startling frankness that he really viewed the guerrilla problem less in terms of jungle warfare than of political infighting, especially with unhappy generals.

Surprisingly, he estimated the guerrilla strength at no more than 16 but said that his armed forces were under severe budget restraints; he hoped that U.S. contributions might ease the pinch. Henderson then received a list signed by the minister of defense that called for an enormous amount "of soft and hard goods to clothe and maintain 1,500 additional reservists . . . and arm [a] sizeable force for extended combat operations." The list included ammunition for 90 days for nine types of weapons from M-1 rifles to 75-millimeter howitzers, 400 parachutes, 100 radios, 10 weapons carriers, and 20 jeeps, among other items.

Henderson promised only that his military advisers would study the request, but his message about the incident to the State Department reveals a great deal about the situation in Bolivia, about Henderson himself, and about U.S. relations with client states in that era. He said:

> Barrientos had previously conveyed to me the fairly clear impression that he was not too happy to see his military take advantage of every reported emergency situation to come up with a Santa Claus list to present to the USG. The following is one not untenable hypothesis which could explain why I got the list anyway. Faced with military leaders who include persons notable for obtuseness and naivete and who are getting increasingly restive under the firm budget limitations put on them by the courageous finance minister, Barrientos simply decided it was necessary for him to shift as much of the military pressure as possible from himself to us by handing over the Christmas list to me in front of a witness [Minister of Government Antonio Arguedas]. His judgement on this may be sound so far as his own position is concerned, but [the] Bolivian military will have to learn that the kind of irresponsibility shown here can have adverse consequences. It would be most helpful if Washington could impress this on Bolivian ambassador Sanjines and on General Ovando, if still available. [Ovando was visiting Washington.][26]

Henderson then sent the list to Washington three days later in the diplomatic pouch, the slowest possible way.

But the Bolivians had no intention of letting things end there. If Henderson's military advisers were studying their requests, then the Bolivians would turn their persuasive abilities on the advisers; thus, the advisers, too, were called in repeatedly to meet with the Bolivian commanders, and they, too, told the Bolivians to "submit requirements in writing." One of the Bolivian requests was to use T-28 aircraft borrowed from the United States and several months overdue for return, plus a supply of antipersonnel bombs.[27] The Bolivian focus on the advisers did not mean Henderson was forgotten by any means, nor for that matter was his deputy, John W. Fisher, who unluckily caught a call from Barrientos once when Henderson was absent. An adamant Barrientos warned sternly of Bolivia's needs. He had visited the guerrilla area and found the situation far worse than he had expected. He did not elaborate except to say there were many more guerrillas than the 16 he estimated originally. The government planned to send 300 troops to the region as soon as possible, he said, and asked in a "peremptory" way whether or not the U.S. government would provide the requested items. Fisher temporized, saying his government was studying the request, needed approvals, these things take time, and so on. Barrientos replied simply that every minute counted.[28]

When reporting the encounter to Washington, the embassy stated frankly, "We are as unconvinced of the validity of the alleged threat and the requirement for US assistance as before," and it speculated that Barrientos was simply responding to pressure from his military chiefs "to get more from the US while the getting is good." But Fisher raised another subject that quickly reverberated between Washington and the embassy with significant effect on the U.S. response to Guevara's rebellion. He said that to establish the facts "on the ground," the Americans would send two officers there, adding that they would go out of uniform to avoid attention.

Explosion in Washington

Out of the numerous meetings the U.S. diplomats and military advisers had with the Bolivians came the inescapable conclusion that they all needed more information about the guerrillas. Consequently, a unit of about 100 men trained in antiguerrilla warfare that had been receiving U.S. equipment would reinforce the army contingent in the guerrilla area, almost doubling it. Meanwhile, MILGP representatives, as Fisher had said, would accompany it into the area and once there see for themselves what was going on. We shall return to the issue of the observers but first should note that the Bolivian armed forces chief of staff added one more request, this one very mundane. He wanted field rations for the new unit while it operated in the area. Many Bolivian contingents still relied upon field kitchens, providing a low level of nutrition for the soldiers and limiting their mobility in antiguerrilla operations, a unit being able to patrol only as far as it could go and still get back for lunch or dinner. All parties in Bolivia, including Barrientos, approved of these plans.[29]

Washington, however, did not. The ambassador had to fight bitterly to get the field rations, threatening to resign, and eventually going to the chief of Southern Command, General Robert W. Porter, Jr., to back his request. The Pentagon did not see itself as a caterer, and field rations were not among the items it sent under military-assistance programs. It saw no reason to change for the sake of Bolivia. Although, under steady pressure, it gave in by the end of the month, the Pentagon's irritation radiates even through official telegraphic language when finally and grudgingly it informed the embassy through the State Department that, considering the urgency of the situation, it agreed to the request; the rations were on their way from Southern Command.[30]

The suggestion that U.S. personnel would accompany Bolivian troops into the combat area, however, became a much more serious issue. The embassy and especially the MILGP felt sure that the Bolivians were deliberately exaggerating the danger to justify requests for preposterous kinds and amounts of weapons. But how could they be sure? The obvious answer was to have a look themselves, sending trained soldiers from the advisory group. The head of the group, U.S. Air Force colonel Lawrence E. Horras, states that he was the one who proposed sending the two observers, soldiers who had once been Green Berets. Henderson agreed, reluctantly some say. Consequently, the idea surfaced again in a communication to Washington. A paragraph in a cable discussing the overall situation consisted of one innocuous-sounding sentence: "Milgrp [*sic*] will perform standard MAP inspection in reported guerrilla area beginning March 27"—that is, six days later. According to Henderson, Acting Assistant Secretary for Inter-American Affairs Robert M. Sayre sent the message to Secretary Dean Rusk. It caused a tornado. Meanwhile, on March 24, the day after the first ambush of Bolivian soldiers, the U.S. officers arrived in Camiri, the site of an army divisional headquarters near the disputed area.[31]

Soon after the message went to Rusk, the State Department's Bolivian desk officer placed a breathless call to La Paz. "Don't ask any questions," Henderson remembers him saying; "if you haven't sent them, don't; if you have, get them back." Next, Horras received a stern letter of reprimand from General Porter. Horras's personnel thereafter were confined almost totally to La Paz, Cochabamba, and Santa Cruz, able to go to Camiri for only limited periods and with special permission; they were not allowed to go anywhere in the "guerrilla area." The new rules particularly galled Horras, especially as he felt that his staff could have trained the Bolivians to handle the insurgency without importing a team of Green Berets, as the U.S. government eventually did. From the time of the reprimand, however, he and his group had little to do with checking the guerrillas, permitted mainly to watch while the Green Berets stole the show. A few months later, Horras—a highly decorated flying officer who started his service during World War II, had received several wounds, and survived almost miraculously—was removed from his post and retired the following year.[32]

Worried about Americans being hurt, killed, or kidnapped and thereby deepening U.S. involvement, the State Department quickly sent Henderson clear orders to keep all U.S. personnel, even members of the Peace Corps but particularly of the armed forces, out of the possible zone of combat. "They did not want another Vietnam-type operation," Henderson said later.[33] In fact, the department shot off a flurry of stern telegrams to La Paz while the initial howl from Washington about the observers was still echoing in the embassy. The cables called forth nervous explanations. For example, Henderson pointed out that he authorized the two officers to spend a few days in the zone simply on a standard inspection; furthermore, they were coming out at once and would not be replaced. Two days later, Washington again snapped at the embassy for even suggesting that U.S. personnel undertake certain rearechelon activities as well as occasional daytime reviews of patrol posts. "U.S. military personnel should not repeat not be in any operational areas," Sayre pronounced unambiguously.

But what area should be banned—where and how many square miles? These became crucial issues, especially as no one knew exactly where the guerrillas operated, how many of them there were, or how widely they were spread out. Responding to the embassy, whose irritation at being managed and scolded by Washington glowed through its polite Foreign Service cablese, Patrick Morris, director of Bolivia/Chile affairs, and his chief, Sayre, patiently, almost patronizingly, provided guidelines. To determine if an area should be in or out of the proscribed zone, ask these questions, they said: Would the individuals involved be in danger? Would the United States be embarrassed if their presence in the area became known? If the operation failed, would the United States be blamed? Would it be possible to distinguish between training advice and operational advice? Finally, the department pointedly reminded the embassy that U.S. personnel had not been assigned within operational areas in other countries where guerrillas were active (meaning only in Latin America presumably, obviously not Southeast Asia).

By the end of the first week in April, the zone had been defined: an area starting south of Santa Cruz and extending to, and including, Camiri. The embassy regretted the inclusion of Camiri, headquarters of Bolivian units trying to cope with the insurgency and a point from which news reporters had begun to cover the story. Nevertheless, U.S. military representatives there, six in all, were "hastily withdrawn."[34]

As anticipated, the major frustration in maintaining the "no-go" area stemmed from the dearth of reliable information about the guerrilla band. The two observers, during their brief mission, had sent back valuable reports, among other things convincing the embassy that a guerrilla band indeed existed and that the Bolivians needed help in coping with it.[35] But more information was needed, especially as speculation about the band's size and movements appeared repeatedly in the media, and Bolivian military estimates of guerrilla strength, patently inflated, continued to be reported to the embassy. The embassy kept pushing to find out the truth, requesting permission, for example, for representatives of its MILGP to go just to Camiri, far from any known guerrilla activity, and just for a few days.

Furthermore, intelligence was only part of the problem. The Bolivian units in the area could not use the equipment the Americans had provided, especially communications gear; in addition, according to the press and returned visitors, confusion reigned within the supply and command functions at Camiri. Consequently, the embassy received permission to send U.S. military advisers there, at first only after receiving case by case permission from Washington, but soon the rules were relaxed slightly. Advisers could go at the ambassador's discretion, but only after consulting with the chief of Southern Command.[36]

No South American Vietnam!

On May 5, the Pentagon drafted and the State Department approved a statement that guided the U.S. military response to the insurgency throughout its duration. The following are the two most significant paragraphs:

2. USSOUTHCOM [Southern Command] regulations make clear that US military personnel are not authorized to assist host country military personnel or units which are actively engaged in counterinsurgency combat operations against armed insurgents.

3. Advisory activities by US military personnel are intended to *prepare* host country military personnel or units to carry out combat and related support operations. US military personnel must be careful to avoid the assumption, either directly or indirectly, of functions that should be performed by Bolivian military personnel *during the conduct* of counterinsurgency combat operations and related support activities. (emphasis in original)[37]

Although at times Washington may have seemed overcautious and occasionally sanctimonious regarding the "no-go" area, in principle there was no disagreement. Charles Grover, says Henderson realized intuitively that the guerrilla leader, whether Guevara or not, wanted the United States enmeshed in a Vietnam-style conflict. "He wasn't going to fall into that trap," said Grover; "he was going to compel the Bolivians to . . . be out front." British journalist Richard Gott also recalls Henderson telling him Bolivia would become a second Vietnam "over his dead body" and that not a single U.S. Marine would come there to fight if he could help it.[38]

The question of military involvement had always been a sensitive one for Henderson, who frequently had prickly relations with the U.S. military, whether in Bolivia, Panama, or Washington. Patrick Morris remembers "a lot of real friction" between Southern Command and the ambassador, who, he said, "was always on the military mission; if it wasn't one thing it was another, and the military mission was always complaining to SouthCom about the ambassador." Morris said whenever he went to Bolivia or Chile, he had to spend one day in Panama "to hear all the complaints from Porter about our ambassadors in both countries. . . . I think there was turf involved to some extent."[39]

Grover recalls that in that era, the "U.S. military had all kinds of fancy gear because it came out of the Vietnam engagement," remembering particularly some air-force officers whose uniforms included cowboy-style hats. Henderson, who found well over 100 U.S. military personnel in Bolivia when he arrived, worked hard to keep their numbers down so that, in Grover's words, their "flamboyance didn't become overwhelming."[40]

With the Americans still trying to determine the scope of the guerrilla operation, the Bolivian foreign minister called in the ambassadors from Brazil, Paraguay, and Argentina to warn them of the danger; it stemmed from a band of some 70 guerrillas with modern arms, he said. Shortly thereafter, Bolivia's vice president, Luiz Adolfo Siles Salinas, passing through Buenos Aires, reiterated the warning in the chambers of the Argentine foreign office, but he almost doubled the number of guerrillas, to 130, and claimed they used modern communications equipment. But at home for public consumption, the Bolivian government denied that a guerrilla force existed, a hard position to maintain especially after the international news media had discovered the story. On March 21, for example, United Press International (UPI) reported a skirmish in which one Bolivian soldier was killed and three captured. UPI speculated that the guerrillas, whom it said were well armed, were entering Bolivia through Paraguay and being directed by radio from Cuba. In its public response, the Bolivian government grumbled that the guerrillas "existed only in the imagination of the press."[41]

Bolivia's neighbors, especially Argentina, took the warnings very seriously. The Argentine government alerted its border guards and at the same time wondered how it could possibly identify guerrillas dispersed throughout its wilder border areas. With reports of the band continuing, concern in Buenos Aires mounted swiftly as the government there recalled an insurgency only three years before in a remote northwest region of the country. That uprising had taken place not far from the present guerrilla area and had been led by Guevara's friend and colleague, Jorge Masetti, and backed by Cuba. Government forces defeated the rebels and killed Masetti, but now it seemed that that had not ended the matter. Here again was the same thing apparently flaring up on Argentina's doorstep. The Argentine government had no confidence in the Bolivian Army whatsoever and wanted to send its own contingents into the guerrilla region at once. The American ambassador in Buenos Aires, Edwin Martin, had to calm both the government and the army, assuring them that after the Green Berets arrived in Bolivia everything would be all right. While they could understand and sympathize with Argentine fears, policymakers in Washington, just like Henderson in La Paz, wanted to be sure that this did not become a high-profile international battle in the middle of South America.[42]

Henderson Implacable: No Flashy Hardware

When the two Bolivian deserters told authorities about Guevara's band, the local army command, deciding to smash the group quickly, fell directly into the guerrillas' March 23 ambush. When it did, Bolivian calls for extensive U.S. assistance became shrill. American officials trekked repeatedly to the Barrientos residence to hear the same message: "Give us the supplies we have asked for."

But the Americans would not. They continued to believe most of the requests were simply a ploy by the Bolivian armed forces, using the insurgency to get exciting new military gadgetry. In addition, they still believed that with limited assistance the Bolivians could handle the guerrillas; what was more, they believed that the Bolivians knew they could. Finally, they had been after the Bolivians for several years to permit a Green Beret team to come there to help develop a really crack ranger battalion. The Bolivians had resisted, probably because with the country's fragile political system, the unit could quickly become a dangerous political force. When the Green Berets finally did come and develop a new ranger battalion, its recruits were enlisted only for the duration of the crisis; the Bolivian government disbanded them the year after Guevara's death.[43]

The day after the ambush, Barrientos, again calling in U.S. officials, estimated guerrilla strength at 150, adding that one 45-man army unit seemed to be surrounded and in danger of being cut off, a complete fantasy. Meanwhile, troop strength in and around Camiri had been bolstered to a total of 300 men. The decision to call up 1,500 reservists, however, was reversed, despite the fact that the Bolivian Army had a dearth of experienced soldiers. It consisted of 6,200 brand-new conscripts supplemented by only 1,500 men who had served for more than a year.[44]

William Broderick, deputy director of the State Department's Office of Bolivia/Chile Affairs, visited La Paz in March 1967 and remembers vividly one of the meetings with Barrientos, a breakfast featuring "cold fried eggs and misinformation." The president was accompanied by his top military officer, General Ovando, plus a young soldier who told "a fantastic story" about being captured by the guerrillas and held for a few hours after several hundred guerrillas surrounded and captured his unit. They had special pills to satisfy hunger and doctors and nurses to care for anyone who was injured. "We heard the story," Broderick said, and then "the generals looked at us and we looked at each other and the generals said, 'Well, what do you think?' We tried to keep from laughing."

Broderick pointed out later that Washington had provided "some kind of CIA [financial] assistance to Bolivia in periods there," including the Paz Estenssoro presidency, when Barrientos was vice president. These

payments, totally separate from AID's budgetary support, possibly were
in Barrientos's mind during those meetings in March 1967, for it was in
the course of one of these that he proposed something new: direct budgetary assistance for the armed forces in addition to the items on the
"Santa Claus list." The request was "distasteful" to Barrientos, Henderson believed, saying that he beat about the bush for nearly an hour, talking about the latest rumors, reports, and speculations about the guerrillas, before broaching it.[45]

For his pains, the president received an "educational talk" from Henderson, who saw the request as "an emotional-political appeal for more
U.S. grant aid in unspecified amounts to keep his military happy." The
Bolivian Ministry of Defense had wasted resources already available to
it, Henderson told him. For example, after two years of urging, it still replaced most of its army every year, losing its training investment, while
ignoring a U.S. military study on money-saving reforms. He reminded
the president that "extraordinary efforts" had been made to provide $1
million in U.S. funds to control subversion in the mining district, but the
Bolivian government's performance fell "considerably short of its commitments and of reasonable expectations." Barrientos should see if he
could get support from neighboring countries, the ambassador suggested, meaning surely financial support or matériel, not military intervention.[46]

But this was more than just an emergency, Barrientos stressed; it was
a conflict in which Bolivia was "helping to fight for the U.S." He made
his case vigorously, but the whole conversation, Henderson thought,
was a humiliation for him. Still, Barrientos preferred the humiliation to
the consequences of not "sweeten[ing] the armed forces budget to their
taste." Furthermore, he seemed to be suffering "some genuine anguish
over the sad spectacle" of his military's performance against the guerrillas. In reporting this conversation to the State Department, Henderson
repeated an earlier warning that Barrientos might attempt to end-run the
U.S. embassy in La Paz and turn directly to "the lobbying talent of Ambassador Sanjines in Washington," something Henderson worried about
constantly during the guerrilla episode.[47]

Throughout the guerrilla era, and at other times as well, Henderson
followed a nannyish mode of diplomacy common among American ambassadors in much of the Third World, certainly in Latin America, during the Cold War years. One key official concerned with Bolivian affairs
said of him, "He was always giving the Bolivians lectures about what

they should do and what they shouldn't do . . . and since we were really their lifeline they couldn't protest. But it all seemed to me to be completely unnecessary. I don't think he endeared himself to any Bolivians." But the same official characterized the Bolivian response to the guerrilla crisis as "Gee, this is another way we can get more money out of the United States. Here we've got Che Guevara in our country, that ought to be worth something." Most official Americans involved believed this to some degree about the Bolivians, which helps explain Henderson's attitude.[48]

Who Was Henderson?

Whatever his style, Henderson was one of two American officials most responsible for the defeat of Che Guevara. (The other was Major Ralph "Pappy" Shelton, the leader of the Green Beret detachment.) Henderson was a career Foreign Service officer, born in Weston, Massachusetts, now a Boston suburb, in a house partially built by his carpenter father and in which Henderson now lives in retirement. His father joined the army to fight in the Philippine insurrection of 1899–1902 and again to take part in the Mexican border campaign of 1916, when Henderson was two years old. From Mexico he went to France to fight in World War I. He spoke often of other cultures, and although he "had a rather redneck attitude toward them," says Henderson, "he stirred my interest." His mother in turn stirred his interest in reading, much as Guevara's mother had influenced him. An uncle who spent many years in Latin America as a mining engineer stimulated Henderson's fascination with that particular area.

Henderson attended public elementary and high schools, then worked at various odd jobs—hospital orderly, rum-bottling plant employee, and apple picker—for four years. He was a gasoline-station attendant when a high-school teacher convinced him to try to go to college and helped him get a scholarship to Boston University. At the suggestion of a professor there, he went on to do graduate work on a fellowship at the Fetcher School of Law and Diplomacy at Tufts University. In 1941, he took the Foreign Service examination and was notified that he passed on the day before the Japanese attacked Pearl Harbor.

The State Department interceded with Henderson's draft board to have him excused from military service, then sent him to a series of consular jobs in small Latin American cities: Nogales, Mexico; Africa, Chile; and Cochabamba, Bolivia. In Bolivia, he rubbed bureaucratic fur the wrong way for the first of many times. When, for example, the ambassador in La Paz politely asked him how things were going in Cochabamba, he told him in detail—problems, frustrations, everything. The ambassador replied, quoting Charles Talleyrand: "Young gentleman, above all, not too much zeal." Later, the deputy chief of mission advised him to "take problems a little easier. . . . Ambassador Flack does not like excitement."[49]

Henderson was assigned next to Washington, where in response to his request to develop his interest in economics he was loaned to the American Republics branch of the Department of Commerce. In many ways, it seems to have been the happiest and most successful time of his career. His private papers make clear that he reveled in the work, doing the intellectual, analytical tasks that were his forte. During this time, he helped draft point 4 of President Harry Truman's 1948 inaugural address, subsequently transformed into the famous Point 4 Program of technical assistance to developing nations. Henderson's superiors were delighted with his performance.

After the Commerce Department, Henderson served in economic assignments in Switzerland and in the State Department in Washington, then spent a year in a top-level training course called the Senior Seminar. From there, he went to Peru as the chief economics officer. Toward the end of the Peruvian assignment, when the ambassador was called away, Henderson took over the embassy as the chargé d'affaires, bringing him to the attention of the Kennedy administration and leading to his appointment in 1963 as ambassador to Bolivia. By then, his was a life spun from the American dream, which for the purpose of legend made him the perfect opponent to Guevara, the staunch Americaphobe. Nevertheless, although Guevara must have known who the American ambassador was, there is no evidence so far that he gave him a moment's thought.

Henderson began his tour in Bolivia with a confrontation with the president, then Víctor Paz Estenssoro. When Henderson arrived in La Paz in 1964, four Americans from the embassy staff along with some German engineers and Bolivian supervisors were being held hostage in a room over the dynamite warehouse at a major Bolivian tin mine. Their captors were determined to release them only in exchange for two mineworker leaders arrested by the police. After presenting his credentials to the president in the courtly language of diplomatic ceremonies, Henderson finished his remarks by saying, "I have to inform your government that my government will hold your government responsible for the lives and property of its citizens now being held hostage in your country."

Paz Estenssoro was already working on the problem, and so was the new Johnson administration, which considered a rescue mission using Green Berets in helicopters until someone calculated that, at the altitude they would need to fly over the Bolivian mountains, each copter could at most carry one passenger. The actual escape, as Henderson recalls it, was much quieter and more bizarre. Several of his aides and the Catholic cardinal of La Paz held a conference with the miners at the mine, and while they met, Charles Thomas, the embassy consular officer, found the hostages unguarded and simply walked out with them. Whether or not it was quite that easy, the captives were released as a result of the conference, and Henderson was off to a flying start as an ambassador.[50]

Henderson once had the temerity to question an order from Robert Kennedy via the Special Group and even won his case, at least in the short run. In career terms, he was probably more courageous than canny. Bolivia by 1964 had a place on the Special Group's list of endangered countries, and in such cases the group required embassies to report on the local communist threat every three months. Then, if the group believed the danger severe enough, it would take steps to help the control the situation. Believing that the Cuban government routinely sent materials to guerrillas in Peru through Bolivia via the Amazon River system, Henderson requested certain items, including small boats, to check that traffic. Because the group denied his request, he says he decided that "if this program can't provide me with what I say is necessary for achievement of my objectives then I don't see any point to the program." Called on the carpet in Washington by Averell Harriman and Robert Kennedy among others, he stood his ground: Without the materials, the reports were pointless. Furthermore, although Bolivia appeared on the Special Group's list of countries endangered by red subversion, communism in fact posed little threat to Bolivian stability, he stressed, pointing out that he had suggested the boats and other items only to keep supplies from going to underground groups in neighboring Peru. A half hour of heated discussion resolved only that his reporting requirement could be reduced from quarterly to yearly, but the experience added to his growing impression that the State Department "is not inclined to back up its missions. It is more influenced by Washington considerations than field considerations in the establishment of policy." He was far from the first or the last field officer to reach that conclusion.[51]

Henderson's belief that communism presented little menace to Bolivian stability was not held universally in U.S. official circles. He does not remember the exact date of his meeting with Kennedy and Harriman, but it seems to have occurred in August or September 1964. In May 1965, the CIA's Office of Current Intelligence produced a memorandum entitled "Instability in Latin America" that ranked critical countries, placing Bolivia second after the Dominican Republic. Although in the intervening months, Barrientos and his military colleagues had toppled the civilian government, the new regime did not put at rest the minds of CIA analysts. They said that, "partly because of dissention among the military, the political situation is highly unstable and could degenerate promptly into civil war. Communists and leftist extremists are armed and determined not to permit a prolongation of the Barrientos regime."[52] As we now know, Barrientos held precisely this same view.

Despite his guerrilla mystique, Guevara's work as a diplomat, especially as an economic envoy, ranks among his main contributions to Cuba. He is seen here with Soviet premier Nikita Khrushchev during a trade mission to Moscow in 1960. (From the National Archives.)

Che Guevara listens drowsily to delegates at an OAS Economic and Social Council meeting at Punta del Este, Uruguay, in 1961. The conference helped give form to President Kennedy's Alliance for Progress, which Cuba derided. (From the National Archives.)

Since the outbreak of World War II, the U.S. military has fostered close ties with neighboring armed forces. Here, top Latin American officers in 1964 prepare to visit First Army headquarters at Governors Island, N.Y. (From the National Archives.)

Douglas Henderson, U.S. ambassador to Bolivia, played a key role in keeping the insurgency in Bolivia from becoming the new "Vietnam" that Guevara wanted it to be. (From the private collection of Douglas Henderson.)

Bolivia. Guevara's guerrilla band fought skirmishes with Bolivia's armed forces from Muyupampa in the south to Samaipata in the north. The Bolivian Army's Eighth Division headquarters and a CIA post were located in Santa

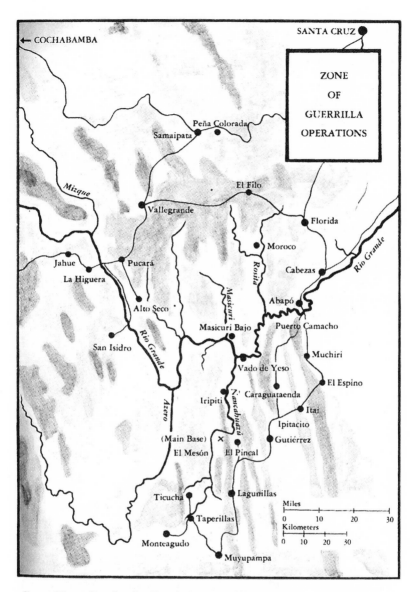

Cruz. (From *Death of a Revolutionary: Che Guevara's Last Mission*, by Richard Harris. Copyright © 1970 by W. W. Norton & Company, Inc. Reprinted by permission of W. W. Norton & Company, Inc.)

Guevara relaxes with fellow guerrillas in November 1966. In order to slip past Bolivian customs officials, he removed most of his hair and all of his beard and mustache, affected eyeglasses and a pipe, and arrived in neat, conservative business clothes. (From the National Archives.)

Bolivian president René Barrientos welcomes U.S. chief justice Earl Warren and his wife, Nina, to Bolivia in 1967. Barrientos cultivated the U.S. alliance even though it sometimes caused him domestic political problems. (From the private collection of Charles Grover.)

General Alfredo Ovando Candia, chief of Bolivia's armed forces, receives a decoration from U.S. Army chief of staff, General Harold K. Johnson, in March 1967, just as Bolivian authorities were discovering Guevara's insurgency. (From the National Archives.)

U.S. Air Force colonel Lawrence Horras, head of the U.S. Military Advisory Group, irritated General Robert W. Porter, Jr., chief of Southern Command, by sending U.S. soldiers into the guerrilla zone to determine what really was happening there. (From the private collection of Lawrence Horras.)

Major Ralph Shelton (*right*) led a Green Beret team in Bolivia. The team was prohibited from entering the guerrilla zone but trained the Bolivian 2nd Ranger Battalion, commanded by Lieutenant Colonel Miguel Ayoroa (*left*), which captured Guevara. (From the National Archives.)

General Robert W. Porter, Jr. (*in peaked cap*), inspects the Green Beret camp in Bolivia. He paid close attention to Guevara's insurgency, sometimes jumping the chain of command to work directly with Shelton. (From the National Archives.)

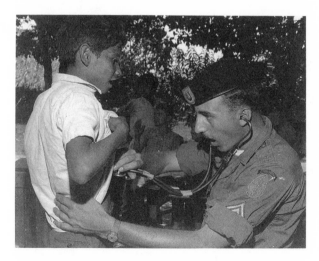

A Green Beret medic examines a Bolivian boy. Regular medical rounds among the civilian population were part of a Green Beret "civic action" program designed to keep the support of the local population. (From the National Archives.)

The Green Berets set up operations at an abandoned sugar mill near the tiny town of La Esperanza. A U.S. aid team working on a nearby road provided a bulldozer and other materials to build part of the camp, including the firing range. (From the National Archives.)

A U.S. captain instructs Bolivian soldiers in the use of a carbine. Bolivia's high command became impatient with prolonged Green Beret training, much preferring to receive U.S. weaponry, including the latest attack aircraft and napalm. (From the National Archives.)

Régis Debray (*left*), a well-connected French intellectual captured leaving Guevara's band, receives a prison visit from Monsignor Andrés Kennedy (*right*) in June 1967. Ambassador Henderson helped persuade the Bolivians not to execute Debray. (From the private collection of Charles Grover.)

Ciro Roberto Bustos, an Argentine revolutionary and artist who was captured with Debray, revealed that Guevara headed the guerrilla operation, drew portraits of him and his men, and made diagrams of their encampment for the Bolivian authorities. (From the private collection of Charles Grover.)

George Andrew Roth, a freelance writer-photographer, discovered Guevara's band, but when he tried to leave in the company of Debray and Bustos, Bolivian soldiers captured them all. Roth was held for over two months, then freed. (From the private collection of Charles Grover.)

U.S. Air Force colonel Ernest Nance, defense attaché to the embassy in La Paz, first informed Washington that Guevara had been captured, after a message from a CIA field agent on the spot failed to be distributed at headquarters. (From the private collection of Ernest Nance.)

Antonio Arguedas (*left*), Bolivian minister of government, and John Tilton (*right*), CIA station chief in La Paz, relax at a U.S. embassy reception. Later Arguedas sent Guevara's Bolivian diary to Castro, then announced he was a CIA operative. (From the private collection of Charles Grover.)

CHAPTER THREE

The Obstacles Accumulate

Guevara and his band were in difficult straits by the time they had
their first firefight with the Bolivian Army, although neither the Americans nor the Bolivians realized it. Food supplies were short, some of
Guevara's men had infected and swollen feet, some suffered from para-
sites. Guevara himself was weak, probably largely the result of his respiratory problems, and morale was low, especially among the Bolivians,
who felt they received second-class treatment. Discipline was becoming
an increasing problem, and worst of all, the local population, what little
there was, was not supportive.[1]

But one of Guevara's most serious problems was political. The uneasy alliance between the Americans and Bolivians was idyllic compared to Guevara's relationship with the Bolivian Communist Party and,
indirectly, with Moscow. The Kremlin had long entertained misgivings
about Havana's strident views of revolution, its determination that the
job of revolutionaries was to make revolution and not wait for favorable
conditions. Furthermore, Soviet leaders were certainly not looking for
confrontations with the United States in Latin America, a potential result of Havana's constant effort to export revolution to the rest of the
hemisphere. In addition, the Cuban implication that the Soviets and their
affiliates worldwide lacked revolutionary zeal was extremely annoying.
A Soviet official and scholar who has spent a lifetime working on Latin
American affairs said that the Communist Party leaders in the Soviet
Union and in parties around the world were used to being attacked from

the right and knew how to respond, but they found it devastating to be attacked from the left.[2]

Soviet leadership took an especially dim view of Guevara's mission to Bolivia, as noted in a CIA field report sent to President Johnson by Walt Rostow. Although the report itself remains classified, Rostow wrote this revealing note when he sent it to the president: "Herewith a fascinating report on a sharp exchange of letters between Castro and [Soviet Communist Party general secretary Leonid] Brezhnev over Castro's sending Guevara to Bolivia without consulting the Soviets. The exchange was one of the reasons for [Soviet premier Alexei] Kosygin going to Havana after Glassboro."[3] (Kosygin met with Johnson at Glassboro State College in New Jersey, June 23–25, 1967, to discuss world problems, especially the war in Vietnam and the crisis in the Middle East. Despite a lack of solutions, the meeting exuded a spirit of détente and improved relations, not at all compatible with a Soviet ally fomenting revolution in South America.)

Still, the Soviets, though not consulted, certainly had an idea that the Cubans were up to something unusual in Bolivia. The CIA claimed that the first secretary of the Moscow-line Bolivian Communist Party, Mario Monje, told the Cuban advance party that he had discussed their project with the Soviets, adding that they promised they "would consider giving their full support." In addition, the undertaking, or at least elements of it, was known in much of the communist world. According to CIA analysts, "Uruguayan communist leader Arismendi . . . had advance knowledge of the plan." Furthermore, government-run Czech and Soviet airlines transported the Cuban conspirators from Havana to Eastern Europe, whence they traveled on to Bolivia. Their administrators must have suspected something extraordinary was in the offing.[4] Finally, as we shall soon see, it is possible, although far from certain, that the KGB had a double agent among the Cuban network in La Paz, in which case the Kremlin had very good information about Cuba's revolutionary preparations in Bolivia.

Sending Guevara to Bolivia threw a challenge in the face of orthodox communism, just as Castro intended, determined as he was to demonstrate the validity of Cuban revolutionary premises and by comparison the sluggishness of the traditional parties. But certain as he and Guevara were of the correctness of their position, Cuban doctrine by 1966 desperately needed validation by a significant military victory, something they had been searching for since they marched into Santiago and Havana in 1959. As CIA analysts aptly put it, "Nothing short of a major success in continental revolution . . . could regain for Cuba its self-appointed role as the leader of the Latin American Communist movement and vanguard status in the 'liberation struggle.' " For that reason, Havana shifted its emphasis from the training and support of revolutionaries in neighboring countries to running an insurrection itself. As the CIA analysts said, "Apart from their disdain of the lethargic Marxist-Leninist parties," the Castro regime felt the need "to seize the initiative directly and provide the example of 'how to do it' in order to sustain revolutionary momentum." Guevara, who played such an influential role in developing Cuban revolutionary thought, was the logical commander because of his international prestige and "the myth of his invincibility among leftist circles in the hemisphere." In addition, the analysts pointed out, he had "seen service in Guatemala, Cuba, and the Congo" and had written a classic Latin American manual on guerrilla warfare.[5]

Reining in Castro

In November 1964, leaders of Latin American communist parties met in Havana at Soviet instigation, mostly to be corralled by the Kremlin into backing its positions vis-à-vis China. Cuban leaders, however, also came under considerable pressure to limit subversion to selected areas and to coordinate their efforts with local communist parties, which were facing dissention in their ranks because of Cuban meddling in their countries, including collaboration with splinter and even noncommunist groups. The local parties, not Castro, henceforth were to decide the major revolutionary issues within their borders, especially whether violent or nonviolent means were to be pursued.

Castro finally consented to restrict Cuban efforts at insurgency in Latin America to three countries—Venezuela, Guatemala, and Colombia—and also to stop aiding and abetting splinter communist groups. In return, the representatives from the other countries agreed that their parties would be more energetic in generating support for the Cuban regime. For example, they agreed to work for the restoration of diplomatic and trade relations between Cuba and the rest of the hemisphere, to expose "CIA-sponsored" subversion of the Cuban regime, and to propagandize the achievements of Castro's government. (Castro had once bitterly complained that the only communist party in the world to demonstrate solidarity after Cuba's humiliation in the 1962 missile crisis was the Venezuelan party, which blew up oil pipelines.)

It was a short honeymoon. Havana soon became restive under these restrictions and, according to the CIA, began "chipping away at the edges" of the agreement during 1965. Then, at the Tri-Continental Conference in Havana in 1966, Castro shook free of it completely and issued a resounding call for continental subversion through guerrilla warfare.[6]

Bolivia had long figured significantly in Cuban revolutionary calculations but at first mainly as a supporting area for action in adjacent countries. Soon, however, it emerged in Havana's planning as both the ignition point and the command post of a South American revolution as well as a training center for continental guerrilla activity. Geography played a prominent role in its selection. Besides the rugged topography of the steep, deeply cut mountain slopes that drop precipitately to midcontinental plains, the nation borders Argentina, Brazil, Peru, Chile, and Paraguay, where new insurrections could be kindled. Many observers believe further that the guerrilla camp's proximity to Argentina made the Bolivian location especially attractive to Guevara because he wanted particularly to see the revolution spread there. Furthermore, Havana believed the Barrientos regime, with its flimsy armed forces and its internal tensions, would be unable to cope with the insurgency.[7]

At this point, Mario Monje again entered the scene in a major way. He attended the 1966 Tri-Continental Conference in Havana, where he appears to have been informed, more than consulted, by Castro of his country's role in Cuba's great push for a continental conflagration. For the next year, he argued with Cuban authorities about what he had and had not promised Castro he would do for Guevara when the latter arrived in South America. In fact, after the whole rebellion ended disastrously, Monje claimed he never even knew it was being planned for Bolivia until the Cubans had already gone a long way toward starting it there. Castro, he maintained, had simply asked him to help Guevara set up an insurrection in Argentina. Régis Debray, who was deeply involved in making the Bolivian arrangements, concurs that originally Bolivia was simply to support revolutionary *focos* in Peru and Argentina. In the summer of 1966, however, Havana concluded that conditions favored Bolivia itself as the *foco*. Monje's central committee, however, had very little intention of being involved in an armed rebellion in their own country and absolutely no intention of being involved in one run by

Cubans. Meanwhile, Guevara's advance team, ensconced in Bolivia by July 1966, was pressing Monje to supply the 20 men they said he had promised them, whereas he claimed he had only promised four. Furthermore, he said they were for an insurrection in Argentina, not Bolivia.[8]

Monje's party obviously held him responsible in large measure for the fact that Cubans were preparing a war in Bolivia, which the party awoke to with a shock during the summer of 1966. Monje's colleagues in the party felt that he should have known Havana's intentions from the start, if indeed he had not. In addition, although he denied it, they suspected Monje may have made careless promises in Havana about the number of men he could provide for the insurgency, regardless of where he thought it would be. Whatever he said, he now found himself torn, his central committee pulling one way and Guevara's advance men another. Finally, after wrangling with the Cubans in Bolivia, Monje flew again to Havana in late November or early December. There, according to a four-and-a-half-page explanation of his conduct that he sent to his central committee, Castro agreed that the revolution should be led by Bolivians; work it out with Guevara, he said. Healthy skepticism is certainly advised here, but we have only Monje's account.[9]

Following his meeting with Castro, Monje's central committee gave him two alternatives: Bring Guevara under party control or give up your post. With that mandate, Monje had an extremely lively meeting with Guevara on New Year's Eve. Guevara described Monje's arrival as "cordial but tense. . . . The question: Why are you here? was in the air." That was soon answered: Monje wanted overall leadership of the movement—political leadership, he called it—with Guevara in a subordinate role as military commander. Not only did the proposal serve Bolivian nationalism, something alive and well even in the Communist Party, but, as Monje later explicitly stated, it also served orthodox communist theory, which held that political leadership could not be subordinate to military leadership, a key point of contention, of course, between the Cubans and Moscow-line communists. Guevara answered clearly and immediately: Monje's proposal was out of the question. As Guevara told it, Monje then put a challenge to Guevara's Bolivian volunteers: They could stay with the guerrilla band or support the party. All chose to remain. The next day, Monje told Guevara that he would resign from the party leadership. Then "he left," said Guevara, "looking as though he were being led to the gallows."[10]

"The Bolivian Revolution and armed struggle must be planned and directed by Bolivians," wrote the Communist Party central committee in La Paz to Castro on January 11, showing much more firmness with him than Monje ever seems to have shown. Guevara considered the letter "evidence of bad faith" and told Castro that Monje was "an enemy." In his diary, he wrote, "The party is now taking up arms against us . . . but it will not stop us and perhaps in the long-run it will prove a good thing." Monje meanwhile resigned as promised and was replaced by Jorge Kolle, brother of the air-force chief of staff. Kolle went to Cuba and told Castro a completely new story. He said that because the revolution in Bolivia was really of "continental strategic magnitude," the party could cooperate after all, even without leading the effort. These words caused joy in Havana, where it was believed that "satisfactory arrangements" could be worked out. But Guevara never shared that opinion; to him, the party remained "two-faced and hesitant, to say the least." And indeed, by May 1967 he had heard nothing from it except, he told Castro, that it had expelled from its ranks those youths who had joined his band. Nor would he hear from it further. Finally, after Guevara's death and far from Castro, Kolle became bolder, telling the press in February 1968 that "we did not invite Guevara; we did not suggest Bolivian territory as a field for his revolutionary operations; nor did we make any commitment except to express our solidarity when the movement had already broken out."[11]

If Guevara really believed that the loss of Communist Party support would "prove a good thing," as he wrote in his diary, he was very mistaken. It hurt him enormously, especially because it denied him the men the party might have recruited in the cities and mines and sent to him in the mountains, just as the July 26 Movement had done in Cuba. It could also have served as a conduit for supplies and communications, making use of urban facilities not available to him. If Cuba still had an embassy in La Paz, the loss of the party's support would have mattered less; the embassy could have provided clandestine assistance. But Bolivia had cut its diplomatic ties with Cuba, complying with an OAS resolution in 1964 after being strongly encouraged by the United States. (Coerced, some would say. The *New York Times*, for example, said Washington threatened the Paz Estenssoro government with a slash in aid if it did not make the break.)[12]

Even when relations between the guerrilla band and the party effectively collapsed in January 1967, however, Guevara still could rely on an urban network of his own. Unfortunately for him, that, too, disappeared before March was out.

The Tania Legends

One key operative in the La Paz organization could be a figure straight out of contemporary spy fiction: a young woman the guerrillas called Tania, who had used several aliases but who began life as Haidee Tamara Bunke. She was born in 1937 in Buenos Aires to German refugee parents who had fled the Nazis in 1935. Her mother was Jewish, born in Russia, and both parents were communists. Tania moved to East Germany with her parents in 1952, and at a very early age, she, like them, became a dedicated communist. She had a fascination with things military and an interest in folk music and linguistics, the latter inherited perhaps from her father, who had supported himself in Buenos Aires as a language teacher.[13]

Tania studied philosophy at Humboldt University in East Berlin, joined the Communist Party, and became active in the official youth movement, principally translating for visiting Latin American delegations, one of which Guevara headed in 1959. Like many others, she found Cuba's revolutionary success fascinating and may also have been fascinated by the dashing young Argentine commandante turned high government official. Two years later, she turned up in Cuba; as is often the case with stories about Tania, there is more than one version about how that happened. Some say she arrived with an East German cultural delegation and stayed after it returned. More likely, the Cuban Ballet, for which she interpreted in Germany, managed to get her to Cuba. Once there, she did several official jobs, including working in the Ministry of Education. She also attended Havana University and served in the Cuban women's militia, which provided the military ambience she yearned for. In 1963 she began training in espionage.

Some say Tania and Guevara became lovers; certainly, they were close. They were reported together at social events, once going together to a costume party in matching outfits.[14] If, however, rumors of an intimate liaison are true, it did not prevent her from being sent to La Paz on a long-term espionage assignment.

Until Tania made a colossal blunder in 1967 that helped destroy Guevara, she was a remarkably effective undercover agent. She arrived in La Paz in 1964, setting herself up as a language teacher and at one point teaching the children of a respected journalist, Gonzálo López Muñoz, who, according to some reports, hired her to work for a magazine he had just founded. Not long thereafter he became Barrientos's chief of information. Meanwhile, Tania married a Bolivian. It was a short liaison, and stories vary about that, too. One thing is certain: From the marriage she gained a Bolivian passport, allowing her to travel freely in and out of the country. By then, she had a nonpaying position with the Ministry of Education, which reportedly helped her arrange for her husband to go on a scholarship to Bulgaria, alone. Here, too, however, the record is clouded; some accounts say he went to study in Israel or in Yugoslavia.[15] Nevertheless, he did leave Tania unfettered in Bolivia. Seven months after their marriage, she divorced him. By then, she was meeting the country's artists, intellectuals, government officials, and people prominent in La Paz society. Her continuing connection with the chief of information served Guevara especially well, enabling Tania to help arrange false credentials for him and his confederates, two of whom— Régis Debray and Argentine artist and revolutionary Ciro Roberto Bustos—gained special notoriety not long thereafter.

The notion has persisted that Tania served two, and possibly three, intelligence organizations. As a young woman she undoubtedly had links with East German intelligence, and some say she was soon recruited by the Soviet KGB and was assigned to get herself to Havana to keep an eye on the worrisome Cubans. Several CIA officials closely involved with these events, while admitting to uncertainty, find the double-spy connection "farfetched," but in the 1960s the agency was not entirely of that opinion. Two agents, who remain anonymous, briefed Benjamin Welles of the *New York Times* on July 22, 1968, on the "Havana-Moscow split." One of the points they used to underpin their thesis that a split existed was "the dispatch of 'Tania' to Cuba in 1961 by the East German Intelligence Service." In their summary of the briefing, they added, "We noted that she was probably but one of many Soviet and Bloc agents run to Cuba to conduct independent operations." That was a view, in fact, that Welles already held: A week earlier he had written a front-page story, claiming that in 1961 Tania had been recruited by Günther Männel of the East German Foreign Intelligence Department to keep Moscow informed of Castro's plans for violent revolution in Latin America. She was, Welles wrote, to "infiltrate the Guevara movement," although in 1961 there was no Guevara movement, certainly none regarding Bolivia. In fact, that was some four years before he went to the Congo.[16]

Nevertheless, writer and Guevara biographer Daniel James, for example, makes this case strongly, based on an interview with Männel, who defected to the West in 1961. James and others who share this view say Guevara eventually became Tania's specific target and that foiling his revolution in Bolivia was her final objective. Some, including James, say her blunder was a deliberate effort to thwart Guevara and his revolution, which the Soviets regarded as ill considered and reckless. To believe that, however, one must accept that the Soviets were willing to see her rusticated to Bolivia in November 1964, more than one year before the Cubans had even formulated a plan for an insurgency there. It was undoubtedly a useful listening post about Cuban schemes on the South American continent, but would that be an adequate use of Tania? One needs also to believe that Tania made her "mistake" deliberately, despite the fact that it would reveal her operations in La Paz, put her in enormous danger, and very likely lead to her execution had she ever returned from her visit to Guevara's camp.[17]

Whatever Tania's motive, what happened is astonishing. Debray and Bustos arrived separately in La Paz in February 1967 and made contact with Tania, who arranged for them to get to Guevara's camp and accompanied them on the trip. It was an arduous journey made by a combination of bus, taxi, and hired jeep. After traveling for more than four days, they arrived on March 5 in Camiri. There, they met a guerrilla named Coco Paredo, who took them to the camp in his vehicle.[18]

Tania lived much of the time in Camiri, keeping a hotel room and a jeep there. She had been to the camp once previously, when Monje had his fateful New Year's Eve meeting with Guevara, but was told by Guevara never to return, the danger being too great that her role would be discovered.[19] She went with Debray and Bustos nevertheless, but, perhaps far worse as things turned out, she waited for Guevara, who was on a training and reconnoitering trip with most of his band and did not arrive for two weeks. We can only speculate why she did so. Was it love? Was it the excitement of military life? Did she enjoy the camp too much to leave, especially before most of the guerrillas and their renowned commander arrived? We do not know. While she was there, however, the Bolivian authorities discovered her jeep in Camiri. Accounts of what they found in it vary, but unquestionably they discovered sufficient documentation to link her to the guerrilla band and the La Paz network. And that brings up the key question about Tania: How could a woman who had been such an adroit undercover agent suddenly be so careless? Many commentators find that so implausible that they believe her actions had to stem from treachery, not fecklessness.

Guevara's diary entry sheds little light on the matter. It says simply that Tania planned to stay only a day in the camp, but "things became complicated." Pombo says if she had not brought her passengers to Camiri, they would have had to wait longer in La Paz. How bad could that have been? Then he adds this intriguing sentence: "Of course, her decision to be the one to take them resulted from the fact that she was unaware that Che was on exploration and not at the camp." Pombo seems to be implying that Guevara was the "draw" for Tania and that had she known he was away, the visitors would have had to get to the camp as best they could.

The discovery of the documents in Tania's jeep created a completely new situation for Guevara, which he summed up on March 27, the day after the government admitted publicly for the first time that it faced a guerrilla threat and that one of its units had suffered losses in an ambush. He said, "Everything indicates that Tania has become known, which means that two years of good patient work has been lost. Departure becomes very difficult now."[20]

That was a considerable understatement. Everything, not just departure, would be very difficult, and victory would be nearly impossible. Guevara was totally isolated, leading a small band, many of whom were already disgruntled, ill nourished, scrounging for food, and sick with diarrhea and swollen limbs. He not only found himself in a hostile area but also now had no supporting organization outside of it—no embassy, no Communist Party, no functioning clandestine network.[21] Although some agents and affiliates remained at liberty for several more months, Guevara never could contact them. In reality, his war was over, and almost before it began, but his enemies did not realize that.

Régis Debray: Reluctant Guerrilla

Régis Debray now assumed enormous importance in the Guevara story. Debray was a very privileged young man with a background in many ways similar to Guevara's, except that his family had not fallen on hard times—far from it. Well-off and influential for generations, the Debray family lived in the swank 16th Arrondissement of Paris, his father a prominent lawyer, his mother a councilwoman of Paris and a nationally known figure. Debray, intellectually gifted, attended the École Normale Supérieure, where he was a brilliant student, studying under the Marxist philosopher Louis Althusser. He was appalled at the French role in Algeria in the 1950s and at the same time attracted to communism, joining the party. He, too, was fascinated by the Cuban Revolution and visited that country in 1959. Several years later, he toured South America and then, back in Paris, wrote a series of articles on Latin America, including one published in Jean-Paul Sartre's review, *Les Temps Modernes.* Thus began his reputation. He was invited to Havana in 1966 to teach at the university and there wrote *Revolution in the Revolution?*, published in 1967, which quickly enjoyed enormous circulation in both communist and noncommunist countries. Essentially, it was a exegesis of the Cuban theory of revolution, which had been developed to a large degree in the Sierra Maestra and already made public to some extent by Guevara in his *Guerrilla Warfare* and other writings.[22]

By mid-1966, Debray was in Bolivia with credentials as a correspondent from a Mexican magazine, *Sucesos,* and the French publishing house Maspero. He was, in fact, however, assisting in the arrangements for Guevara's insurgency, and in September he began a study for Havana of the merits of certain potential locations for the revolutionary *foco.* Those locations he and a group of Cuban colleagues originally considered lay in another region entirely than the spot Guevara eventually chose. The team seriously viewed but quickly discarded one site when it was discovered to be within easy range of a military base, but several other locations had much to recommend them. They lay deep in the mountain range but still much closer to La Paz and Cochabamba than the place finally selected. That site, which has come to be called Ñancahuazú, was far into the wilds of southeast Bolivia near the Ñancahuazú River, where, in fact, the guerrillas already had bought a farm.[23]

Pombo, one of those who made the purchase, says Guevara originally intended the Ñancahuazú location to be a rear base for organizing and training the band, which then would operate "a little farther to the north" in an area of "taller vegetation, a higher population density, and better conditions." When that time came, Guevara planned to move the base camp to the region of the upper Chapare River. He also intended to have a link with Argentina through the eastern ranges of the Andes, says Pombo. Premature discovery of the camp by the army, however, changed those plans completely, locking Guevara into operating further south than he had intended.[24]

Debray says he lamented the decision to go to Ñancahuazú. The site was too far from any urban center that could support the guerrillas and too far from populations with animosities toward the government that might help in the struggle. Nevertheless, Guevara decided on it in October, in large measure, says Debray, because by then the Communist Party knew that Bolivia was to be the center of the insurrection and also knew which sites near La Paz were being considered for the base camp. The party, strongly opposed to the undertaking, became even further irritated because Debray and the Cubans were negotiating for support with a despised radical splinter faction, headed by Moisés Guevara. Fearing that the Communist Party would betray him, says Debray, Guevara opted for the security of the more inaccessible site, which had the added advantage from his point of view of being closer to Argentina.

Monje told Guevara biographer Jon Lee Anderson a different story. He said he selected the site with Guevara's advance team almost arbitrarily because it was near Argentina, where he assumed Guevara was headed.[25]

Guevara arrived in November 1966, entering the country clean shaven, almost entirely bald, and traveling on phony documents provided with Tania's help. By the end of January, all was prepared. "Now is when the actual guerrilla period begins," he said; "we shall test the troops, and time will tell the results and what the prospects of the Bolivian Revolution are." In March, Debray and Bustos arrived in camp to plan ways to help create and spread the South American rebellion. Debray was to serve as a courier to Cuba on his way back to France and then to encourage support in Europe. Bustos was to help organize support and insurrection in Argentina, just as the Peruvian Juan Pablo Chang Navarro, code-named El Chino, was to do in Peru.[26]

Castro suggested that Debray actually join the band; the Frenchman said he wanted to comply but Guevara needed his services elsewhere. Guevara's diary, however, casts doubt on the strength of Debray's ambition to be a guerrilla. As Guevara noted, with the discovery of Tania's jeep, departure became very difficult. Then he added wryly, "I received the impression that Danton [Debray] was not the least bit pleased when I told him so." The next day, Guevara again made Debray the subject of his ironic turn of phrase, saying, "El Frances was too vehement when he mentioned how useful he could be outside." Meanwhile, no one had ever suggested that Bustos stay, least of all Bustos himself.[27]

Debray remained with the guerrillas a few weeks until the band could get him out. Guevara decided to move toward Muyupampa and if possible send Debray and Bustos off from there toward Sucre and Cochabamba. Unfortunately for them all, on the night of April 16 one of the Bolivians in the group disappeared, and Guevara feared that he intended to betray the band. Still, he said, "it was decided to depart in spite of everything so as to get El Frances and Carlos [Bustos] out once and for all."

Botched Escape

When they neared Muyupampa on April 19, events took a new turn. George Andrew Roth, a writer-photographer of English-Chilean background, caught up with them, having tracked them down easily on the basis of considerable information from members of Guevara's band in the rear. Roth's arrival represented such obviously lax security that it left Guevara spluttering with anger. "The same old story, the lack of discipline and of responsibility takes first place," he wrote. But Debray viewed Roth in an entirely different light. He calculated at once that because Roth's documents, mission, and behavior were all legal, Roth could help get him and Bustos past any inquiring authorities, lending substance to their pose as journalists working on a story. Bustos agreed "unwillingly," says Guevara, "and I washed my hands of it." Nevertheless, urged on by Debray, all three left that afternoon. The following day, all three were arrested in Muyupampa, and therein began a major drama within the overall episode of Guevara in Bolivia.[28]

Roth's ability to smooth the group's way past suspicious Bolivian authorities obviously proved nonexistent. In fact, they wanted to put Debray and Bustos to the wall at once and nearly did. Fortunately for the two captives, however, they were caught just as a heated debate concerning the fate of prisoners in general was going on between the Americans and the Bolivians. Two days after their capture, Henderson cabled Washington saying that Barrientos had told him informally "that every guerrilla falling into the hands of his people should be liquidated." The president maintained that prisoners "of this ilk" never came to justice in Bolivia but instead got out of custody promptly, renewed their subversive activities, and encouraged others by their example. Henderson disagreed. "Extra-legal" methods of dealing with prisoners, he believed, created martyrs internally and stigmatized Bolivia internationally. Furthermore, through summary executions, the army lost any evidence that might be gained from captured guerrillas. Barrientos was unmoved. He could not afford to keep prisoners, he said, and their disappearance, far from causing problems, would go unnoticed by the public.[29]

In the midst of this discussion, the Bolivians found themselves with not only three new prisoners but also foreigners, one of whom they suspected was Debray. Their execution, certainly his, most assuredly would not go unnoticed. First reports indicated that Debray had been killed; in fact, Henderson received "excited telephone calls" from both Barrientos and Ovando on the day he was caught saying the army had killed him. Soon that was in doubt, then clearly untrue. Upon learning that he was alive, U.S. embassy officers urged clemency on "high Bolivian officials" but still could not be sure they would prevail. They asked Washington if they should press the Debray matter further. Could the State Department suggest additional arguments they might raise against "extralegal actions" (meaning executions)? Might it not help if the department also raised the issue with Ambassador Sanjines?[30]

The department indeed took the matter up with Sanjines, who said, in effect, yes, extralegal executions were not in Bolivia's best interest, but he understood that no prisoners had been taken, although several guerrillas had been killed. Sanjines was wrong, of course—perhaps deliberately to dodge a tough question—but he may have really been confused because Guevara's band fought skirmishes off and on with the army for about a week beginning on April 20, the day Debray and the others were caught.[31]

Although the government placed a news blackout on the Camiri area, newspapers and anonymous embassy sources still reported that Debray was alive, contradicting high military officials who continued to insist that he was dead. It did not matter much at that point which report was accurate, the embassy feared, because even if he had not already been executed, "his future [did] not appear to be promising." About the time that assessment was being written, Washington told the embassy that it had made the case for clemency adequately; "further representations at this time not advisable."[32]

Within a week of his capture, it became clear to everyone that Debray was alive. Barrientos finally admitted it to Henderson, and the media were permitted to report on his captivity. Henderson used the opportunity to stress the need for better intelligence in the combat area. He believed, for example, that the embassy should have had firmer information about Debray and about all of the confrontations between the Bolivian armed forces and the guerrillas during the preceding week.[33]

Prisoner Extraordinaire

Soon Debray's capture, like his eventual trial, became an international media circus, causing Bolivian officials, often cast in the light of inhumane troglodytes, acute embarrassment. The French government joined the Americans in putting pressure on the Bolivians for fairness and clemency. French President Charles de Gaulle wrote Barrientos, and the French embassy in La Paz did everything it could. The Vatican weighed in discreetly, and Debray's mother arrived in Bolivia to plead his case.[34]

This enormous pressure, especially by the American government to whom the Bolivian regime was so beholden, paid off at least temporarily. The prisoners would get a trial, although the Foreign Ministry made it clear that because Bolivia was not at war with any nation and because the guerrillas were trying to overthrow the government, thereby causing the deaths of both Bolivian soldiers and civilians, the prisoners must be treated as common criminals rather than prisoners of war. Nevertheless, they would come before a military court in Camiri. Barrientos, however, who declared publicly that the Frenchman had come to stain Bolivia with blood, was far from happy about the trial. Furthermore, he was unhappy with the American ambassador for urging that the prisoners be spared, even before other voices had been raised on their behalf. If they could have been dispatched quickly, as the military wanted, those other voices, faced with a fait accompli, would have been raised only in a futile lament. Henderson, who said later that his relationship with Barrientos was noticeably cooler after the Debray affair, obviously had put the president in a very difficult position. Either he had to turn down a strong request by the United States, a patron upon which so much depended, or he had to risk antagonizing his military, a highly perilous thing for a Bolivian president to do, especially in that era.[35]

If Barrientos was angry, members of the Debray family in Paris were frantic. While Mme. Debray, a friend of de Gaulle's, tried desperately to influence the Bolivians to save her son, the family in Paris urged the U.S. government, through its embassy there, to exert its influence in Bolivia to gain him clemency. The State Department cabled the Paris embassy: "U.S. Mission in La Paz has used every opportunity [to] impress on GOB [the government of Bolivia] desirability [of] extend[ing] humane treatment to prisoners. . . . You may inform family . . . we will continue, where appropriate, to urge Bolivians [to] apply acceptable standards of due process, including fair trial, and to point out benefits of doing so to GOB."[36]

Debray was questioned by Cuban exiles employed by the CIA and then put on trial, but he maintained steadily that he was a journalist covering a story, nothing more, although he did not try to hide his sympathies, which were, of course, internationally known by then. Guevara had asked both Debray and Bustos not to reveal that he was in Bolivia, but during their incarceration, which lasted some three months before the trial began, both revealed it—"under military interrogation," according to DeBray. He also told his lawyer, Walter Flores Torrico, about Guevara's presence, and Flores subsequently made it public.[37]

Although Debray benefited by legal counsel, life was not easy even for his lawyer. By June, the entire guerrilla operation had become so unpopular that the attorney required police protection in Camiri, where youths roamed the streets calling for Debray's death.[38]

Bustos went even further than Debray in describing the guerrilla movement, telling a press conference in July not only that Guevara was in Bolivia but also that he was there to lead a continental rebellion. He added that Guevara had only about 40 or 50 men, many of them foreigners. According to one writer, Bustos's press conference probably resulted from a deal made with the army, because soon after that his wife was permitted to visit him and he began to receive better treatment than Debray.[39]

Their treatment, in fact, became a matter of international comment. With the three prisoners held incommunicado since they were captured in April, rumors began circulating that they were being mistreated. As a consequence, the Bolivian high command permitted a prominent clergyman, Monsignor Andrés Kennedy, an American who was chaplain to the Bolivian Armed Forces, to interview them on June 21. The military did this reluctantly, however, according to a U.S. embassy cable, requiring repeated intercessions by Barrientos before agreeing to the meetings. Three days later, Kennedy appeared in a photograph in *Presencia* with a very fit looking Debray, and he told the newspaper that he found all three prisoners to be in good health.[40] In early July, however, an Associated Press reporter who interviewed Debray said he had a new scar, a lump on the right side of his forehead, and lumps near his right eye. The reporter added that Debray feared for his life in Camiri and wanted his case moved to La Paz.[41]

Regardless of the military's treatment of Debray, and it was undoubtedly rough at times, and its treatment of the press, which it irritated enormously, especially by expelling it from the courtroom when Debray testified, it nevertheless permitted Debray ample access to media. He made public statements and held interviews throughout the trial, including one to rebut the president, who hailed Guevara as "a revolutionary who fought for his ideals" but called Debray "an immature bourgeois in the trappings of a revolutionary."[42]

At the end of the three-month trial, which lasted until November 17, Debray and Bustos received 30-year sentences, of which they actually served only three years in relative comfort in a former officers' club at a military base near Camiri. Roth had been released early in July.[43]

Strengths and Weaknesses, Real and Perceived

When Guevara moved toward Muyupampa on April 17 to get rid of Debray and Bustos, he divided his force. Planning to refocus his operations and center them in the Muyupampa region, he sent a vanguard in that direction the day before. Unfortunately for his plans, however, Tania and one of the guerrillas had fallen ill, both running fevers, and Moisés Guevara suffered a severe gall-bladder attack. They remained behind with several other guerrillas under the command of one of Guevara's lieutenants, Major Juan Vitalio Acuña Núñez (code-named Joaquín). Guevara planned to rejoin them after launching Debray and Bustos; then he would try similarly to get El Chino and Tania out of the band. But the reunion with Joaquín never took place. The requirements of combat forced Guevara to move in a direction different than the one he had planned and eventually also forced Joaquín to move his group. Despite searching constantly for each other, the two columns never met again.[44]

The difficulty of his position, especially vis-à-vis the local population, impressed itself increasingly upon Guevara. On April 16, his group bought food from some campesinos of whom he wrote, "They are very poor farmers and are frightened of our presence here." In his monthly summary, he described what was in effect a stalemate. The Bolivian forces, because of their immobility and weakness, he said, had not been able to control his band: "They disturb us but they do not prevent us from moving." Still, he said, "the isolation continues to be complete; sickness keeps undermining the health of some of the comrades, obliging us to divide forces, which lowers effectiveness. . . . The peasant base is still undeveloped, although it seems that through planned terror, we can neutralize most of them; their support will come later. Not one person has joined up with us." Later in the summary, he returned to the question of the campesinos, this time speaking disparagingly of their collaboration with government forces: "Peasant mobilization does not exist, except for their work as informers, which annoys us somewhat. They are neither very rapid nor very efficient; they can be neutralized." Soon, however, in collaboration with U.S. intelligence experts, the peasants and their information constituted one of the most powerful forces working against him.

In this same diary entry, in an almost hopeful tone, Guevara adds, "It seems certain that the North Americans will intervene with force here and are already sending helicopters and, apparently, Green Berets, although they have not been seen here." He was right that the Americans supplied helicopters but very wrong about their intervention with force; nor would he ever see a Green Beret.

Finally, he again sneered at Debray and Bustos, who he said "fell victims of their own haste, their near desperation to leave, and my lack of energy to stop them, so that communication with Cuba has been cut off (Danton) and the plan of action in Argentina (Carlos) has been lost." Debray was supposed to go to Cuba on his way to Europe and presumably report on the guerrilla band, its problems, and its needs. Other means of communication from Guevara to Havana (although not vice versa) obviously had been lost. In fact, the group's ability to transmit may have collapsed as early as January, when they retrieved radio equipment stored in the caves and found much of it to be wet, rusty, and broken.[45] At the end of May, Guevara noted a "total lack of contact with Manila [Havana], La Paz, and Joaquín, which reduces the group to 25 men." Although Havana sent radio messages to him until the end, he could not respond, and his communication with La Paz was nil.

If Guevara's situation was beginning to look problematic to him, it looked very different to the Bolivian government and military staff, who found the guerrilla band more menacing every day. Shortly after the first armed encounters, air force chief of staff Colonel Leon Kolle Cueto made a trip to Argentina, Paraguay, Peru, and Brazil to request assistance. Although the contributions of the others remain unclear, Argentina—which had a military advisory mission in La Paz (the only country besides the United States to have one)—provided rations, radios, ammunition, and other supplies. Furthermore, the Bolivians, who had received napalm from Argentina previously, now asked for more. The Americans were appalled. They had removed all U.S.-owned napalm supplies from Bolivia in 1965 and wanted to be clearly disassociated from its purchase or use in that country. Furthermore, they suggested that the Argentines deny the request. An American diplomat told the London *Times:* "We are certainly not going to supply the means for Bolivian hotheads to start bombing and napalming villages or even suspected guerrilla hideaways. Civilians would inevitably be killed and we have a long experience that this inevitably produces a stream of recruits for the guerrillas." The lessons of Vietnam again, as often, affected the guerrilla war in Bolivia.[46]

Despite enormous concern in Washington about the Bolivian insurgency, the State Department, at least INR, took a fairly relaxed, and as we now know, accurate view of events there, an attitude not shared throughout the government. In a short study, INR noted that the Bolivian armed forces found it difficult to keep in contact with the guerrillas and had a long way to go before they stamped out the movement. Nevertheless, it believed that rumors that several guerrilla fronts might develop, a prospect that haunted the Bolivian government, were unrealistic considering the size of the guerrilla band, which it put with great accuracy at about 60. The authors of the report pointed out that they had seen no evidence of successful recruiting by the insurgents and then added an extraordinary observation: They had heard that the Soviet-oriented Communist Party had begun "classroom training" in guerrilla warfare for its members. Considering Guevara's caustic wit, fury at the party, and the ludicrous circumstance of the party's practicing revolution in the classroom while eschewing it in the field, one yearns to know if he heard the same reports, and if he did, what he said about them. We are, alas, denied the pleasure. Finally, INR concluded that the guerrilla band could probably evade and harass the Bolivian Army indefinitely, but that it did not in its present size "constitute a serious threat to the government."[47]

Bolivian Forces Improve

In some matters, the Bolivian armed forces made improvements. Almost as soon as they confronted the guerrillas, they concurred in the long-standing U.S. recommendation that enlistments be extended to two years and be staggered instead of lasting only one year with each year's recruits entering at one time. The new system would ensure that at least 50 percent of the armed forces' personnel would have at least a year's experience at any time. Previously, new conscripts, almost the entire force, entered in January and did not complete basic training until April. Unfortunately for them, in 1967 they were called upon to face Guevara's men in March. As they did, their morale was low; they were short of rations, radios, and hand weapons; their line officers were too few; they had received only a bare minimum of weapons training; and those units not supplied by the United States carried weapons that were largely defective. Moreover, perverse though it may seem, many U.S.-assisted units remained out of the combat area because the government was becoming nearly obsessed with the possibility of even greater flare-ups closer to the capital, especially in the mining areas. Consequently, it kept the stronger forces nearer La Paz to cope with that eventuality, a strategy in which U.S. military advisers concurred.[48]

Today, the Bolivian government's fear of a multifaceted rebellion seems to verge on paranoia, but the specter reached as far as the White House, which took it seriously, even if INR dismissed it. National Security Adviser Rostow sent President Johnson a summary of the situation, saying that the guerrillas so far had "out-classed" the government forces, which, however, still were able to keep them "on the run," preventing them from being "an immediate threat to Barrientos." But, Rostow added, if they should be "quickly augmented," enabling them to open new fronts in the near future, as rumored, "the thin Bolivian armed forces would be hard pressed and the fragile political situation would be threatened."

Johnson thereupon told Rostow to meet with CIA, State Department, and Defense Department representatives on the "whole guerrilla problem in Latin America," which Rostow did the next day, June 24. Reporting that it was "a good meeting," he made a list of seven countries by "degree of urgency." Rostow put Bolivia first, "more because of the fragility of the political situation and the weakness of the armed forces than the size and effectiveness of the guerrilla movement," which he put at 50 to 60 members but said "may run up to 100." Then, he added, "there are indications that six other bands, totalling 100–200 men may be organizing in other parts of the country. President Barrientos is hard pressed coping with the active band. If other fronts were successfully opened, the situation could get out of hand." That in a nutshell was Barrientos's nightmare.

In both memoranda, Rostow pointed out that the 17-man Green Beret team, which by then had arrived in Bolivia, was training a new ranger battalion. In addition, his brief description of the guerrilla band makes clear that the CIA's leadership by then had revised its view that Guevara was dead, undoubtedly because of the revelations of Debray and Bustos. "CIA," he said, "believes that 'Che' Guevara has been with this group."[49]

With training and experience, the Bolivian troops had become somewhat more effective by the end of April. Guevara noticed the difference and wrote that at least some of its units had improved.[50] The army then had some 600 men in the counterinsurgency effort, supported by air force units, and Bolivia's high command had developed something of a strategy to cope with the guerrilla menace. It consisted simply of maintaining contact with the insurgents and blocking their escape, while the special ranger unit was being trained to move into the area and eliminate them.[51] In succeeding months, however, the army, with improved techniques and confidence plus greatly increased numbers, took more initiative than that.

CHAPTER FOUR

The Green Berets

Bolivia was the best thing we ever did," said Major Ralph "Pappy" Shelton, leader of a Green Beret Mobile Training Team (MTT), the Pentagon's traveling groups that helped train friendly armed forces, mostly in the arts of counterinsurgency. The U.S. embassy had been prodding the Bolivian government for at least two years to bring such a team to help its military cope with uprisings in the hinterlands, which, like Guevara's uprising, were always a possibility, especially after Cuba began exporting revolution to the continent. The Bolivians had been reluctant. National pride made them balk at having Americans develop their armed forces—military hardware was one thing, but a group of trainers was quite another. Furthermore, a well trained ranger battalion could be almost invincible in the Bolivian context and therefore not only a major military force but also a major political force. Nevertheless, the Bolivians finally agreed to schedule a team for 1968. Then, in March 1967, under pressure from the U.S. embassy and with insurgency a reality, they agreed to bring in the team earlier, advancing its arrival to the following month.

Southern Command agreed completely about the need for a Green Beret team in Bolivia. No element of the U.S. government led it in concern over the insurgency. Officers of general or admiral rank made some half-dozen visits to Bolivia during the eight months between the discovery of the guerrilla band and Guevara's death; General Porter himself came twice. In addition, soon after the shooting began, the command invited Ambassador Henderson to its headquarters in the Panama Canal Zone to brief its chief officers on the guerrilla situation.

The ambassador, however, was preceded by his formidable antimilitary reputation, a worrisome matter to Porter. It "frightened" the general, according to one high-ranking officer on Porter's staff, who added that Henderson really "wasn't antimilitary, he was just antistupidity, and we had a surplus of it."[1]

General Tope's Fact-Finding Mission

Whatever he thought of the military in general, Henderson liked and admired an air-force brigadier general on Porter's staff, William A. Tope, the director of planning. Shortly after the shooting began in Bolivia, Porter planned to send down a 16-officer team to study the situation. Henderson would have none of it. The whole thing was developing too high an American profile. No military team, he said; just send one man, no more, and that should be Tope. The general did not speak Spanish, but Henderson waved that objection aside, certain that he very quickly would be on a first-name basis with Barrientos, who spoke English and was a fellow air-force officer. Tope finally convinced the ambassador to let him bring along one aide, a Puerto Rican officer fluent in Spanish, but that was all.[2]

Henderson stressed to Tope the importance of keeping the American reaction to the insurgency "small" and assistance to the Bolivian government limited. He knew that Guevara by then had been driven out of his base encampment, and he was convinced that the situation mainly required, as he put it, "a highly trained group which will concentrate on the one operation and not fan out and look for guerrillas behind every mountain peak." Tope agreed, but the Bolivian high command did not see things exactly that way.[3]

Tope visited Bolivia from April 18–30 and had three meetings with Barrientos, the first two including cabinet members and top military officers, the third alone with the president. In each meeting, the Bolivians made clear that they wanted high-powered, up-to-date military equipment. Given that, they could defeat the guerrillas, they maintained, despite the shortcomings in their armed forces. For one thing, better firepower would boost the morale of the armed forces, and once that happened, even marginal soldiers could prevail by "fill[ing] the air with lead," as Tope put it. The Bolivians did not want to wait for a unit to be trained. They needed a victory, and they needed one quickly. Once again, they made no secret of their fear that they might soon face a hydra-headed revolution creating havoc throughout the country. As Tope reported, they expressed "strong concern over the political and psychological impact of recent army reverses on the rest of the country, particularly on other dissident groups who they feel are just waiting to strike."[4]

But "unfortunately, all of their quick fixes are unsound," Tope said, and he told them so. Still, before the crisis ended, the United States might have to reinforce that message with "some very firm approaches," he reported, using all of the "leverage" it had. Meanwhile, he pointed out to the Bolivians that "an untrained conscript will drop a modern weapon just as quickly as he will a Mauser," and he underscored the point that the Viet Cong supplied themselves largely by picking up U.S. equipment dropped by South Vietnamese soldiers.[5]

Tope sent a detailed report on his trip to Southern Command and a summary to the State Department for dissemination among the foreign-affairs agencies in Washington. In both versions, his assessment of the Bolivian military establishment was so critical it was almost comical. In his view, it scarcely deserved to be called an organization of any kind, much less a military one. The demand for a quick victory only made things worse, "creating chaotic conditions in the operational areas," where, he said, units were sent into combat haphazardly with no overall plans. Furthermore, there was no field intelligence, almost no communication, poor command arrangements, no individual or unit training, incompetent leadership, and inadequate equipment. In addition, because commanders played down losses and exaggerated successes, it was nearly impossible to assess the real situation in the field. In that regard, he recommended easing the restrictions that kept U.S. military advisers from entering the combat area and thereby "bringing order out of chaos." He added that "assistance to units now in the guerrilla area could be effective only if accompanied by advisers on the spot. . . . U.S. failure to be present where help is needed the most is inexplicable to the Bolivians."

Tope pointed out, by way of explaining the condition of the Bolivian military, that the revolutionary regime in power from 1952 to 1964 had nearly abolished the armed forces. Consequently, they were to a large extent less than three years old. In the meantime senior commanders and staff officers had received key assignments on the basis of "personal loyalty and political patronage," and hence, he said, "military thinking at the higher levels is generally archaic, impulsive, and self-aggrandizing."

The State Department copied its version of Tope's report to the National Security Council, among other agencies, and there William G. Bowdler, in charge of Latin American affairs, sent it to Walt Rostow, calling it "a grim report" and saying the problem was with not only the troops but also those at the top, "including Barrientos."[6] The problem, in fact, seemed at times to rest especially with Barrientos, who pushed the hardest for fancy military equipment, including a type of high-performance, close-support aircraft. The Americans said use of the plane would only cause serious repair and maintenance problems and offered instead to refurbish Bolivia's World War II–vintage fighters. Furthermore, Tope pointed out that the Bolivians had used excessive amounts of bombs and aircraft ammunition, which Barrientos said stemmed from an effort to compensate for the army's inactivity. Tope asked how targets were selected, pointing out that indiscriminate bombing not only wasted munitions and often killed friendly forces but also killed friendly civilians with "obvious adverse effects." The president dismissed all of this, said Tope, and pointed out the efficacy of bombing: it had, he said, killed one guerrilla and five of their mules in the Muyupampa area.

General Ovando, at least in conversations with Tope, proved more amenable to reforms in the armed forces and enthusiastic about the Second Ranger Battalion to be trained by the Green Berets. The army units then in the operational area, he said, would continue to isolate and confine the guerrillas until the battalion could come into service, and while Tope was in Bolivia the MILGP and the Bolivian government signed a three-page "memorandum of understanding" regarding their cooperation in training and equipping the battalion. The document's tacit purpose was to lock up Bolivian support and provide details in writing for an agreement previously made. Shelton and three other Green Berets had, in fact, already arrived from Panama on April 11 to begin preliminary arrangements for the U.S. training team.[7]

Still, despite this emphasis on countering the guerrillas in the backlands, first priority even among the Americans went not to training the new ranger battalion but to equipping and training rapid-reaction forces in the mining regions. Both U.S. and Bolivian military commands considered the situation there to be "highly volatile." Tope stated that threats in the urban areas and the mines remained very real and said that "their immediate impact on both the economy and the government could be much more disastrous than the present guerrilla activity."

While Tope formulated many of the divergent views on security issues that vexed U.S.-Bolivian relations, he also identified some closer to home. MILGP personnel understood the problems afflicting the Bolivian armed forces and knew the steps needed to correct them. They did not know, however, how to get the Bolivians to take those steps, "a cause of intense frustration and disappointment." "It was the ambassador's oft-expressed opinion," Tope said, "that the fault lay with MLGRP [*sic*] personnel failing to be firm in their dealings with the Bolivians and operating too much on the basis of a desire to be liked. As a result, he feels they gain a superficial rapport and friendship with their counterparts but fail to establish the firm position necessary to have their advice heeded."

Although possibly true in some cases, said Tope, in general it was not that simple. Something more needed to be done than just changing the attitudes of the group's officers. "Elements of reward and punishment will have to be brought to bear," he said, supported by all levels in the U.S. government, and he recommended that before any significant military support was forthcoming from the United States, Washington should have a written memorandum from the Bolivians stating how they intended to achieve the "contemplated improvements." It was in this spirit that he extracted the memorandum of understanding regarding Shelton's team of Green Berets.

All elements in a military operation had to be handled capably, the Americans emphasized, including intelligence, training, logistics, chain of command, maintenance, and appropriate weaponry. But this implied a gradual, methodical approach to the guerrilla problem. The Americans, for example, talked of a training period of up to six months for the Second Ranger Battalion, while Barrientos sensed that the public was clamoring for quick success. And, of course, he always had to remember the military commanders. Would they be as patient as the Americans wanted him to be, especially if he could not deliver a new up-to-date inventory? In short, the Americans seemed to him to be far more relaxed about Guevara's insurgency than he was. Certainly, he wanted to alarm them enough so that they would provide the hardware he asked for, but he also had reasons to be genuinely worried about the guerrillas, and he took exception with the MILGP's appraisal that they could be contained until the Second Rangers could confront them.[8]

Barrientos gave Guevara credit he did not deserve for cleverly starting offensive operations at exactly that moment in every year when Bolivia had almost no military capability at all, when all of the one-year
conscripts had been mustered out and the new ones had just been
brought in. Henderson could not convince the president of the accuracy
of earlier reports that said fighting had been thrust upon the guerrillas
and not vice versa. Furthermore, Barrientos felt that Henderson was too
conservative in his estimates of guerrilla strength and downplayed the
seriousness of the threat. He pointed to the effectiveness of the guerrilla
organization, its control of the operational area, its incursions outside
that area, the rapidity of its movements, and its recent release of a communiqué, published in a Cochabamba newspaper, that demonstrated its
confidence and spirit of superiority. It was, in fact, the only communiqué published during the insurgency.[9]

During a meeting with Tope, Henderson, and their aides, Admiral Horacio Ugarteche, commander of the navy, supported Barrientos's assessment. (Though landlocked, Bolivia maintained a navy to operate on
Lake Titicaca and the country's rivers.) The admiral maintained not only
that the guerrillas had the initiative and were conducting harassing actions but also that they were ready to extend their activities to other
areas. The American assistance policy, Ugarteche said, was overly rigid,
as demonstrated by U.S. denial of radio and other communications
equipment to the Bolivian Navy. On the other hand, the guerrillas were
well equipped, he said, and if they were not stopped, democracy would
lose, reflecting badly on the U.S. military mission, not only in Bolivia
but also in all of Latin America. And again, the Bolivians pushed a list
of desired new weapons.[10]

Uneven Attrition

Did the Bolivians believe what they said about the guerrillas' strength?
Perhaps partially. It was beginning to seem as though the army could at
best contain the threat but could not eliminate it. Guevara had scarred the
army in a series of clashes and ambushes, one of the most notable occur-
ring near a small town called Iripiti, where, according to Guevara, the
soldiers fell twice into the same ambush. The fight resulted in nine Bolivians being killed, including two officers and one noncommissioned
officer. Although the army claimed that it killed at least four guerrillas, it

seems more likely that it killed one, a Cuban captain, Jésus Suárez Gayol (code-named El Rubio), who had been in the Sierra Maestra campaign and held high administrative posts in Cuba before coming to Bolivia.[11]

The clashes with the guerrillas caused the government to place four new provinces under military control, in addition to one already declared a military zone.[12] The increased level of conflict also convinced the government to outlaw both the Bolivian Communist Party, which must have amused Guevara when he heard about it, and the Revolutionary Workers Party. Meanwhile, throughout May and June, the clashes and skirmishes continued, with the army consistently taking heavier losses than the guerrillas, suffering at least 25 dead by May 10.[13]

But Guevara, too, was taking casualties. By the end of March, he had only some 40 men, and in April he suffered what he called "two great losses." One was El Rubio, the other Captain Eliseo Reyes Rodríguez (Rolando), two of his best fighters, both of whom had fought in the Cuban Revolution.[14] He had no new recruits to fill the empty ranks, and because he had been forced out of his base encampment, he had to keep moving. In addition, he spent considerable time and effort in a fruitless attempt to find Joaquín and reunite his forces.

Unfamiliarity with the territory hampered Guevara continually. Despite the fact that many writers about guerrilla warfare, ironically including Guevara, have stressed the need for guerrillas to know the territory in which they operate very well, and despite Bolivian Army claims that the guerrillas had excellent knowledge of the area, they, in fact, had very little grasp of the local geography.[15] It was rugged, complicated terrain to which most had come in late 1966; not even the Bolivians in the group were from that part of the country. Their total area of operations extended from north to south for approximately 120 miles, along an axis starting just south of Santa Cruz and ending just north of Camiri. The zone, a heavily wooded territory with numerous small rivers and precipitous ravines, extended east to west for about 65 miles.[16] Guevara was determined to become familiar with the region, but his attempts were cut short. He had been conducting a long orientation expedition in March when the Bolivians first became aware of the group and the fighting began.

In contrast to the extraordinary prowess the Bolivians attributed to the guerrillas, Guevara bemoaned their lack of discipline and skill, even if they were superior in those respects to the enemy. For example, on April 22, while Tope and Henderson wrote gloomy assessments of the

Bolivian armed forces, Guevara wrote of his own band, "The errors began early in the morning." He then described a botched attempt to get supplies, involving the band in a useless skirmish. One man went missing, merchandise they had purchased was lost, and a wad of money, which fell during the fighting, was never found. "There is still much to do to turn this into a combat force," he said, "although the morale is quite high."

The Americans seem to have judged the situation accurately, at least for the time being. They believed that the two forces could prowl around each other, the army prodding the guerrilla band into moving more or less constantly but unable to close with it and finish it off and probably unwilling to try. They also believed, as Tope stated, that the only "real hope" for the army rested with the newly formed Second Ranger Battalion.[17]

Guevara took quite a different view of the new Bolivian military developments. Hearing of the planned arrival of the battalion's Green Beret trainers, he wrote on April 13, "Perhaps this is the first episode of a new Vietnam."

"Pappy" Shelton, Green Beret

Despite Guevara's hopes, there was to be no new Vietnam in Bolivia. The U.S. soldiers who arrived there stayed in a training camp, simply teaching the Bolivians how best to cope with the insurgency. Directed by Shelton, they molded the new two-year conscripts of the Second Ranger Battalion into an effective fighting force, and consequently Shelton, in his role as teacher of soldiers, had more responsibility for the way the struggle developed than any other American except Henderson.

Shelton's life, like Henderson's, is the kind that perennially fuels the American dream. Born in Corinth, Mississippi, into a poor family whose father had left before Shelton's birth, he would later join the military as a private and retire as a major. He would then receive bachelor's and master's degrees from Memphis State University and eventually become a federal-government executive with the Office of Personnel Management in Memphis.[18]

Shelton attended public schools until tenth grade, when he left to help support his family. He then held various jobs in southern Tennessee, where the family had moved the year before he left school, working as a logger, saw-mill worker, tractor operator, and shoe-factory employee. At age 17, he moved to Detroit to work in an automobile plant, staying there for some four months. When the company began a round of lay-offs, he turned to the army for educational opportunities and upward mobility. Enlisting for five years, he was sent first to Japan, as he had requested, and was promoted to sergeant before the Korean War began in 1950. He was among the first U.S. soldiers to go into combat in that conflict, being rushed to Pusan, where he fought less than two weeks before being hit by a mortar shell and evacuated to Japan. Within about three months, he returned to the war and received the Silver Star for destroying an enemy machine-gun nest. After some four months of continuous combat, he received another wound, this one from a hand grenade, and was sent back to the United States.

When Shelton's five-year enlistment ended in 1953, he decided to help his father on his farm in Mississippi. He put most of his savings into cotton and corn seed, but a drought-ridden growing season changed his mind about farming in less than three months. The army permitted soldiers who left the service to return to their same rank if they did so within 90 days. Shelton returned on day 87. By then he was married and had two children. During the next five years, he served in assignments in the United States and Germany, and he and his wife had another child.

In Germany, Shelton went to school for noncommissioned officers, graduating first in his class, then applied for Officers Candidate School. Admitted to the school just before his 28th birthday, the cutoff age, he seemed to be "an old man" to his classmates and hence became "Pappy." It was, like "Che," the affectionate nickname of fellow soldiers. He graduated as a second lieutenant in 1958, then went through ranger and paratrooper training. Following assignments in the United States, he returned for a year to Korea, then at peace, and in late 1961 joined the Special Forces, or Green Berets, being built up by the Kennedy administration following the Bay of Pigs debacle to help the United States fight limited wars and especially to combat insurgencies. Unfortunately, by this time his marriage was beginning to deteriorate.

In 1962, he went with a mobile training team to help fight an insurrection in Laos. When he returned, he tried "to put things back together in his marriage," a union which by then had produced two more children. Meanwhile, he told military career planners from Washington that he wanted Spanish-language training followed by an assignment to the Eighth Special Forces in Panama or an assignment to Germany. He received the Spanish training and went to Panama, where his wife joined him; after some three months, however, she returned to Tennessee, effectively ending the marriage.

Shelton went to the Dominican Republic in 1965 with another mobile training team when American troops entered that country during an insurrection there. He stayed for eight months. In March 1967, when a Bolivian Army patrol fell into Guevara's first ambush, Shelton was back in Panama. Suddenly, the mobile training team scheduled to go to Bolivia sometime the following year was needed immediately. Shelton was available and had the required qualifications—besides speaking Spanish, he was a field-grade infantry officer with ranger and airborne training. Because the officer next in line to command a team received an assignment to Vietnam instead, Shelton was sent to Bolivia.

Shelton Sets Up Camp

In the second week of April, Shelton traveled to Bolivia from Panama with another officer and two sergeants to survey the situation. They met the recruits already signed into the battalion and Colonel Joaquín Zenteno Anaya, commander of the Eighth Division, of which the rangers were a part. They also looked for a suitable place to train, choosing a tiny settlement called La Esperanza, a town with "15 or 20 families," according to Shelton's deputy, Captain Edmond L. Fricke, with a few dirt streets over which cowhands occasionally drove thundering herds of cattle that raised huge clouds of dust. La Esperanza seemed to have been made for a western movie. "Close your eyes," Fricke said, "and think of Tombstone."

The Green Berets set themselves up outside of town at an abandoned sugar plantation and mill, once the recipient of an ill-considered Alliance for Progress loan, as one AID official stated frankly. It lay approximately 45 miles north of Santa Cruz, the region's principal center, itself a town of dirt roads and adobe buildings about 55 miles from the scene of the guerrillas' northernmost operation. That was as close as Guevara and the Green Berets would ever be to one another, roughly 100 miles.

On April 29, Shelton and his team of 16 trainers, all Spanish speakers, flew into Santa Cruz aboard two large C-130 cargo planes, also loaded with food and supplies. A convoy of Bolivian Army trucks hauled everything, men and materials, to La Esperanza.[19] On May 8, the Green Berets began training the men of the Second Ranger Battalion. The course, distressingly slow in the view of the Bolivian government, lasted until September 19. The Bolivians learned how to march, shoot, move at night, detect booby traps, fight hand to hand, go through barbed wire, and operate effectively as units: platoons, companies, and battalion. They underwent physical training, practiced firing at silhouettes, learned how to avoid ambushes, and were taught how to build latrines. They were very proud of the latter and preferred to use the bushes rather than soil them.[20]

AID happened to be assisting the Bolivians in building a road near the camp, and the American in charge of it, Harry Singh, put his crew and machinery at the service of the Green Berets. His bulldozers helped immeasurably in building a firing range and in cutting out a road from the camp to the larger road Singh was working on, which provided a connection to the outside world.

In the 1960s, doing good works or "civic action" was part of American counterinsurgency strategy. No one was better at it than Shelton and no recipients more appreciative than the rural Bolivians around him. His new friend Singh, with his construction capability, helped him greatly. As soon as Shelton's team had the camp at La Esperanza organized, they began building a school for the community, which they had finished by the time the rangers graduated in late September.

Shelton seems to have a populist streak, perhaps a result of his rural southern background, which served him well in Bolivia. He also knew when he came to Bolivia that he would retire when the assignment ended, and that gave him a dashing kind of freedom from the caution, especially regarding superiors, that constrains many soldiers and diplomats who still anticipate advancement. In addition, although Shelton was only a major, Porter knew who he was, respected him, and at least once had an extended interview with him in Panama about the team in Bolivia. Such was the seriousness with which Southern Command viewed the Guevara insurgency.

On paper, Shelton reported to the MILGP representative in Cochabamba, Lieutenant Colonel Joseph P. Rice, who in turn reported to the commander of the advisory group in La Paz and so to Panama. Shelton, in fact, almost never saw Rice, and the last time he did, Porter was talking to the battalion. Shelton recalls that Rice believed for some reason that the translation of the remarks into Spanish was not being done properly, whereupon Shelton told him that they could not both run the battalion. "When you know you're going to retire you can be pretty abrupt," Shelton said, looking back on the event. It was the last time he saw or heard from Rice. He also had almost no dealings with Colonel Horras, the advisory-group commander in La Paz.

Shelton had few if any contacts with Henderson either. He claims to have met the ambassador once, at a party, when he asked if Henderson could provide some funds to get a roof for the school at La Esperanza. According to Shelton, the ambassador replied in impeccable Spanish— why he used Spanish is not clear—"You don't need a roof unless it rains, and if it rains you don't need to have school." The story is at best a case of confused identity, according to Henderson, who says he never met Shelton. Either way, it is clear that the embassy and the ambassador simply did not figure in Shelton's life in Bolivia.

The presence of Shelton's group, however, caused Henderson to figure more prominently than before in the concerns of Southern Command, and behind some of his brittle contacts with its top officers lurked an issue of control that looms very large to both ambassadors and military commanders. Post–World War II presidents, including both Kennedy and Johnson, had issued clear statements that the ambassador in any country is the chief U.S. official there, exercising authority over representatives of the many Washington agencies that have become involved in foreign affairs, from the CIA to the Library of Congress. But if there were a war in a particular country requiring the involvement of U.S. troops, the situation could be different, and the military commander could act independently in the best interests of the American forces. Which situation described Bolivia?

The participants worked out the answer informally on the ground: Henderson was the boss, but he left Shelton alone. Shelton reported directly to Panama and sometimes to Porter himself. Porter, in fact, on one of his trips to the battalion asked Shelton how he could help; give him money for the school roof, Shelton said, and he got it very shortly thereafter. On another occasion, Shelton, a major, and his second in command, Fricke, a captain, went to Panama to discuss supplies with Porter. According to Fricke, the general was very concerned with the quantities of materials requested and the costs involved, until finally Shelton placed his elbow on the general's desk, looked him directly in the eye, and said, "You wouldn't want to lose that battalion, now would you, general?" and got everything he wanted.[21]

Shelton, in fact, never lacked supplies, which once even included a refrigerator for a political contact. He used a powerful sideband radio during the day to handle much of the team's business with Panama headquarters, including its requests for matériel, and the men used it at night to talk to their families.

On a very simple level, Shelton mixed intelligence gathering and civic action extremely effectively. Approximately every other Saturday, he and his medical officer traveled to a school somewhere in the La Esperanza area and held sick call for anyone in the community who wanted medical attention. (Guevara, when he could, did the same thing in the guerrilla area.)[22] Meanwhile, Shelton, who always brought his guitar, would go to a neighboring bar and play one song—which, he says, was about the only song he knew—and then pass the guitar around. Any number of cowboys would come by, drink beer, play the guitar, "and talk about what was going on." Shelton developed a network of farmers, cowboys, and youngsters who told him anything they noticed that seemed different or suspicious. "Nothing happened around there that we didn't know about," he said, adding that the Green Berets "had a perfect net. The troops liked us, kids loved us." In fact, most of Bolivia seemed to love them. In Santa Cruz, they would sit at a sidewalk café where everyone seemed to know them. Newspapers and radio stations frequently featured them, especially their colorful leader. Bolivian radio, for example, broadcast nationwide his remarks at the battalion's graduation, a decision the government probably made, but nevertheless they received good publicity and hospitable treatment throughout their time in Bolivia.

Shelton and Fricke both speak with enormous satisfaction about their mission in Bolivia. Part of it unquestionably stems from their popularity, which for Shelton contrasted very favorably with his experience in the Dominican Republic, where much of the population viewed the American forces as intruders and let it be known that they thought the Americans should go home. In addition, in Bolivia the Green Berets had a clear sense of achievement. As Fricke said, it was a wonderful feeling to be assigned a mission and accomplish what one set out to do. There were no loose ends. The job had been done and done completely.

The Green Berets, and especially Shelton, reciprocated the friendliness they found. Relations became very close between the trainers and Bolivians in the ranger battalion, and Shelton seems to have had an affection for the population in the area beyond simply realizing that their goodwill was tactically useful. While he was at La Esperanza, the former owners of the abandoned sugar mill decided to sell the property to Japanese ranchers, thus displacing Bolivian farmers who had moved onto some of the land. Shelton remembers that the Japanese came with "this fat bald-headed guy from New York, trying to sell them that land." He, however, explained to the agent, "If they drive these Indians off of here, all their cattle might die, anything might happen." The deal fell through, very possibly in part because of Shelton's veiled threat.

Top Priority: Field Intelligence

Both the Bolivian armed forces and their American patrons had a desperate need for intelligence. The Bolivians needed it in the field; the Americans needed it in order to know how to help them. The embassy relied largely on the Bolivian government to appraise the guerrilla situation, especially after the wrangle with Washington about Americans in the combat zone, but as Tope reported, "the Bolivian Armed Forces do not possess a sound, or even workable, military intelligence system."[23] Meanwhile, the embassy believed that the Bolivians readily filled in with fiction wherever data were lacking. It once told Washington, "Due [to the] inadequacy [of the] BAF [Bolivian armed forces] intelligence system and felt need [to] exaggerate alleged AF successes, we are inclined to take communiqué claims at [a] considerable discount."[24] Even Secretary of State Rusk once weighed in on the need for intelligence, telling Bolivian vice president Siles that experience in Vietnam, Laos, Greece, and elsewhere had taught the United States that an information-collection system among people living in guerrilla areas was indispensable to controlling insurgencies.[25]

The arrival of the Green Beret team, however, changed the intelligence picture very quickly. The Americans and Bolivians soon had a glut of information about Guevara and his guerrillas. Shelton's intelligence methods, of course, kept him well informed of things that happened in his area, but he was far from the combat zone. To get information from there required other means, and soon after the establishment of the training camp, intelligence experts began flocking to La Paz, La Esperanza, and Santa Cruz. U.S. Air Force general William K. Skaer, Porter's head of intelligence in Panama, came down to help set up the networks. Arthur Maloney, a CIA officer assigned to Porter's command to work with Skaer, helped get things started and visited occasionally. Maloney traveled throughout the Andean area, concerned with insurgencies in three countries besides Bolivia: Venezuela, Colombia, and Peru. Two American CIA agents arrived in Santa Cruz to set up a communications center, remaining there for the duration of the crisis, and several Cuban exiles, plus an American case officer, came to assist at various levels in the process of gathering and analyzing intelligence, including serving in the Ministry of Government in La Paz. In addition, the station in La Paz, which had responsibility for this effort, regularly consisted of four intelligence officers.[26]

But key to the intelligence operation was the presence of two of the Cuban exiles who could go into the area of operations or anywhere else in Bolivia they chose. One member of the team was Bay of Pigs veteran Félix Rodríguez (code-named Félix Ramos). He had been trained by the CIA in intelligence techniques and methods and had served the agency in Indochina and Latin America. In 1989 he wrote a book about his adventures with the CIA entitled *Shadow Warrior* and in the 1990s surfaced in the news because of his involvement in the Iran-Contra episode during the Reagan administration. He worked with Gustavo Villoldo, code-named Eduardo González. Both spoke English, but González was especially fluent, a talent that would have surprising repercussions before he left Bolivia. He, too, had done CIA jobs since 1961. Remarkably, someone in the CIA involved with Bolivian affairs clearly had not noticed or had forgotten the ruckus about Americans in the guerrilla area. When arrangements were under way for Rodríguez and González to operate with the Green Beret advisers, the CIA made the preposterous suggestion to Southern Command that they wear Green Beret uniforms, which, of course, was rejected out of hand.[27] Americans were not to be in the area, and American uniforms were not to be there either, even on Cuban exiles. In fact, when the time came, the two agents wore the uniforms of Bolivian Army captains, something that would figure significantly in Rodríguez's account of the death of Guevara.

The new intelligence establishment quickly created a network among the Bolivian campesinos in the general region of the guerrilla operations. It linked the villages on at least a weekly basis with Santa Cruz and La Paz. Cooperative villagers traveled on horseback or by jeep or, where possible, used telephones to inform local authorities of guerrilla activities, who in turn informed military officials. Almost any time Guevara went to buy supplies, for example, this network reported it to the army.[28]

By mid-June, however, Bolivian anxieties had not diminished, Green Berets and CIA operatives notwithstanding. The government's fears drove it to appeal once more to Buenos Aires for the kind of help the Americans refused to provide, including napalm. One Colonel Molina Pizarro, according to a secret informant to the U.S. embassy in Buenos Aires, told Argentine officials that the guerrillas numbered between 200 and 300 and were making progress. They might soon have support from miners, students, and opposition parties, Pizarro said, and would be able to cause uprisings in almost any area. Meanwhile, he indicated on "a top secret level" some dissatisfaction with the Green Berets. He reportedly said their training was completely theoretical, that they had no experience in Vietnam, and that much they were teaching had no relation to Bolivia, all of which was false.[29]

Meanwhile, another Bolivian security notion had emerged that the Americans thought misguided and refused to support. Barrientos wanted to form an elite "hunter-killer" group, maybe 50 or 60 young officers, with intelligence, motivation, and drive, who were highly trained to find and destroy guerrilla movements. That is how Bolivian ambassador Sanjines explained the idea to William G. Bowdler of the National Security Council, whom he asked to the Bolivian embassy specifically to hear the plan. Barrientos had tried the idea out on Tope back in April, saying that the group was to be the nucleus of an antiguerrilla force. The idea was, in fact, entertained briefly in Southern Command, where the group was to receive part of its training, but rejected firmly by U.S. officials in La Paz. The proposal simply did not ring true to them, especially as the president earlier had approached the embassy for carbines for a 50-officer guard, which he said was to prevent coups d'état. Tope believed that therein lay the key to the whole idea: The unit now being proposed really was to be a palace guard. Nevertheless, both he and Bowdler answered the request in terms of controlling insurrections and emphasized that the Second Ranger Battalion was being trained for exactly that purpose. Regarding support for yet another elite unit, both temporized.[30]

Rebellion in the Mines

The mining area had always been a scene of trouble and disaffection for Bolivian governments, even after the revolution of 1952. Tension increased enormously after the military seized the government in 1964 and quickly made it clear that it would not tolerate "extremist" labor leaders. In May 1965, the regime jailed and exiled many leftist union chiefs and killed at least one, César Lora. Troops occupied the mines, as they often had in recent Bolivian history, unleashing a bloody confrontation between miners and the army that raged for several days throughout the mining area and on the outskirts of La Paz. By the time a truce was reached, at least 48 people had died and 284 had been wounded, according to army estimates, which were undoubtedly conservative.

In June, fighting flared again for about a day in La Paz between the armed forces on one side and miners and factory workers on the other after the government shipped principal labor leader and ex–vice president Juan Lechin out of the country. Local press on that occasion reported some 40 people killed and scores wounded. Afterward, the soldiers remained in the mines, and in September another bitter confrontation erupted as the miners tried to break their occupation. According to the *New York Times,* 32 people died and 105 were wounded in four days of fighting, although one historian, clearly sympathetic to the miners, puts the dead at 200.[31]

With the outbreak of Guevara's insurgency, the miners required even closer scrutiny, in the opinion of government officials in La Paz. Students, often allies of the miners, now made efforts, albeit feeble, to unite with them in support of the insurgents. In addition, a handful of men from the area had gone with Moisés Guevara to fight with the guerrillas, though many were the worst fighters in the band, doing far more damage than good through their desertions and confessions. Moreover, a radio station belonging to the miners' trade union continually praised the guerrillas, the only one to do so.

American officials involved with Bolivian affairs maintained almost as keen an interest in the political situation in the Bolivian mines as did the Bolivian government. In a report entitled "Crisis Management in Bolivia: Government Flounders but Keeps Its Footing," INR analysts pointed out that continuing unrest among miners had been unable to spark general opposition to the government. It noted that Barrientos, while retaining the support of the military, had resisted temptations to respond to the miners with violence, and meanwhile, the elements in Bolivia that could threaten public order—guerrillas, miners, students, and leftist political groups—had failed to coalesce.

That report implied that Guevara would have gained little by proximity to the miners. The INR writers stated that "the best efforts of extreme leftist agitators have apparently failed to spark any massive, violent move against the government or to weld the miners to the guerrillas. . . . The rank and file miners seemed little inclined to cooperate with the guerrillas." Leftists' efforts were complicated, the report said, because they were at odds among themselves and harassed by the government, and while university and high-school students sympathized with both the miners and the insurgents, they showed no signs even of demonstrating solidarity with them.[32]

The INR report, written on June 23, 1967, made one major mistake when it tried to predict the future. It said that "harshly repressive measures" might cause groups capable of violence to coalesce but that Barrientos had not authorized such measures against the miners, "and his chances of avoiding drastic action seem somewhat better than ever." Within fewer than 24 hours after those words were written, Bolivian troops entered one of the principal mines, touching off a conflict that left scores of people dead or wounded.

On a midsummer night, the eve of Saint John's feast and a major holiday in Bolivia as in many Christian countries, the miners at the large Siglo XX mine celebrated long and hard. They were joined by leftist political and union leaders gathered in a conference to call for a restoration of wages and a reinstatement of miners fired since May 1965. The government, desperately fearful that another insurgency would erupt in the mining region, moved troops into the area in the early hours of the morning of June 24, when the miners, their families, and the conferees were sleeping off the effects of the previous evening. The result has often been referred to as the San Juan massacre. Fighting broke out as the miners put up what resistance they could to the occupation, but their struggle was to no avail. In the end, the Bolivian government listed 16 dead and 71 wounded, although other sources put the figure as high as 87 killed, including women and children, and many more wounded. During the melee, troops knocked the miners' radio station off the air, killing one broadcaster in the process.[33]

When Guevara heard what happened, he had high hopes that if the news could be "proclaimed widely" it would be a great help to his cause. He quickly produced a communiqué to rally the miners behind the revolution, but like all but one of the guerrilla's communiqués, it remained unknown until after his death. Whether or not it would have helped him, we can never know, but we do know that despite the government's harsh repression, leftist forces did not coalesce.[34] The only discernible effect on the insurgents' fortunes occurred after they and the army had a major firefight near the town of Florida on June 27, leaving three soldiers dead and two wounded. Following the clash, the army planned to mass troops in the guerrilla region and surround the insurgents, but in the words of an embassy cable, "Due [to the] situation in mines, no army reinforcements expected in area."[35] Beyond that, the bloodshed at Siglo XX did little to help Guevara.

For better or for worse, the U.S. government was complicit in the suppression of the miners. In the 1960s, planning documents for American military assistance in the hemisphere frankly pointed out what all observers had long known—that internal security, not collective hemispheric defense, had first priority for U.S. military aid. In the terms of one document, "internal security" included "Communist infiltration, uprising, other threats of violence, and the movement of armaments and men across borders."[36] In 1966 a Southern Command report, speaking of the U.S. Military Assistance Program (MAP), stated:

> The MAP-supported units of the Bolivian Army and Air Force have definitely contributed to the political stability in support of the Military Junta. Although all military units were mobilized in May, 1965, and again in September, 1965, to deal with the miners' resistance to governmental reforms, the key units in suppressing the resistance were MAP-supported units of the Bolivian Army and Air Force.[37]

Furthermore, as we have seen, in 1967 Tope and the embassy approved of maintaining U.S.-supported military units in the mining areas. In addition, the embassy applauded the government's response to the problem at Siglo XX.[38]

Rostow sent President Johnson a three-page report from La Paz on the situation, saying the crisis precipitated by the mines intervention apparently had run its course. The student demonstrations were spluttering, and the miners seemed to have capitulated. It attributed success to Barrientos's firmness but restraint, except for the occupation; his avoidance of undue repression that might have created martyrs; and his willingness to discuss the issues with all parties concerned. Furthermore, the possibility of a successful threat from any other quarter had been prevented because the government and armed forces remained unified, which, the embassy pointed out, constituted "the elemental fact of political life in Bolivia." In a very brief note to Johnson, Rostow called the attached report encouraging and said that Bolivia was returning to normal but that the remaining problems were a "fall in government revenues" and "the guerrillas."[39]

Guevara heard on his radio that the workers eventually had signed an agreement with Comibol, the government-run company that managed the mines. "This means total defeat for the workers," he wrote.[40]

"Is Guevara Alive? In Bolivia?"

That Guevara was alive and operating in Bolivia had long been widely assumed in the Bolivian high command, but significantly not by Barrientos. By the end of June, however, General Ovando made it very difficult for anyone to believe anything else. In a press conference, he revealed to national and international media the statements of Debray to his lawyer, affirming Guevara's presence at the head of the guerrilla band and describing the group and its activities. Reports stated that Debray first made the statement to military authorities and that his lawyer then revealed them to the press. Guevara heard Ovando's statement on his radio, including his claim that the Bolivian Army faced perfectly trained guerrillas, among them Viet Cong commanders who had defeated the best U.S. troops. The general based his remarks, said Guevara, on statements by Debray, "who apparently has spoken more than is necessary, although we cannot know the implications of this, nor the circumstances in which he said what he has said."[41]

In July, the artist Ciro Roberto Bustos also told the press that Guevara was in Bolivia and made sketches from memory of various individuals in the band, including Guevara. In addition, he stated that Debray had helped indoctrinate its members, something the Frenchman hotly denied.[42]

These developments forced CIA headquarters to revise its view that Guevara was dead. Back in May, when Henderson went to Washington, he had a talk with Desmond Fitzgerald, director of the CIA's clandestine operations, who, according to Henderson, said it could not be Guevara causing the problems in Bolivia because he had been killed in the Dominican Republic and buried in an unmarked grave.[43] Also in May Rostow told Johnson that Washington had received the *"first credible report"* (emphasis in original) that Guevara was "alive and operating in South America" but added: "We need more evidence before concluding that

Guevara is operational—and not dead, as the intelligence community, with the passage of time, has been more and more inclined to believe."[44] In late June, however, after the capture of Debray and Bustos, Rostow told the president that the CIA then believed that Guevara *had been* with the guerrillas in Bolivia.[45] Nevertheless, as late as July the defense attaché's office at the embassy added to the impression of Guevara's demise. It forwarded to the Defense Intelligence Agency (DIA) an informer's report saying that following a "run-in" with Castro, Guevara had been shot in Cuba in the presence of Castro and some "henchmen."

The embassy's political section entered the discussion on July 12 and, after weeks of wrestling with all of the information it could lay hold of, wrote a two-page study entitled "Is 'Che' Guevara in Bolivia?" The answer: "We're not sure," as the chief of the section put it. Bolivian observers who said that Guevara was there had not known him before, so their testimony was questionable, as the writers pointed out. In addition, Ovando, who also maintained that Guevara was in Bolivia, had an ulterior motive: The presence of the formidable guerrilla leader helped explain why the armed forces had such difficulty in putting an end to the insurgency. "The government," the political section said, "is reportedly pressuring 'witnesses' to claim they have seen Guevara with the guerrillas."

As is the nature of political reports, this one came down on both sides of the debate. After casting considerable doubt that Guevara was in Bolivia, it admitted that, of course, he just might be there and concluded, "Whatever the case, the guerrillas are obviously led by a man of professional caliber. While this leader may not be Guevara, he is certainly someone who has studied and absorbed his insurgency doctrines and techniques."[46]

Guevara heard of the Debray and Bustos statements on his radio at least by July 10, the day he commented on them as he camped probably about 20 miles south of Samaipata—he was not sure himself where he was. The day before, he says, "we lost our way," and this day the road that he believed led to the tiny settlement of El Filo instead simply ended, leading "nowhere." Meanwhile, he had nearly run out of medicine for his asthma and thought the group might have to return to Ñancahuazú to get more, presumably from the caves where they had hidden supplies. The confessions of the captives found him in the midst of these predicaments. He wrote, "The statements by Debray and Pelado [Bustos] are not good; above all, they should not have confessed the international purpose of the guerrilla band, something they did not have to do."[47]

CHAPTER FIVE

Guerrilla Triumph and Trouble

With the new intelligence webs, the Bolivian Army began to have some idea of Guevara's movements, but it still overestimated both the size of his band and his capacity to do damage. They were fooled in part by the accidental split in the band that set Guevara and Joaquín searching desperately for each other and in part by the fact that at least once they encountered several guerrillas on a special chore and consequently separated from the main unit. Contacts with guerrillas at widely separated points gave the army the impression that the band could operate on several fronts at once, exactly what the government feared most.[1] In short, Guevara's very weakness had created an illusion of strength.

Guevara's movements and all of the clashes between his band and the Bolivian armed forces have been detailed by a number of other authors. One of the better accounts is that of Luis J. González and Gustavo A. Sánchez Salazar, Paraguayan and Bolivian journalists who use Guevara's Bolivian diary, media accounts, and interviews with combatants to provide a generally accurate description of Guevara's campaign in Bolivia. Here, I will retell only enough of that story to make the American-Bolivian response understandable.

The Firefight That Impressed the World

Guevara greatly reinforced the illusion of the power he commanded when, on July 7, he staged the most spectacular action in the entire campaign; the capture of the town of Samaipata. The guerrillas carried it out with such elán and coordination that observers could not help but be impressed with their skill. Late in the evening, Guevara blocked the road leading from a combination farm/sawmill to Samaipata, then commandeered a bus, loaded with students, and a truck that happened to pass by. Next, the guerrillas telephoned Samaipata from the sawmill, reportedly ordering the town officials to gather together at a police post at the edge of town, using the hostages' safety to guarantee compliance. They then proceeded to Samaipata in their newly acquired vehicles.[2]

At Samaipata, they took hostage nearly all of the town's principal officials, plus two soldiers and a lieutenant. They forced a druggist to open his store, bought medical supplies with cash, and then forced the lieutenant to let them into an improvised barracks in a schoolhouse. Here, some 15 soldiers slept while most of the local detachment of about 50 men were out on a patrol. The guerrillas killed one soldier who tried to resist, the only casualty in the operation, then took weapons (mostly the infamous Mausers), plus ammunition, blankets, clothing, and 10 hostages. Back at the police post, which adjoined a small grocery stand, they bought food, again paying cash, then left town, taking the 10 hostages with them for about a half mile and leaving them naked there so they could not immediately follow the raiders. Back at the sawmill, they returned the borrowed bus and truck, released the remaining hostages, and disappeared.

Despite the panache of the operation, Guevara considered it only partially successful because El Chino, in charge of buying supplies, got nothing of "any use," especially not the medicine that Guevara desperately needed, one of the major reasons for the raid. In late June and early July, his asthma took a turn for the worse; according to reports of defectors from his band, he also suffered from arthritis, but that is not certain.

The Samaipata raid resulted from the band's dire need for supplies while living under circumstances that kept it constantly on the move. It was evidence of its weakness, not its strength, but most observers interpreted it exactly the opposite way. In fact, Guevara and his guerrillas had become a vagabond band, pushed out of their base at Ñancahuazú, wandering pointlessly through the rugged countryside of southern Bolivia with no strategic objective and no means to make their revolutionary dreams prevail. They could only hope to survive a little longer, until the attrition of continual small combats eventually ground them away.

To Guevara, there still seemed to be some point to their travails, but each day it became increasingly futile. He hoped that somehow, if they could survive, he might find a way to contact the city, to get help, and especially to attract recruits who could still turn his movement into something bigger, even something international. "Our most urgent task," he said in his analysis for June, "is to re-establish contact with La Paz, to be resupplied with military equipment and medicine and to incorporate 50–100 men from the city even though the number will be reduced in action to 10–25." Spiteful as it may seem, one cannot help but remember his arrogance toward the city guerrillas in Cuba. Now he needed nothing so much as contact with someone like Frank País and his urban July 26 operatives. Every month, he lamented the lack of peasant involvement and in July repeated the remarks of June, saying, "The most urgent tasks are: to reestablish the contacts, incorporate fighters and obtain medicine." Establishing contacts, however, would not be easy. Although the guerrillas still received coded radio messages from Havana and occasionally communicated through couriers, the group's radio transmitter was inoperative.[3]

In August, Guevara repeated the July summary in nearly the same words but added the poignant remark: "1) We continue without contacts of any kind and without reasonable hope of establishing them in the near future. 2) We continue without recruiting any peasants, logically enough if we take into account the little contact we have had with them in recent times." The remarks in the analysis for September, the last full month of the diary, are even more pessimistic.

But Samaipata did not seem to the Bolivian high command to be the work of weaklings, nor did the fact that the guerrillas could fight on two fronts, Guevara's and Joaquín's. The command renewed its call for first-class equipment from the Americans, and now it wanted the Second Ranger Battalion to enter the fray immediately—enough of its dawdling in training camp. Samaipata represented the northern extreme for Guevara, putting him only 55 miles away from Santa Cruz, headquarters of both the Bolivian Eighth Division and American intelligence operations for the combat zone. That was uncomfortably close, thought the Bolivians; the battalion was needed to defend the town. But the Americans held firm; the battalion did not budge.[4]

Nevertheless, Samaipata also jolted American confidence, with effects felt all the way from the embassy in La Paz to the White House. The ambassador and his key aides, known as the "country team," immediately began "restudying Bolivian army capabilities" and the measures the United States should take in view of the "situation." At the same time, the embassy complained again to Washington about its inability to observe the operational zone "first hand," adding that reports from Santa Cruz and visiting nongovernment personnel were "disquieting."

The embassy believed that the guerrillas could move freely around the countryside, as demonstrated by the unopposed occupation of the "garrisoned town of Samaipata," and spoke to Washington about a "reported lack of aggressiveness, slow reaction time, and low morale among Bolivian army units (not including 2nd Rangers)." On-site training in the combat area, it had heard, consisted largely of close-order drill with no meaningful counterinsurgency training. Finally, it perceived an aura of pessimism pervading the Bolivian high command, which continued to seek a "miraculous solution." "The sad fact is," the embassy concluded, "that [the] guerrilla force, while not appreciably larger than it was three months ago, has for all practical purposes relative freedom of movement within western and southern provinces of Santa Cruz." The situation did not pose an "immediate" or "grave" threat to Barrientos's government, especially because, in the embassy's estimation, his firm handling of the mining crisis strengthened the regime in the short term more than Samaipata weakened it. But clearly the embassy for the first time felt very uneasy about the guerrilla threat.[5]

One cannot help but wonder what the results might have been had Guevara been able to stage a few more showy operations like that at Samaipata. Might he have gotten more support? Would recruits from the cities and mines have sought him out? Would the Americans have become more involved? The fact is that, although the Americans and Bolivians feared the worse, Samaipata was Guevara's last hurrah. There would be many more fights, but none in which he took the offensive. After that night, he was back on the run and never stopped until he was caught.

Bolivian Achievements, U.S. Scorn

Throughout the guerrilla episode, the Americans were relentlessly disparaging about the Bolivian armed forces, and certainly there was much to criticize. Still, the Bolivians were controlling the insurgency more effectively than American communications between La Paz and Washington suggested. In June and July, Guevara began operating further north, in the province of Vallegrande, much of the time in territory that was both more barren and more rugged than the area where he began his operations. He had been forced into the region, which proved less able to support his band and harder to traverse, by the Bolivian Fourth Division, headquartered at Camiri, which had maintained continuous pressure on him farther south, around Ñancahuazú.

Unquestionably, the Bolivian forces benefited from many kinds of U.S. assistance as they faced Guevara's guerrillas. Besides invaluable help with field intelligence, they received substantial amounts of new equipment. Although it fell well below the initial hopes of the Bolivian high command, it included automatic weapons to nine companies besides the Second Rangers, plus field rations, communications gear, and several helicopters. Some of this arrived a year or two before the insurgency broke out in anticipation of trouble, some was on order for future years but delivered early, and some was provided specifically to meet the emergency.[6] Certain units that received U.S. supplies were sent to the guerrilla zone to reinforce the troops already there, although by far the greater number stayed in the cities and the mining area. Finally, many of Bolivia's officers had undergone counterinsurgency training at Fort Gulick in the Panama Canal Zone or in courses given by Americans in Bolivia. (One of the less successful graduates of the latter was the major captured leading the ill-fated ambush on March 23 that opened the fight with Guevara.)[7]

The Bolivians thus had begun to create real problems for the guerrillas, although they received little applause from their allies. By May, the army's new recruits had been trained and had begun to get field experience, and while on the whole Guevara did not give the Bolivian Army much better reviews than the Americans did, he noted some changes. "The army has improved its technique," he reported even as early as the end of April; "they surprised us at Taperillas and they were not demoralized at El Mesón." The following month, however, the army slid in his estimation. It "goes on without being organized," he said, "and its technique does not improve substantially." In June, he continued to be unimpressed with Bolivian military capability but noted its intelligence-gathering activities. "The army continues to be nothing militarily," he wrote, "but it works on the peasants in a way that must not be underestimated, because it transforms all the members of the community into informers, whether by fear or by lying to them about our objectives." By the end of July, the month that began with the Samaipata raid, he recorded that "the army keeps on without making head or tail of the situation, but there are units which seem to be more aggressive."[8]

On July 8, after Guevara had left the area, the Fourth Division began a sweep of the Ñancahuazú basin, where the guerrillas had located their original headquarters. It was the army's first organized effort to find guerrillas, camps, and hidden caches, and although it never confronted Guevara, the force had two encounters with Joaquín's contingent, resulting in the wounding of a Bolivian soldier and the death of Moisés Guevara. A report from the U.S. defense attaché to the DIA says, "Even though they were not successful in capturing a guerrilla unit the experience obtained by the Bolivian troops has certainly enhanced their morale. For the first time, upon being fired at, they did not drop their weapons and run." Interestingly, as the soldiers searched one camp abandoned by Joaquín, they found a piece of paper inside an empty toothpaste tube that identified the members of his group, but they seem not to have recognized what it was.[9]

Ironically, at this moment, with the Bolivian Army responding more capably and Guevara's band, including Joaquín's splinter group, on the defensive, the U.S. House of Representatives released transcripts of Henderson's testimony made before a subcommittee more than two months earlier, on May 4, 1967. It caused a brief crisis in U.S.-Bolivian relations. The House Subcommittee on Inter-American Affairs of the Committee on Foreign Affairs had begun hearings on communist activities in Latin America and asked Henderson to testify. He said, "I would judge only from the evidence available to *all of us* that the guerrilla activity *was* in it first stage, that it *had not yet* taken the shape of an activist direct attack by violence against the Government" (emphasis added). The La Paz newspapers, basing their reports on an Associated Press dispatch, changed Henderson's observations from the past to the present tense, perhaps because it was unclear what time period he referred to. They also changed "all of us" to simply "us," thus losing the sense of information publicly available and implying that Henderson meant embassy, and probably U.S. intelligence, sources. They also carried his additional observation that the guerrillas were "hard-core" people who would not be eradicated easily and that the effort to do so would take resources away from other purposes. This, said Henderson, was the "long-range meaning of the threat."[10]

Bolivian media stories ran Associated Press speculation that the situation might be uncontrollable as though it represented Henderson's opinion and gave similar treatment to other U.S. press commentaries. One came from *U.S. News & World Report*, saying that Barrientos had "lost prestige" because of the failure to oust the "terrorists" and that as long as the guerrillas continued to operate, the country faced the danger of "skidding into another military coup." Another stinging commentary came from the *New York Times*, which Latin American journalists and politicians often regard as quasi-official. A major article in "The Week in Review" section of the June 18 Sunday edition described a Bolivia in shambles. Students and miners, it said, were "acting up," leftist politicians were being arrested at an increasing rate, capital was drifting out of the banks, and the army was fumbling ineffectively against the guerrillas. Meanwhile, Barrientos, who had imposed a state of emergency, presided over a shaky government that would almost surely be overthrown but for the armed forces' loyalty to Ovando, who was in turn loyal to Barrientos.[11]

Three weeks later, in the same well-read section of the paper, the *Times* returned to the charge, this time calling the Barrientos government a "grossly inept" regime that was viewed by the United States as only the best of grim alternatives. The issue appeared two days after the Samaipata raid and dwelt extensively on the guerrilla problem. "Intelligence experts," it stated, "say that the guerrillas are getting stronger and bolder daily," and it described U.S. military experts as being "appalled at the poor quality and poorer motivation of the Bolivian foot soldier. . . . Merely by continuing to exist the guerrillas are 'winning' militarily." Finally, the story made the stunning claim that the Bolivian government secretly had asked Argentina to send troops to pin down the guerrillas. While acknowledging that both governments denied any such request, the *Times* said that actually Buenos Aires turned it down, but only "for the time being." The source or the accuracy of the *Times* story remains unclear, but seasoned observers of the Bolivian scene believe such a request, especially if granted, would have been the kiss of death for an incumbent government in La Paz. The paper also quoted Argentine military sources in Bolivia as saying 10,000 Argentine troops would be on the border "before long." And again, it speculated upon the possibility of a coup d'état, this time giving it more credence than it had three weeks earlier.[12]

Bolivian reporters quickly asked Barrientos for his reaction to all of these comments, many of which seemed to come from Henderson and to be based on his private sources of information. Obviously angry,

Barrientos nevertheless controlled his remarks admirably, leaving room for the situation to improve.

> Just as Mr. Henderson has his opinions based upon some information, so can I assure each Bolivian citizen absolutely that the guerrillas are not going to succeed in this country. Everything Mr. Henderson says, if it is as reported, is completely false. But I doubt that he would have said such things . . . because I do not believe Mr. Henderson talks nonsense.

This episode was perhaps a tempest in a teacup, but it provided an added irritant to the already sensitive U.S.-Bolivian relationship. Eventually, however, with fast and careful work on the part of Washington and the embassy, the waters were calmed, the American journalists' commentaries were separated from Henderson's remarks, and an exact text of those remarks was presented to Barrientos. He then declared, "I want to make clear that Ambassador Henderson is my good friend and I do not believe he would have said those things which I call nonsense."[13]

Pep Rally in Havana

On August 1, despite the dwindling force of Guevara's insurgency—the major rebellion in Latin America—or perhaps because of it, Castro hosted a meeting of Latin American revolutionary parties and some that were not so revolutionary, such as the Bolivian Communist Party. Describing itself as the first conference of the Latin American Solidarity Organization (LASO), it opened its sessions under a banner that shouted Cuba's challenge to world communism, "The Duty of All Revolutionaries Is to Make Revolution." It then drove the point home by naming Guevara honorary chairman of the conference. The gathering was a pep rally for revolution and an effort to strengthen Cuba's influence in leftist radical politics in the hemisphere. The conference organizers declared its purpose to be "to strengthen the bond of militant solidarity among the Latin American anti-imperialist fighters and to draw up basic bonds for the development of the continental revolution"—stirring phrases for a fading cause.[14]

Even in the revolutionary milieu of Havana, however, visitors from traditional communist parties challenged Cuban views. According to one report, they resisted not only the notion that revolution can succeed before the "objective and subjective conditions" call for it but also what they perceived as Havana's effort to make Castro the leader of revolution throughout the continent.[15]

Regardless of criticism from other quarters, Aldo Flores, representing the Bolivian Communist Party, surprisingly tried to align it with the guerrillas, proclaiming that Guevara's fighters were simply doing their patriotic duty in opposing the U.S. advisers and matériel sent to aid "oppressive forces" in Bolivia.[16] Guevara heard of this on September 5 in a radio message beamed to him from Havana. According to his diary, the message said in effect:

> LASO was a triumph but the Bolivian delegation was a pile of shit; Aldo Flores of the B.C.P. [Bolivian Communist Party] pretended to be the representative of the E.L.N. [Spanish initials for National Army of Liberation, the rather grand name Guevara gave his group] but he was proven to be a liar. They have asked one of Kolle's men to discuss the matter.

Despite the fragile reality of revolution in Latin America, the LASO conference caught Washington's attention, especially as it showcased black activist Stokely Carmichael, who, in the words of CIA director Richard Helms, made "excessive comments . . . about 'guerrilla activity' in American cities." Among Carmichael's statements was his remark that "we are moving toward guerrilla warfare within the United States since there is no other way to obtain our homes, our lands, and our rights." Venerating Guevara and echoing his call for more Vietnams, Carmichael declared that "when the U.S. has fifty Vietnams inside and fifty outside that will mean the death of imperialism."[17]

The CIA Misled

The events in Havana moved Helms to ask President Johnson to read a CIA report on the Bolivian insurgency that was written, Helms said, "to point up the nature of the guerrilla movements which Castro is generating throughout Latin America." He added that Carmichael's statements demonstrated "the desirability of a better understanding among us of what these revolutionaries are talking about."[18]

The CIA report, an "interim assessment," bore the date August 8, 1967, and obviously incorporated much reporting from the embassy at La Paz to the State Department and from the U.S. defense attaché in Bolivia to the DIA. In addition, CIA analysts surely had Tope's report at hand and, of course, relied upon covert reporting from Cuba, Bolivia, and elsewhere. They also certainly reviewed worldwide media reaction provided by their overt monitoring network, the Foreign Broadcast Information Service (FBIS). Nevertheless, despite this wealth of data, their assessments were skewed in ways that leap out at a reader today, with knowledge not available then, especially from Guevara's Bolivian diary.

Guevara's stunning ploy at Samaipata, although not mentioned specifically, had left a deep impression upon the analysts regarding his capability, the size of his force, and the possible length and effect of his insurgency. Furthermore, the CIA study reflected very clearly the extremely negative official U.S. reporting from La Paz on the Bolivian Army, assuming that Guevara was much more in control of events than he was and that the Bolivians were almost totally ineffective in containing him. And yet when this report went to the White House, Guevara's band numbered 22, "three being crippled," including himself, to use his own words.[19] Meanwhile, Joaquín, whom he still could not find, had nine guerrillas at the most, including Tania, who had no combat training.

Guevara proclaimed August 7, the day before the CIA report was completed, to be the nine-month anniversary of the band, obviously regarding it as beginning in Ñancahuazú when he arrived in November 1966, despite months of earlier preparation. Speaking of its members, he said, "Out of the first six, two are dead, one has disappeared and two are wounded; I have asthma which I do not know how to stop." Finally, almost as if they were being mocked by fate, one of their two horses died that day.[20]

The CIA report claimed that all five states on Bolivia's borders shared U.S. doubts about the Bolivian military's ability to control the insurgency. Furthermore, agency analysts said they had information that if Barrientos were overthrown, presumably by the guerrillas and/or their allies, Presidents Ongania of Argentina and Stroessner of Paraguay had agreed to consider military intervention.

The CIA noted that the insurgency, strongly influenced and supported by Cuba, seemed more "sophisticated and professional than similar efforts elsewhere in Latin America," and LASO was seen as providing propaganda assistance. Because of the "alleged presence of Che Guevara" and the capture of Debray, the CIA predicted that the insurgency would remain in the "public eye" and "could become a focus for the continuing polemical debate in the Communist world over the wisdom of political versus militant revolutionary action." The analysts added that in contrast to pro-Castro insurgents in Venezuela, Guatemala, and Colombia, those in Bolivia stood out because of their ability to seize the initiative in encounters with the military. The guerrillas were "well-trained and disciplined" and "well-schooled" in Guevara's insurgency techniques, the study stated, whether or not he was with them, as, it noted, some reports alleged. The analysts ascribed the guerrillas' success to "totally inept" Bolivian counterinsurgency operations and pointed out Barrientos's need for a quick victory and his belief in the efficacy of simply massing greater firepower.

The CIA also believed that "leaders and individuals within the pro-Moscow Bolivian Communist Party" were directly involved in the insurgency and working in liaison with the guerrillas. Almost certainly, they had been taken in by Flore's remarks at the LASO meeting but missed Havana's message to Guevara characterizing them as "a pile of shit."

Interestingly, the CIA analysts also felt that local garrisons tended to alienate the populations around them, terrorizing local inhabitants, molesting women, "and opening themselves to unfavorable comparison with the well-disciplined guerrillas." This view directly contradicts that of Charles Grover, who believes the inhabitants in the guerrilla area disliked both groups but especially the insurgents. Again, the question of which campesinos and which region becomes important. Campesinos in the guerrilla area may have had less sympathy for the army than elsewhere, but still, as the writings of Guevara and his colleagues unquestionably show, the population there harassed the insurgents until the day they left.[21] The campesinos' relations with the army may indeed have been strained in places where local garrisons existed and soldiers had too much time on their hands, but it seems that the CIA had interpreted all aspects of the conflict in a manner that was far too positive regarding the guerrillas' prospects and too critical of the army.

Outside the southeast, campesinos often had a high regard for the armed forces, if only because they provided recruits with rudimentary education and boots. In addition, U.S. military advisers and embassy officers in Bolivia believed the armed services were popular with many of campesinos because of their civil-action programs, building roads, bridges, and schools. Colonel Horras, for example, regards this work and the positive attitude it engendered to be a major contribution to the defeat of Guevara. These, of course, are partisan views of individuals who were themselves involved in the civil-action programs. Nevertheless, we can be sure that, whatever their feelings about the armed forces, many campesinos in the Cochabamba Valley and the Altiplano not only believed their lot to be improving but also formed a solid bloc of political support for Barrientos. Consequently, members of those communities never made the slightest effort to seek out Guevara in the wild southeast.[22]

According to the CIA, the guerrillas were "reportedly in contact with one of the larger political opposition parties in Bolivia, the opportunistic Bolivian Socialist Falange (FSB), which received 12 percent of the vote in 1966." The band, said the report, offered to collaborate with the party if it would begin guerrilla activities in the cities. Considering that in his summaries for May, June, and July, Guevara wrote of "total lack of contact" with the party and La Paz (as he would do also in August and September), it is hard to imagine what the CIA had gotten hold of in this instance, but the report's facts certainly seem questionable.

Speaking of LASO, the CIA's writers said that "no particular emphasis has been placed on the success of the Bolivian guerrillas during the proceedings; their continuing progress, however, has certainly raised the morale and affected the outlook of the delegates." They added that the worldwide play given to "the Guevara theme" and to Debray's capture would help keep the Bolivian guerrillas in the public eye long after the LASO conference ended. The CIA logically assumed that the "Guevara theme" plus widespread speculation that he headed the guerrillas in Bolivia would strengthen the rebellion there and amplify its effect. Yet Guevara, for reasons he never makes clear, wanted to keep his location and connection with the Bolivian struggle a secret; as we have seen, he was irritated with Debray and Bustos for revealing that he was in Bolivia.

The most striking aspect of the CIA report, however, is its assumption in early August that the guerrilla campaign was succeeding. Although it said that the Second Ranger Battalion might turn things around, its final sentence stated, "On the other hand, should the guerrillas *continue succeeding* in Bolivia, their experiences and methods are certain to be emulated in other Latin American countries" (emphasis added). The effect of one well-staged offensive, Samaipata, even though born of a desperate need for supplies, especially food and medicine, is stunning. American assessments of the guerrilla strength and Bolivian ability to control the affair were much closer to the mark in March, when the insurgency was discovered, than in August, when it had in fact dwindled. In March, the embassy spoke of 60 to 100 guerrillas and believed that the Bolivians could control them if they persevered, even before plans were laid to begin training the Second Rangers. Now, with Guevara's force reduced by casualties and desertions by at least one-third from its maximum strength of some 50-plus combatants, the CIA reported that last estimates indicated "about 100" guerrillas operating in Bolivia.[23] More impressive, however, than the numbers, which were easy to misjudge, especially in such small increments, is the belief in mounting guerrilla success. Apparently in guerrilla warfare, as in so much else, showmanship plays a prominent role. Guevara, however, seems never to have realized the full psychological impact of the Samaipata raid as he returned to small skirmishes and elusive actions, evading the army in the southeastern Bolivian hills; even if he had understood its full effect, it is far from certain that he could have done much about it.

Not all American intelligence analysts came as heavily under the spell of Samaipata as those at the CIA. On the contrary, the State Department's director of intelligence and research, Thomas L. Hughes, told Secretary Rusk that the guerrilla threat in Bolivia would remain "less than critical for some time." He pointed out that although the terrain in the guerrilla zone protected the insurgents very well, it also isolated them, making recruitment, resupply, and communication extremely difficult. He added that health hazards and disease were prevalent. The guerrillas could probably survive, he concluded, but only if morale stayed high and problems of sickness, personnel replacement, and logistics could be solved.[24]

Incriminating Cache

In the first days of August, it became clear beyond reasonable doubt that Guevara was, or at least recently had been, in Bolivia and that Cuba backed the rebellion. Bolivian Army patrols began making sensational discoveries in the caves created by the guerrillas around the original base camp at Ñancahuazú. They found stocks of weapons, medical supplies, massive documentation on the members of the guerrilla group, lists of their contacts in Bolivia and elsewhere, deciphered radio messages from Havana, codes, and even a cigar butt. Passports with false names showed pictures and gave travel histories of many of the guerrillas, including a disguised Guevara.[25] In addition, snapshots of the guerrillas abounded. In fact, their proclivity for photography, with all of its incriminating potential, was "unbelievable for a guerrilla group," as one CIA official put it.

The guerrillas had abandoned the base, but they still used it as a storage facility, returning to it from time to time to get supplies. On August 14, Guevara wrote in his diary:

> A black day. . . . At night a radio announcer reported the taking of a cave which our runners [*enviados*] were to go to, with details so precise that it is not possible to doubt it. Now I am doomed to suffer asthma for an indefinite time. They also took all types of documents and photographs. It is the hardest blow they have ever given us; somebody talked. Who? That is what we don't know.

Somebody had talked, indeed! Bustos not only talked but also drew a set of detailed maps of the Ñancahuazú base, including its storage areas.[26] The authorities immediately arrested Loyola Guzmán and, from information gained from her, rounded up 11 others and identified 8 more as sympathizers. "The photos must be to blame," Guevara wrote on September 15, when he heard of the arrest. He again suspected the photos on September 18, when the radio brought news of Guzmán's attempted suicide because it said, she feared reprisals from the guerrillas. Guevara was right; the photos led the authorities to Guzmán, who had been in charge of finances for the network. After giving useful information to investigators, she threw herself from an upper story of the Ministry of Government but survived.[27]

The arrests isolated Guevara further, if anything could. Even after the debacle of Tania's jeep, the group still had sympathizers in La Paz, although Guevara's diary makes clear that he could never manage to reach them. Now there would be no one to reach even if he found a means of communication. But it was a slight loss. However much the persons arrested sympathized with Guevara, it would be a considerable exaggeration to view them as a support network. One of them once had tried to organize a teachers' strike in sympathy with the guerrillas but failed, and none of them had ever managed to send the band recruits or supplies.

The cache of materials, valuable as it was to the U.S.-Bolivian cause, sowed discord within the American bureaucracy. First, it created enormous friction in the U.S. embassy between Henderson and the military representatives and also between Ernest Nance, the defense attaché (who, like all U.S. defense attachés, reported to the DIA), and the CIA station, something that occurred more than once during the Guevara insurgency. The materials then caused sparks to fly in Washington between the CIA and the DIA, often rivals at home as well as abroad, and even between the Bolivian high command and the embassy.

The troubles began when the U.S. military representatives—the attachés and the new head of the MILGP, who had replaced Horras—learned of the find from the Bolivian Army but said nothing, at least not to Henderson or to the CIA station. The station learned of it later from its own sources and told the ambassador, who, needless to say, was furious with the military representatives for not informing him. Apparently, the Bolivians did not want to release the material for fear of losing it, and the U.S. officers were playing their game. The CIA, of course, wanted the items, and, according to Henderson, raised a tremendous storm with the Pentagon about the way the military had handled the matter.[28]

Soon, the Americans prevailed upon the Bolivians to allow the documentary materials and one or two other items to go to Washington for analysis, especially to try to determine whether or not the partially bald, clean shaven, bespectacled individual on one of the passports was indeed Guevara. The articles, which filled two large sacks the size of mailbags, went off to the CIA, accompanied by an American warrant officer and the chief of intelligence of the Bolivian Army. Nance had hoped that the latter could have been brought into the intelligence analysis as a means of training, but in fact he was ignored in Washington, making Ovando furious and resulting in Nance being cut out of the intelligence loop in Bolivia, he says, for weeks.[29]

The final contretemps verged on farce. The Bolivians, who wanted everything back, itemized all of the materials very carefully. Upon their return, the Bolivian officials notified the embassy that an item was missing—the cigar butt. The embassy queried the State Department, the State Department queried the CIA, and soon a somewhat enigmatic answer came back: "Consumed in analysis."[30]

Word of the find went all the way to President Johnson. With it went a note from Rostow revealing why the Bolivians wanted the materials back so badly: they wanted to use them as evidence against Debray.[31] A little more than two weeks later, on September 22, Barrientos and Ovando made the find public in a press conference in which Ovando documented the Cuban involvement while also assuring the press and the Bolivian people that victory was near. Two days later, he stated, accurately, that Guevara's capture was "imminent."[32]

The materials from the caves served more than intelligence purposes; the Bolivian government, again with considerable help from the State Department and the CIA, used them at a meeting of foreign ministers of the OAS in September. They enabled Bolivian foreign minister Walter Guevara to demonstrate that his namesake was alive and well and in Bolivia and that the insurrection there was essentially a Cuban operation. Before the meeting, the State Department sent a circular telegram to all of its diplomatic posts in Latin America, telling them to let the local governments know of the planned Bolivian presentation at the OAS and to request their support. If those governments asked about U.S. involvement in the presentation, American diplomats were to say that Washington had been informed of the materials and was prepared to provide Bolivian authorities with whatever "technical assistance" might be needed.[33]

Patrick Morris remembers a potential embarrassment regarding "technical assistance," although, in fact, no problem arose. When the day for the presentation arrived, September 25, Walter Guevara made his speech accompanied by slides of the documents from the caves, but the cardboard mount of each slide bore very un-Bolivian initials: CIA. At the end of the day, Morris cleared a telegram to La Paz saying the foreign minister made his speech accompanied by "slides of photos, passports, handwriting samples, etc.," all of which helped the minister make his point that Cuban-inspired intervention needed to be dealt with on a regional basis. However, the telegram said, the presentation was "somewhat marred by poor organization and operation of slides." Perhaps some of the problems occurred because Morris and his aides cut "CIA" off as many slides as they could, which could not have made them fit very well in the projector.[34]

A Column Wiped Out

Guevara suffered one of the worst defeats of the campaign on August 31 when Joaquín and the nine other guerrillas in his column walked into an army ambush. They were sent to their destruction by a farmer living near the Masicurí River named Honorato Rojas.

The guerrillas knew Rojas, first encountering him on February 10 when they were exploring the area. Guevara became wary of the man at once, describing him in his diary as "potentially dangerous."[35] A married man in middle life with eight children, he was a farmer who once had trained horses for one of the wealthier men in the region. Two years later, however, in 1963, he was caught slaughtering one of the man's oxen and was imprisoned for six months for cattle theft. He maintained a small country store, the stock of which included items purchased during trips to Vallegrande. The guerrilla band became part of his small clientele; in fact, it made a significant difference in his business.[36]

A guerrilla survivor, the Bolivian José Castillo Chavez (code-named Paco, or sometimes Paquito),[37] maintains that Rojas came to the attention of the army because of his improved life-style, particularly his smarter clothes. Paco says Rojas was arrested twice, once taken to Vallegrande, where he was tortured, and once to Santa Cruz, where a CIA agent, Irving Ross, bribed him with an offer of money and a chance to move with his entire family to the United States, where he could "live like a prince." However, if he were to avoid punishment for his past cooperation with the guerrillas, he must let the army know the next time the guerrillas appeared. We have only Paco's word for Rojas's links with the army and the CIA, but we do know that Rojas, due either to greed or coercion, betrayed his guerrilla clients.

Many sometimes fanciful variations exist concerning the details of Rojas's betrayal of the guerrillas, but the essentials are clear.[38] Arriving at his farmhouse, the guerrillas asked his advice about crossing a nearby stream, almost certainly the Vado del Yeso, because fast currents can make such a crossing dangerous unless done at the right time and place.[39] Rojas said that he would investigate the stream's conditions, but instead he slipped away to a nearby army unit headed by Captain Mario Vargas Salinas, where he described the guerrillas' plans. When Rojas returned home, he recommended that Joaquín's band spend the night near his house and wait until the following day to cross the stream.

During that night, August 30–31, while the guerrillas rested, an infantry patrol of 31 men arrived at the far side of the stream, setting up an ambush early in the morning. Then they waited most of the day. Late that afternoon, the guerrillas, guided to the crossing by Rojas, waded into the water and, being either extraordinarily confident or careless, left no one on the bank behind them to provide covering fire if needed. The leader of the column, a guerrilla named Israel Reyes Zayas (code-named Braulio), reached the opposite bank while the remaining nine guerrillas, including Tania, still slogged through the water, heading toward a horse-shoe formation on the opposite bank. There, the Bolivian infantrymen waited. Just as Braulio reached the bank, the soldiers opened fire. At a stroke, Guevara lost about one-third of his remaining force.

Seven of the insurgents died in that ambush, though Braulio exchanged fire with the Bolivians, killing a soldier before being killed himself. The army executed another guerrilla who was badly wounded and took one prisoner, Paco, who also was wounded. Two of the bodies drifted downstream, Tania's and that of a guerrilla and cardiologist called El Negro (identified variously as Gustavo Rodríguez Murrillo and Restituto José Cabrera Flores), said by some to be Cuban, by others, including Guevara, to be Peruvian. El Negro was only wounded at Vado del Yeso and eventually reached shore, but he was killed in a firefight a few days later. Tania's body was discovered a week after the ambush.[40]

Guevara and his group arrived at Rojas's house on the evening of the following day, September 1, but without learning about the fate of their lost colleagues. Although a lighted fire flickered inside, the house was deserted when they arrived. Nevertheless, they decided to spend the night. Mule drivers whom the group encountered there said Rojas's wife complained that the soldiers beat Rojas and ate all of their food. The soldiers also had built some barrack rooms onto the house.

Guevara first heard of the ambush in a radio newscast September 2 but did not believe it because it was broadcast by the U.S. government's station, the Voice of America, and not by local stations.[41] The next day, he heard on the Voice of America that Paco had been taken prisoner, but again he did not believe it, and on the following day he heard of the death of El Negro, identified by Bustos. He believed finally that someone had been killed but thought there was something peculiar about the reports overall, and even on September 7 and 8, when he heard of the discovery and burial of Tania's body, he remained skeptical.

The news Guevara heard was accurate each time. Yet by the end of September, although he believed there might be some truth in the reports and that Joaquín's unit could be "considered liquidated," he continued to hope that a small group still wandered about avoiding the army; he continued to think the news of the simultaneous death of "all seven" had to be false. It is unclear whether or not Guevara realized the death toll eventually was even greater than seven, that it was nine out of ten.

Although the news of the disaster at Vado del Yeso was hard for Guevara to believe, La Paz and Washington believed it at once and welcomed it. It raised hopes and gave not only the Bolivian troops but also government officials in both capitals a new spirit of confidence. "After a series of defeats at the hands of the guerrillas," Rostow wrote to Johnson, "the Bolivian armed forces finally scored their first victory—and it seems to have been a big one." It should "do much" to boost morale in the Bolivian Army, he added, and he pointed out that the Second Ranger Battalion would go into operation late that month.[42] But here again, even while praising the Bolivians, Rostow's message shows how hard the Americans were on their allies—in this instance, calling the ambush their first victory. In fact, the Bolivian Fourth Division, in a drive it called Operation Cynthia, had pushed both Guevara and Joaquín north, out of the area of its jurisdiction. Meanwhile, in the north of the combat zone the Eighth Division, which ambushed Joaquín, began a sweep of its own in late August, named Operation Parabanó after a town in the area. By the time Joaquín's band was destroyed, all of the guerrillas were caught in a vise between the two divisions.

The victory eased many anxieties, not the least of which were felt in Buenos Aires and Asunción. Recognizing this, the State Department, with a clear sense of relief, sent news of the episode to all of its Latin American embassies, expressing its belief that "this successful action" by the Bolivian Army would help "to cool off any Latin American interest in intervention in Bolivia" to stop the guerrillas.[43]

To capitalize quickly on the victory and the pervasive new sense of optimism, Barrientos attended Tania's burial in Vallegrande, then went to Rojas's house.[44] There he congratulated Rojas and declared that any Bolivians cooperating with the guerrillas would be pardoned if they surrendered. This was a major departure, as the U.S. embassy put it, from the former unofficial armed-forces policy of killing all guerrillas, defectors or not, and one the embassy had long been urging. U.S. officials only hoped the armed forces would heed the presidential words. Unfortunately for Rojas, by highlighting his betrayal Barrientos inadvertently set him up for assassination in 1969 by remnant sympathizers of Guevara's movement.[45]

Barrientos added another facet to the new policy when, on September 11, he stated that he had evidence that Guevara had been in Bolivia and offered 50,000 pesos ($4,200 in 1967) to anyone who captured him. Newspapers and radio stations carried his statement, and airplanes dropped leaflets announcing the offer throughout the guerrilla area. Barrientos had changed his mind several times about Guevara's presence in Bolivia, and this new policy flowed from his most recent view of the matter. When the guerrillas were first discovered, he refused to believe that Guevara led them; in July, he decided differently, but in early September, when visiting the guerrilla zone, he returned to his original view, saying not only that he doubted the guerrilla chief was there but also that he felt certain he was dead. Now, again, he was sure Guevara was leading the insurgents.[46]

The Fabric Unraveling

Guevara's men were becoming discouraged, especially the Bolivians. With notable exceptions, they had always lacked the motivation of the Cubans, who to a large degree were dedicated, high-ranking members of the Cuban revolutionary movement. As the weeks wore on, Guevara began referring to many of the Bolivians as the "dregs" (*resaca*). By mid-August, two of them, Orlando Jiménez Bazán (Camba) and Jaime Arana Campero (Chapaco) wanted to leave, to Guevara's extreme annoyance. Camba said he could see no future in their struggle. "A typical case of cowardice," Guevara wrote angrily, and he would have let Camba go except that he knew the route Guevara planned to take in his effort to join Joaquín. Obviously, Guevara feared treachery if he released him, but as soon as the two groups were reunited, Camba could leave, Guevara said. Chapaco, on the other hand, agreed to stay for six months to a year because to do otherwise would be cowardly, but he talked so disconnectedly that Guevara wrote, "He is not well." At the end of that month, Guevara wrote that the group's morale and fighting spirit had declined.[47]

A month later, the guerrillas took over the town of Alto Seco, dominating it for three days with no opposition. They collected together the terrified townspeople, while Guevara and Coco Paredo lectured them on the purpose of the insurgency, the value it could bring to Alto Seco, and the evils of the Bolivian military regime and Yankee imperialism. They also urged the citizens to join their ranks, an appeal ignored by everyone except for one young man, who when he tried to enlist was told quietly by one of the group, "Don't be silly; we're done for."[48] A few days later, at the end of September, Guevara himself wrote that by then the most important thing was to pull out, find a more propitious area, and reestablish contacts, despite the fact, which he noted, that the La Paz network had been ripped apart.

By now, the Bolivian government, too, began to realize the desperate condition of the guerrillas and to exude confidence, Ovando announcing publicly, for example, that Guevara would soon be captured.[49] Not long after, one of the most disastrous battles of Guevara's Bolivian insurgency flared up in the village of La Higuera three days after the guerrillas left Alto Seco. After being well treated in a small village at daybreak, the band moved on to La Higuera and into an eerie atmosphere of unrealistic calm. Only a few women were to be seen. At the telegraph office, the group learned that the day they moved into neighboring Alto Seco a message had arrived saying guerrillas had entered the area, and if they were seen at La Higuera, the mayor should inform authorities in nearby Vallegrande. The mayor, in fact, had disappeared. His wife remained behind, however, and she assured the insurgents that no message had been sent that day.[50]

Guevara, uneasy, nevertheless sent a "vanguard" toward a neighboring town to arrange for some mules and medical help for one of his men. "And on one of those barren hills, in full light of day, the advance guard began to march as though the army didn't exist," said Castro later, believing that Guevara, deeply affected by the deaths of Joaquín and his comrades, acted recklessly.[51]

Not long after the advance party set out, just as Guevara and the rest of the group began to follow, they heard weapons firing up and down a nearby ridge. They knew at once that the vanguard had fallen into an ambush. Guevara quickly arranged defensive positions in the town and awaited the survivors; when they arrived, he would head for the Rio Grande. Soon three of his men returned, two wounded, but they brought the news that three had been killed, one Cuban and two Bolivians, including Coco Paredo, one of his most able men. He was one of two Bolivian brothers, the other being Inti, who were among the first of the conspirators, helping with preparations for the insurgency in 1966, months before Guevara arrived.[52]

Coco's death was the worst blow, Guevara wrote, but the other two men were "magnificent fighters," and the loss of the three was "incalculable." Adding to the calamity, two Bolivians deserted. One was Camba, the other Antonio Domínguez Flores (code-named León). Responding to Barrientos's offer of clemency, they fled, turned themselves in to the authorities, and confirmed Guevara's presence in the area. They described the Alto Seco raid and again said Guevara was extremely ill with what they described as arthritis. This may have been simply the result of an amateur diagnosis; Guevara himself, a physician, does not mention arthritis, but he was suffering greatly from asthma and traveled mostly by mule at that point because of his disability.[53]

Guevara heard news of the two deserters on his radio. He noted that they gave information about his illness "and everything else" and assumed that they said even more that was not made public. "Thus ends the story of two heroic guerrillas," was his bitter conclusion. In addition to the information given the Bolivian authorities by the two deserters, Paco, the survivor from Joaquín's column, had been turned over to CIA agent Rodríguez, to whom he poured out information regarding names of Guevara's men and the band's methods of operating. Consequently, he identified the dead in the battle of La Higuera and knew, according to Rodríguez, that they were part of the vanguard. From that, it was easy to make rough calculations concerning the location of the rest of the force.[54]

By now, the Bolivian high command was nearly issuing victory statements. It made a series of comments about Guevara's "desperate" plight, while Ovando stated that the entire group would be exterminated shortly. Guevara was caught in a narrow jungle valley, the Bolivian authorities maintained, with 1,500 troops advancing from both ends, "a trapped man who is ready to fall."[55]

The deserters worsened not only Guevara's situation but Debray's as well, testifying that he had carried arms during his time with the guerrillas and had given them ideological lectures. Debray replied to the charges in the course of an interview that the army permitted a university student to conduct in the presence of the press. If he were a guerrilla, Debray said, he "would shout it from the rooftops," because being a guerrilla was "a thing of honor and glory." But, he added, he had not been, nor had he taken up arms, and he wanted to be tried on facts, not on his intentions. "I left the guerrillas," he said, "precisely because I am not one of them. . . . My departure is proof that I am innocent." Regulations, he pointed out, prohibit a guerrilla from leaving the battlefield.[56] Guevara mentions the episode in one sentence dripping with caustic irony: "An interview with Debray was heard, very courageous when faced by a student provocateur."[57]

But in these last troubled weeks, Guevara turned his greatest scorn and anger not toward the Bolivian armed forces or the "Yankee imperialists" or the weaklings and deserters that plagued him but toward the mainline communists. On September 8, he noted that a Budapest daily newspaper called him "pathetic and irresponsible" and hailed the "practical attitude" of the Chilean Communist Party by comparison. That, of course, hit a nerve, with Guevara by then forced to anticipate the collapse of his revolutionary dream, to say nothing of his own probable demise, and surely bedeviled by the certainty that his failure must strengthen the hand of all of those who counseled caution and prudence.

By then, with the discovery of the documents in the Ñancahuazú caves and the annihilation of Joaquín's column, the whole world knew that Guevara was badly wounded. The orthodox communists with their media mouthpieces must have seemed to him like a pack of circling jackals. Their remarks, which he heard on his radio, goaded him into a snarling response in his diary, extremely unusual for a man whose written expressions of anger rarely went beyond the restrained sarcasm he aimed at the deserters and Debray. "How I would like to come to power," he wrote in his lonely reply, "if only to unmask the cowards and lackeys of every kind and rub their snouts in their own filth."

But toward the end of the month, although Guevara could not know it then, annoyances like these would become insignificant. After his first successful ambush on March 23, he wondered if the "famous rangers" would come the next day. They did not. But on September 25, the Second Ranger Battalion, part of the Eighth Division, entered active service in the guerrilla zone.[58]

CHAPTER SIX

The Kill—and After

Hey, Limey, you want some news? We just got Guevara. . . . You better get your ass in gear and get out to Vallegrande." The Green Beret who yelled this to Brian Moser, a British documentary film director, was celebrating the event with colleagues at one of the team's favorite watering holes in Santa Cruz, to the side of the town's main plaza. Moser, passing by that Sunday, October 8, had come to Bolivia to do a film for Granada TV. He and Richard Gott of the *Manchester Guardian* were enjoying a quiet stroll when they heard the news about Guevara, whereupon they immediately dashed to Eighth Division headquarters. There Gott "chatted up" the soldiers at the door while Moser slipped into the code room. "It was wild in there," Moser said; "we knew something was happening."

By the time they left, they knew what it was. A firefight was under way; Guevara had been wounded and taken to the village of La Higuera. The next day, he would be flown to Vallegrande, a town where dead and wounded soldiers had sometimes been transported, the bodies of the dead lashed to the skids of helicopters. Moser and Gott spent most of the next eleven hours arranging transportation to get to Vallegrande. Finally, with Christopher Roper, a Reuters correspondent, they clambered into a hired jeep shortly after four o'clock Monday morning. They bounced through the darkness over rough mountain roads, had engine trouble along the way, and eventually arrived in Vallegrande at about 10 A.M.,

October 9. Their reports were to influence greatly the way the world has viewed the events of those days in Bolivia.[1]

Painful Finale

Guevara's men, although ragged, sick, and emaciated, with tattered clothing and ruined boots, were still a dangerous band on October 8, 1967. But by then, just sustaining life was difficult. On October 5, Guevara said that one of this men "made a scene, crying for a mouthful of water." The following day, finding a creek that had not dried up, they camped and cooked a meal, but Guevara felt uneasy. In their hunt for water, they had moved past populated areas in daylight, and now they were in a hollow, vulnerable to attack by the soldiers they had begun to see with increasing frequency.

The vise was closing. The Second Ranger Battalion was very near, searching for the group. When it went into action at the end of September, Colonel Zenteno moved his command post deeper into the guerrilla zone, from Santa Cruz to Vallegrande.[2] Meanwhile, the Fourth Division had just moved its advance headquarters from Lagunillas north to Padilla, almost to the edge of its jurisdiction and halfway into what had once been called the "guerrilla area."

The guerrillas cooked supper at 6:00 P.M. on October 6 and in the morning set out to follow a creek and see where it led. October 7, the day before Guevara's last fight, was free of complications, even bucolic, said Guevara, until an old woman herding goats stumbled upon them. They "apprehended" her, questioning her about troops in the region, but she knew nothing about them, or so she said. The guerrillas did not believe her. They asked about their location. They were approximately one league (some three miles) from La Higuera, she told them, and then they released her.[3] That evening, however, they searched her out again in her home where she lived with two daughters, one crippled, one "half-dwarfed," Guevara noted. They paid her to say nothing about them to anyone, but Guevara said they had "little hope that she would keep her promises."[4]

The guerrillas headed toward the confluence of two small streams, the Churo and the San Antonio, between three and four miles from La Higuera. The rangers, meanwhile, had taken up positions along the San Antonio to help contain them, continually restricting their area of movement. On September 28, the rangers captured Camba, who had deserted the band during the fight at La Higuera two days earlier. (Guevara had said that he could leave when they reached La Higuera. There, with rifle fire crackling in his ears, Camba skipped farewells and fled.)[5]

Camba's bedraggled appearance heartened the rangers enormously. According to a report to the DIA his capture had an immediate effect on the troops' morale. "Previously they had thought of the Gs [guerrillas] as very strong and clever," the report said, "but after seeing 'Gamba' [*sic*] without shoes and suffering from malnutrition, they gained confidence in their ability to destroy the G band." In addition, Camba was "very contrite," which also "sparked confidence and courage among the troops."[6] But he had been dissatisfied for weeks, yearning to flee, so his contrition, added to his shabby appearance, was misleading. Guevara's troops retained a high degree of fighting spirit and were still to inflict a number of casualties upon the army.

The units of the ranger battalion now knew they had almost made contact with the guerrillas; still, closing with them was not easy in an area one journalist described as "an infernal, desolate countryside of high peaks and deep valleys."[7] They patrolled the region continually, moving time and again within a few miles of the guerrillas and, as they did, sending out intelligence teams dressed as civilians. One of these teams learned from a farmer that voices had been heard in the Churo ravine.[8] Then, on the morning of October 8, Company A received word that 17 guerrillas had been spotted in the ravine.

The company called for support, especially mortars. It received it and an additional platoon. Then the combined forces moved toward the ravine, blocking possible exits as they went. One platoon entered the ravine where the Churo and the San Antonio creeks joined. From there, it set out after the guerrillas while Captain Gary Prado Salmón, commander of Company B, shelled them with mortars. But when the platoon came within range of the guerrillas' fire, it lost three men almost at once. Prado quickly ordered another platoon into the ravine to bolster the first. According to the DIA, it "immediately encountered a group of 6 to 8 guerrillas and opened fire." In the exchange, two Cuban guerrillas and one Bolivian soldier were killed, and another soldier was wounded.

Guevara, who was among this group, and a Bolivian, Simón Cuba (code-named Willy), began to scramble up the side of the ravine, but just as they started, a burst of machine-gun fire brought Guevara down, wounding him in the leg and destroying his rifle. Willy dragged him out of the line of fire to a spot where they could rest for a few minutes. Then, inadvertently, they moved directly in front of Prado, who ordered several soldiers to catch them. With Guevara wounded, unarmed, and supported by Willy, they were easily caught.

Although Guevara was a prisoner, the battle did not end. Fighting continued into the evening, and, in fact, survivors clashed on and off with the soldiers for days afterward as they began an odyssey out of Bolivia. But the revolution was over.[9]

Guevara a Prisoner

Guevara was in the army's hands. The soldiers took him and Willy from the ravine to a schoolhouse in the tiny adobe town of La Higuera. From that point until Guevara was laid out dead on a slab in Vallegrande, the stories of what happened to him vary greatly, often to serve the interests of the individual or organization presenting the so-called facts. Nevertheless, there can no longer be any doubt about the major events. He was taken to La Higuera, and there he was questioned to little effect by Bolivian officers. The following day, CIA agent Rodríguez arrived, talked with him, and photographed documents in Guevara's rucksack, including his diary. Guevara was executed that day, October 9, at about 1:00 P.M., not at the orders of the CIA, as has sometimes been charged, or of anyone in the U.S. government but at the orders of the Bolivian president and high command. The Bolivians never informed the Americans of Guevara's capture, believing that they wanted him alive and knowing that they objected to executing prisoners. The Bolivian high command also remembered clearly Henderson's interference in the Debray case. Now, with Debray still on trial, the Bolivian government was being portrayed by much of the world's press as a collection of military "gorillas" and Debray as an innocent victim.[10]

Still, the Americans knew Guevara had been captured. They did not learn that as soon as might have been expected, and not without bureaucratic flurry and communications lapses, but nevertheless, by the evening of the day he was caught—the day before his execution—they knew.

As we view the U.S. foreign-affairs apparatus at work in this period, the ways officials in Washington seem not to have heard the news become as interesting as the ways in which they did. For example, the CIA agents working in the Bolivian government should have known about the capture almost as soon as the Bolivian officials in La Paz received the word, but the testimony of various members of the embassy make it clear that they did not, perhaps because it was Sunday. Furthermore, at least one CIA agent "assumes" that the station in La Paz had high-powered radio equipment that could easily pick up and read Bolivian Army transmissions, which were sent in a "very, very simple code." The transmissions apparently went undetected.

The embassy learned about the capture from Rodríguez, who heard the news while rigging radios in government aircraft on October 8. He then flew over the battlefield with a Bolivian pilot, and, talking to the soldiers on the ground with the new radio he had installed, he confirmed the news, returned to the Eighth Army's forward command post in Vallegrande, and relayed the word not to La Paz but to CIA headquarters in Langley, Virginia, near Washington. He describes his own radio equipment as relatively simple and states that the towering Andes Mountains prevented him from reaching La Paz with his signals. Consequently, he had an arrangement with a CIA station in a neighboring country to stand by twice a day to receive his messages and relay them to Langley, which in turn sent them back to La Paz, all in a matter of seconds. Rodríguez could also request the neighboring station to stand by continuously in a crisis, and he did so on the day of the capture, but the station refused. Rodríguez does not know why, but he believes the reason was simply that it was a weekend.[11]

One other thing went slightly wrong: Rodríguez's message got to Langley and was quickly relayed to La Paz, where a Marine on duty at once called a CIA officer in from a party to see it; for some reason, however, the message was never distributed to officials in Langley. The station spread the word among the chief embassy officers but said nothing to headquarters, assuming it had already seen the message. Meanwhile, according to the CIA version of the events, Colonel Nance, the military attaché, immediately passed the word to the DIA, which as a matter of course relayed it to the CIA.

Nance tells the story differently. No one from the CIA told him anything, he says. Instead, the embassy public affairs officer happened to be lunching at the same club that Sunday as General Ovando and members of the Bolivian high command. Suddenly, the military commanders all jumped up from their lunch and dashed out. (Reports vary regarding the exact time of Guevara's capture, but it did occur at approximately midday.) The embassy official did not know what excited the officers so much, but he thought Nance should know. Nance quickly confirmed the cause, and he sent a message to Washington that afternoon saying, "This is the first notification to the world of the capture of Che Guevara." He admits he did not share the information with the ambassador or the station. Because it was a Sunday, they would not see such a message until the next morning at the earliest.

Whichever version is correct, no one denies that Nance was the first to send the information, and his cable, to a large extent, earned him the Legend of Merit. With the message sent, he says, he went at once to talk to Ovando and the air force chief of staff, General Jorge Belmonte Ardiles, and urged them to spare Guevara. Both smiled pleasantly but said little.[12]

In Washington, DIA officials very quickly realized to their enormous satisfaction that they had scooped the CIA. The next day, officials in the CIA's Latin American section of the Directorate of Operations were far less amused. They scorched the La Paz station for letting them learn via another intelligence agency a report that they presumed came from their own agent, Rodríguez.[13]

The U.S. Government Watches Silently

Regardless of bureaucratic wrangling, the important thing was that Guevara was alive and in captivity, and both Washington and the embassy knew it.[14] Now what?

Washington was silent, and the embassy seems to have been frozen. Perhaps it did not realize how little time Guevara had left, how swiftly the Bolivians would dispatch him. Perhaps it did not want to know. Throughout the following day, the embassy continued to relay reports, rumors, and bits of information to Washington, but it seems never to have asked, "Should we intervene to save Guevara?" Pontius Pilate seemed to have been its model as the hours ticked away.

The question has been posed, including by one CIA officer involved in Bolivian affairs, Why should the United States have tried to save Guevara? If it was willing to forgo the information he might have provided, why antagonize Barrientos and his armed forces by insisting on clemency? Above all, why put Barrientos's presidency in danger of overthrow by outraged military officers? Barrientos was well disposed to the United States and staunchly anticommunist. Furthermore, he cooperated readily in the application of development aid that Washington hoped could show significant results, thereby helping undermine communist appeal throughout the hemisphere.

The capture of Guevara was then and has ever since been a matter of enormous pride to the Bolivian military. If he were whisked away to some safe house in northern Virginia, the Bolivians would not only lose their prize but also appear to be puppets of the Americans. Furthermore, his fate could not have been kept a secret, and one can imagine the frenzy of criticism that then would have been leveled at the U.S. government from around the world, including from Americans, already sharply divided over Vietnam. Was that something the Johnson administration needed in late 1967, beleaguered as it was by widespread, often violent, opposition to its foreign policy? Somebody, perhaps Henderson himself, decided it was not. Or perhaps there was no overt decision but simply the quiet observation of unfolding events until it was too late.

There is no record of any discussion about the subject, or at least none that has ever been released, although we do know that within the CIA there was more than one opinion. John Tilton, the station chief in La Paz, who was away on leave when Guevara was captured, doubts that Guevara would have talked but thinks that interrogating him would have been worth a try. On the other hand, a key official in Langley closely connected with the case states that Guevara "would have been hopeless to debrief" because he was such a "committed, dedicated man." Had he remained in Bolivia, "the pressures on the Bolivian government would have been horrendous," the official said, but wherever he was held, Guevara's imprisonment would have been "a rallying cry for the left everywhere." He added that even the pope might have gotten involved.

Tilton and Nance both say that at various times they urged Barrientos and his high command to spare Guevara when they eventually caught him, but their informal representations had no effect. For Guevara to be saved, the U.S. president's representative in Bolivia, Ambassador Henderson, would have had to ask for it, and Henderson points out that he never received a word from the Bolivians about the capture. What could he do? And indeed why should an American ambassador have saved Che Guevara? In short, the U.S. government took the position tacitly, if not explicitly, that Guevara's fate should be left to the Bolivians, and its officials had few illusions about what that would mean.

Falsehoods from High Places

The Bolivians not only did not inform the Americans that Guevara had been captured but also put out a series of confusing stories about his death. The first misleading report came from Barrientos himself, who told reporters at 10:00 A.M. on October 9 that Guevara was dead but said the news should be withheld until "further notice." The specific time is important because Guevara was then alive and would be for another three hours, which is perhaps the reason Barrientos asked the journalists to hold the news. An hour later, an embassy cable was on its way to Washington, reporting the news but with "no further confirmation or details." This message worked its way through Washington's official labyrinth, arriving in President Johnson's office shortly after 5:00 P.M., La Paz time. By then it was true. Rostow pointed out to Johnson that "the Bolivian unit engaged is the one we have been training for some time and has just entered the field of action." That evening at about 10:00 P.M., the embassy sent another cable passing on a report that Guevara had died of his wounds that day.[15]

That day, after the Barrientos news conference, Colonel Zenteno picked up the theme and made his own public statement, reaffirming that Guevara had died in the battle in the Churo ravine. He repeated those remarks at a press conference in Vallegrande the following day, this time adding that Guevara said to soldiers taking him to La Higuera, "I am Che Guevara; I have failed," a highly doubtful quotation that has enjoyed considerable currency in accounts of these events. Then, said Zenteno, Guevara lapsed into a coma from which he never recovered.

In fact, according to Prado, Zenteno relayed to his troops the order from La Paz to execute Guevara, then returned to headquarters in Santa Cruz and announced at 1:45 P.M. that Guevara had been killed in combat.[16] That was about 35 minutes after Guevara had been shot in the schoolhouse. General Ovando soon repeated the Zenteno line, and the army chief of staff, Colonel Marcos Vasquez Sempertegui, joined the chorus and told the press that evening in La Paz that he was 90 percent certain Guevara died in the fight. Publicly, the Bolivians never budged from that pretext, with even Prado adding to the myth in his own press interviews after the battle. In secret debriefings, however, forwarded to the DIA shortly after the conflict, he and other Bolivian soldiers frankly admitted that Guevara had, in fact, been executed.[17]

Prado, writing about these events some three decades later as a prominent Bolivian diplomat, admitted publicly that Guevara had been executed. The reasons, he said, were fourfold:

[1.] It was felt more important for internal public opinion to show Che defeated in combat and dead than taken prisoner.

[2.] Debray's trial was becoming an annoyance because of its international repercussions. Those would definitely increase if the guerrilla chief were tried.

[3.] Security problems with Che during his trial and after his certain conviction would be difficult. . . .

[4.] If Che were eliminated, a heavy blow would be struck at Castroism, setting back its doctrinaire policy of expansion in Latin America.[18]

Varying accounts of Guevara's last days reflect various personal interests. Rodríguez, extrovert, soldier of fortune, and above all Cuban exile and Bay of Pigs veteran, gives a highly dramatic account of his own involvement with Guevara on October 9, suggesting that he could have saved him but instead honored the Bolivian wish to execute him. Rodríguez, who was using the cover of a Bolivian captain at the time, even affirms that he was considered to be in command of the Bolivian contingent when Guevara was executed; no one else has substantiated this claim, but true or not it is surely the stuff of dreams for a Cuban exile whose friends Guevara had put to the wall after the rebel victory in Cuba in 1959.[19]

Prado will have none of it. He says that although he himself had returned to the ravine, Zenteno was at La Higuera and in command at the time of the execution. Rodríguez, Prado says, identified Guevara, took pictures of him, and photographed his diary, nothing more, just as the CIA had very little to do with the campaign in general. He says Rodríguez returned to Vallegrande after a few hours, which if true would mean that he could not have been involved in the execution the way he says he was.[20]

This is more than a historical quibble. In Prado's view, Rodríguez is grandstanding, claiming undue credit not only for himself but also by extension for the CIA and the United States. He is walking off with Bolivian glory. Prado wants it clear that the Bolivians and nobody else caught—and executed—Guevara. That sensitivity did not take 30 years to develop; it was alive and well, even raw, before the smoke had cleared in the Churo ravine.

On October 10, when a reporter asked Zenteno if the CIA was helping the army investigate captured guerrilla documents, he replied, "Only national elements have been aiding us. I am unaware of the presence of any others." Maybe he was just the maintaining the CIA's cover, but at the same time, Barrientos, while praising the Bolivian armed forces for their achievement, denied that the army had received any special help from the United States beyond a shipment of dry rations. Again, on October 13, he made the same point when, stressing the victory of Bolivian arms, he is reported to have said that it was achieved with no foreign military or economic aid.[21]

Media Reactions

The people of Vallegrande knew on October 9 that a battle had taken place. In the past, they had seen helicopters coming in with dead and wounded but never quite this many, not even after Joaquín's column had been wiped out and the bodies brought there. They crowded around the landing field—schoolchildren, townspeople, a few clergy, a handful of journalists, some officials. The weather was bright and clear, "a great day for a spectacle," said Richard Gott. Brazil's TV Globo had a crew there at Moser's suggestion (he hoped to share footage), and a Swedish newspaper and Bolivia's daily, *Presencia,* had reporters there. This small band had the better part of a day to cover Guevara's death and his body's arrival in Vallegrande before other journalists arrived from La Paz on October 10, using a plane arranged for them by Barrientos.[22]

A helicopter with Rodríguez in the passenger seat and Guevara's body strapped to the landing skid put down at the Vallegrande airport, at about 5:00 P.M.[23] Rodríguez at once disappeared into the crowd and soon left town. Soldiers immediately unstrapped Guevara's corpse, put it in a van, and went speeding away. As they did, the British journalists leaped into their jeep and followed in hot pursuit. The van roared through the great iron gates of the Nuestro Señor de Malta Hospital with the jeep right behind it, while a crowd of people flooded in before the gates could be closed. The van stopped and out jumped a man in a Bolivian captain's uniform who shouted in American-accented English, "Let's get the hell out of here"—meaning, Gott believes, the back of the van, where he had been riding with the body. Gott heard it clearly and knew that the man was one of the Cubans the CIA had brought to Bolivia.

The captain was the American-born Cuban exile code-named Eduardo González, although it remains unclear to whom he was talking and why he spoke in English. Gott recounted the event in his stories for the *Manchester Guardian*, which were also carried in that paper's news service to media around the world. He said an agent from "one of the U.S. intelligence agencies" apparently accompanied Guevara's body from the combat zone. At the hospital, the agent made "desperate efforts" to keep the crowds back and was seen talking to "the senior officer on familiar terms." Gott had really described the actions of two agents—Rodríguez, who accompanied the body, and González, who took over at Vallegrande—but in essence he was correct: The CIA was involved.[24]

Roper also mentioned the incident on the Reuters wire, and Moser showed González in his TV film, identifying him as a CIA agent. From the moment Roper and Gott filed their stories, the news spread around the world that the CIA was involved in the death of Che Guevara, a story that quickly mutated until the CIA was held responsible.

The question remains unanswered: Why was González making arrangements for Guevara's body? Surely, one would expect that with Guevara dead and his documents copied, CIA agents would vanish. Why had González not? One agency official involved in these events said emphatically that he should have but he simply wanted to be in on the action, an opinion shared by Tilton and Rodríguez. Nevertheless, González insinuated himself to such a degree that both Gott and Moser stated that he seemed to be in charge, trying, among other things, to send the press away.[25]

Despite British coverage of CIA involvement, the mainstream American press did not report it for months. Gott once asked a *Washington Post* editor why his paper had not covered that aspect of the story, especially as the *Post* subscribed to the *Guardian*'s news service. The editor replied that the paper simply did not believe it. In addition, the *New York Times*, according to Gott, used Roper's dispatch but deleted the paragraphs about the CIA agents' involvement. An American press official stated later that the U.S. press tended to be skeptical about reports from European news bureaus in Latin America because many of them originated with stringers whose accuracy they questioned and who were perceived as holding strong leftist biases. Roper, although a full-time Reuters employee, once described U.S. assistance to Bolivia as part of the "international imperialist network," a fair indication of his political position. Gott, although his reports were accurate, was nevertheless a stringer in a sense; he was a *Guardian* reporter on leave in Chile while he worked on a book. He was also "a left-wing activist" in the 1960s, as he himself put it in 1994 when allegations about his close links with the KGB caused his resignation from the paper.

Gott repeated his report about the CIA agents in the *Nation* in November 1967, but for months the story got little, if any, further airing in the United States.[26] In March 1968, however, a half year after Guevara's death, the story that the CIA killed him finally appeared in U.S. newspapers. French journalist Michèle Ray, who had covered the Vietnam War and had been highly critical of the United States, had gone to Bolivia to try to buy Guevara's diary manuscript for Parisian publisher Jean-Jacques Pauvert. She gave up that idea, she said, because the diary, having fallen into the hands of the Bolivian military and the CIA, had lost all credibility. She stayed in Bolivia, however, to write the story of Guevara's last days, interpreting them in terms of official American perfidy.

Ray's story appeared in the radical American magazine, *Ramparts*, on March 5, the cover of which presented a striking photograph of the dead Guevara, macabre but remarkably Christlike, hair matted, mouth slightly open, one visible eye glazed and staring at the camera. A box superimposed on the photo showed Ray, a former fashion model, posed before jungle foliage, looking lovely and sad with eyes gazing heavenward. Over it all ran the title, "IN COLD BLOOD: How the CIA Executed Che." Inside, the famous photo of Guevara in his Cuban rebel beret took up a full page under the words, once more, "IN COLD BLOOD." And again, a picture of Ray, this time a full page, shown in a striking miniskirted dress, photographed from below, as though to reinforce our suspicions that sex, death, and war have a deeper bond than we may want to believe. In an age when youth and beauty were often portrayed, with some accuracy, as being on the side of protest, the beautiful woman lamented the handsome, young "martyred revolutionary hero," to use her own words.

In a way, *Ramparts* had produced a contemporary *Pietà*. It had such a powerful effect that this far-left, countercultural magazine managed to do what neither Reuters nor the *Manchester Guardian* had been able to do: get major American media to focus on the story of the CIA's role in Guevara's defeat and death. The article itself, entitled "The Execution of Che by the CIA," stated incorrectly that González (rather than Rodríguez) visited Guevara in La Higuera, but, more significant, Ray stated that after several weeks in Bolivia, she left "assured" that the CIA was responsible for Guevara's death.[27]

On March 6, 1968, the day after Ray's article appeared, the *New York Times* ran a story by reporter Juan de Onis headlined "Disclose CIA Agent Interviewed Guevara before His Execution," which said it was pieced together "from Bolivian and American sources" interviewed in December 1967. The piece, also run on the *Times* news service, was picked up by papers around the country. It gave lengthy coverage to the *Ramparts* story but contradicted Ray, stating that "there is no evidence that the CIA had any part in the decision to execute Guevara."

Confusion in Washington

During the days immediately after the capture, the White House displayed none of Ray's certainty about what had happened to Guevara. Was he really dead? And if so, how did he die? On October 10, Bowdler told Rostow that there was "no *firm* reading on whether Guevara was among the casualties of the October 8 engagement" (emphasis in original). He indicated that word had been received that there were no guerrilla survivors, whereas the day before it was believed that "two were seriously wounded, but alive. One was possibly Che." On October 11, Helms wrote to Rostow, the secretaries of state and defense, and the assistant secretary of state for inter-American affairs. He said:

> 1. You are aware of the published accounts concerning the death of Ernesto "Che" Guevara which were based in essence on the Bolivian Army press conference on 10 October attributing Guevara's death to battle wounds sustained in the clash between the army and the guerrillas on 8 October 1967. Guevara was said to be in a coma when captured and to have died shortly thereafter, the heat of battle having prevented early or effective treatment by Bolivian soldiers.

The rest of the message, two short paragraphs, remains censored by the CIA, but obviously Helms goes on to correct the impression that Guevara died in battle. We know this because of the subject line the censor omitted to strike out: "Capture and *Execution* of Ernesto 'Che' Guevara" (emphasis added).[28]

Rostow passed on the information to the president the same day.

"This morning," he said, "we are about 99% sure that 'Che' Guevara is dead." Although on his note the source is blacked out, we know from the message above that it was Helms. Furthermore, the phrase "Helms says" would fit perfectly in the blanked out area in a line that then continues

> that the latest information is that Guevara was taken alive. After a short interrogation to establish his identity, General Ovando—Chief of the Bolivian Armed Forces—ordered him shot. I regard this as stupid, but it is understandable from a Bolivian standpoint, given the problems which the sparing of the French communist and Castro courier Régis Debray has caused them.

Rostow added that Guevara's death carried "these significant implications":

> —It marks the passing of another of the aggressive, romantic revolutionaries like Sukarno, Nkrumah, Ben Bella—and reinforces this trend.
> —In the Latin American context, it will have a strong impact in discouraging would-be guerrillas.
> —It shows the soundness of our "preventive medicine" assistance to countries facing incipient insurgency—it was the Bolivian 2nd Ranger Battalion, trained by our Green Berets from June [*sic*]–September of this year, that cornered him and got him.[29]

Washington remained keenly concerned with Guevara's fate during the days and weeks immediately after his capture. An interagency meeting, including the National Security Council staff, discussed it at length on October 12. Officials there believed that Guevara's death "triggered Debray's confession of guilt," overlooking the effect that the discovery of Guevara's diary, with all it might reveal, must have had on Debray's decision. Those attending the meeting assumed that the events represented a serious setback "to Castro's theory and practice of promoting guerrilla warfare in this hemisphere" but thought it too early to know how his position in Cuba, his efforts at subversion in Latin America, and his relations with the communist world might be affected. The group worried, however, that his loss of face in Bolivia might cause him to try some "spectacular act" against American installations or personnel to prove he had not "lost his punch." The State Department, Bowdler told Rostow in his report of the meeting, "was asked to send a cable to embassies putting them on alert." Rostow passed on this information to the president the following day.[30]

On October 20, the CIA hedged a little more than Rostow had on the matter of the execution. Nevertheless, in an internal memo it reported that "circumstances surrounding his death are still clouded but it is probable that Guevara, injured in the fighting, was captured alive and later executed by the army."[31]

Really Guevara?

The matter of Guevara's identity loomed large in the days immediately after his death. Few people involved had ever seen Guevara alive. Some voices from distant corners of the world even cried out that it could not be the Argentine revolutionary, reviving the old theory that Castro killed him in 1965. Not surprisingly, Guevara's family also hesitated to believe the news. His father, an uncle in Caracas, and his brother Roberto all expressed their doubts publicly, even though the Bolivian government immediately sent fingerprints to Buenos Aires, where police officials declared them Guevara's. At the CIA also, experts confirmed that the fingerprints matched those previously recorded by the Argentine government and those in the Uruguayan passport, presumed to be his, that was discovered in the guerrilla cache in August. Furthermore, the agency reported on October 20 that handwriting and photograph analyses supported the identification.[32] Meanwhile, Guevara's body was placed on view for journalists to see on October 10, and they were allowed to take fingerprints if they wished. Several did. Then, on October 13, Barrientos made the gruesome announcement that Bolivian authorities would put a thumb, amputated from Guevara's body, at the disposition of investigators.

But what happened to the body after October 10 remained confused for 30 years. Ovando announced on October 11 that Guevara had been buried in an unmarked grave in Vallegrande, and Barrientos told Henderson that all of the dead guerrillas would be cremated, even those already buried, to avoid the creation of future shrines. With observers still trying to clarify the confusing reports, Roberto Guevara flew to La Paz to ascertain the truth about his brother's death. But as if to add to everyone's doubt about the entire matter, Bolivian authorities prevented Guevara from seeing the body. He told the press that, unable to get government officials to take his telephone calls, he went to the home of General Ovando, who refused to see him. Finally, Guevara sent word to the general that he planned to return to Argentina and state that he had been refused permission to see his brother's remains. Then Ovando finally received him, was "friendly and even cordial," and urged Guevara to go to Vallegrande as soon as possible because the body would soon be cremated. Meanwhile, on the same day, October 12, Barrientos told journalists that the body had already been buried.

When Guevara arrived in Vallegrande, military officials told him that unfortunately his brother's body had already been cremated. Some observers speculated that the Bolivian regime was determined that the family should not have the body, fearing again that its last resting place would become a shrine. Finally, as if to blur the truth totally, Ovando in November said the body was, in fact, not cremated but buried in a secret place.[33]

One last ghastly rumor has subsequently proven to be accurate: that the Bolivians cut off both of Guevara's hands. Various motives have been given: They went to Argentine authorities for identification, to the CIA for identification, to one or another Bolivian high official for souvenirs, to a Bolivian ministry whence they were stolen along with Guevara's death mask or, alternatively, whence they were sent surreptitiously to Castro.[34]

In November 1995 Mario Vargas Salinas, whose unit had wiped out Joaquín's column, announced that Guevara's body lay under the landing strip at Vallegrande. The hands and death mask, he said, had indeed been smuggled to Cuba. After searching for some 18 months, Bolivian authorities found a grave containing several skeletons whose clothes indicated they were the skeletons of former guerrillas. One of them, which had no hands, was surely Guevara's, and the Bolivians sent it to Cuba to be buried at Santa Clara, the site of his greatest civil war victory. CIA agent Eduardo Gonzáles, located years later in Miami, says he oversaw the removal of the hands and burial of the body at Vallegrande, but under whose orders, if any, remains unclear.[35]

Despite the confusion about the state and whereabouts of Guevara's body, by the end of October 1967 few people doubted that he had been killed in Bolivia, especially after Castro publicly acknowledged on October 15 that the news was "painfully true." Cuba observed three days of national mourning, during which Castro declared October 8 (the date he believed Guevara died) to be "The Day of the Heroic Guerrilla Fighter," an annual day of commemoration. He also delivered a long and glowing speech in memory of Guevara before a mass meeting in Havana's Plaza de la Revolucion. With virtually every major political figure in Cuba on the platform standing under huge photomurals of Guevara illuminated by floodlights, the crowd saw a film that eulogized him throughout his revolutionary career, showed sinister U.S. military personnel in Bolivia and Vietnam, and ridiculed the Alliance for Progress. Following a recorded Guevara speech, a 21-gun salute, and a bugler's rendition of taps, Castro began his talk. He not only praised Guevara lavishly but also tried to send a message of hope to continental revolutionaries despite the disaster in Bolivia. "We are absolutely convinced," Castro said, "that the revolutionary cause in this continent will not be defeated by that blow."[36]

To the State Department's Bureau of Intelligence and Research, much of the speech seemed to be an attempt "to explain how the Revolution's 'most experienced and capable chief' could have been defeated by a Latin American army not celebrated for its military prowess." Bad luck, difficult terrain, government spies, Green Berets, and 1,500 Bolivian soldiers were part of the equation Castro formulated, said the bureau. It concluded that the Cubans feared that their followers in Venezuela, Guatemala, and elsewhere might now turn to the Soviet thesis of delaying armed insurgency until the required "objective conditions" came about.[37]

Flight of the Survivors

After capturing Guevara on October 8, the rangers moved out of their positions at about 7:00 P.M., but the guerrillas stayed. After the shooting ended, they regrouped, ascertained who was left, and tried to return some structure to their ranks despite the stunning reality of Guevara's capture. At 4:00 A.M., the battle resumed. A mortar squad blocked the ravine at the confluence of the two streams, while an officer and six men pursued the rebels. In the exchange of fire that followed, two guerrillas died, including El Chino. Despite their perilous situation, the surviving guerrillas managed to escape. Prado sent patrols throughout the area but to no effect. At nightfall, the soldiers returned to La Higuera. Meanwhile, with Pombo in command and Inti Paredo as their guide, the surviving insurgents headed west toward the high plateau.[38]

For the next three days, the soldiers searched for the survivors. They heard, correctly, that the guerrillas had broken into two sections, and on October 12 they spotted a group moving along a ravine with the help, they believed, of two young guides. The army units tried to trap them in the ravine, but according to a report of the action, "when Espinoza and his men opened fire on the guerrillas they began to leap about. This confused Espinoza's soldiers though they continued to fire." They did not hit any of their targets. The guerrillas escaped, but in their haste, they abandoned their rucksacks containing food, documents, drugs, and surgical tools. Several hours later, the guerrillas and the soldiers clashed again, this time leaving two soldiers dead and an unconfirmed number wounded. The following day, the rangers made another effort to trap the fleeing rebels, encircling them, but again they failed. The insurgents made a powerful attack on one point of the circle, broke out, killing two soldiers as they did, and disappeared. "By noon of the 13th," says the DIA, "the company had lost contact completely with the guerrilla force," which the army believed was headed in a "southerly direction."[39]

Nine Bolivian soldiers and one civilian guide had died and at least six soldiers had been wounded since the rangers and the guerrillas met on October 8. Five of the deaths occurred in the firefights with the fleeing remnants of Guevara's band. The Bolivian armed forces were "quite elated," according to the U.S. defense attaché, after the confirmation of Guevara's death, but their losses in two days at the hands of the survivors made it clear that the "guerrilla situation" was not over. Nor would it be easy to eliminate the remnants of the band, the attaché pointed out, because the area where the fighting was taking place was one of small hills and valleys with dense jungle growth, making close combat difficult. Yet if Paredo or Pombo were "captured or eliminated," he speculated, the rest of the group would surrender or disperse. Unfortunately for the army, that did not happen.[40]

The guerrillas and the rangers met one last time. On October 14, one of the insurgent groups, four men, collided with Company C, which had not yet faced the enemy. In a sharp fight near El Cajon, the fleeing rebels were not nearly as lucky as they had been in the preceding days: All four died in the exchange. Of the 17 guerrillas who first faced the rangers on October 8, six remained.[41]

Reports reaching Bolivian and U.S. authorities indicated that the Cuban survivors had disarmed the three remaining Bolivians and kept them under guard, but the information must be considered very suspect, especially as Paredo, a stalwart of the rebellion and one of the advance team that set it up, was among the Bolivians and was helping lead the group. A farmer at whose home the fugitives ate said the Cubans kept the Bolivians separate from them and watched them closely. The Bolivians, he said, had no weapons. Finally, he added that all of the guerrillas had shaved and cut their hair, which was probably true.[42]

Other intelligence was equally questionable. The networks that had functioned so well in countering the guerrilla band proved defective in capturing the survivors, as the fugitives left the area quickly and without contact with the population. After the last clash, the army believed that the survivors intended to move out of the area to the east, possibly through Abapo or Cabezas, and prepared to intercept them.[43] Nevertheless, no official ever saw or heard of them again for months, although the search continued. To help, the CIA brought in another two-man team of Cuban exiles, replacing Rodríguez and González, who were rotated home.[44]

The American military adviser to a Bolivian battalion recalls patrolling with that unit and hunting for the survivors in southeastern Bolivia as late as February. As they searched in the Rio Grande area, they believed themselves to be within 20 miles of the fugitives; one day, however, they heard that in fact the guerrillas were in Chile. The adviser, incidentally, not only was engaged in a futile exercise but also was in clear violation of the rule that Americans should not enter the guerrilla area, to say nothing of taking part in a military sweep that might have resulted in combat. "The embassy," he admitted, "would not have been too pleased" had it known.[45]

In fact, the survivors headed west, not east, avoiding population centers, roads, and even major trails, while eating by hunting and gleaning whatever they could from the land they passed through. They traveled for three-and-a-half months, resting only for several days when one of the Bolivians could no longer continue. During that pause, he died from fatigue, according to his colleagues, although Pombo declared in Chile that the Bolivian had been killed in a firefight with the army. Ovando immediately denied that. No such clash ever took place, he said, and suggested that the guerrillas killed their colleague and then made up the battle story. Indeed, Pombo said later in Cuba that the firefight story had been made up. His puzzling explanation was simply "to confuse things."[46] Was the guerrilla's death "assisted" after he became infirm? Was Ovando right and Pombo's story concocted to explain a bullet hole if the body were ever found? Yes, says Rodríguez, who claims that informants in Havana told him so later. The fugitives had an agreement, he says, to kill any one of them who became too incapacitated to travel.[47]

Somewhere on the high plain, a Bolivian Indian named Tani joined the fugitives to guide them to Chile. Their first chance to rest, refit, and supply themselves came when they stopped at Catavi. A mining center and the scene of bloody confrontations between miners and the government, Catavi remained occupied by the soldiers who had taken over the mines in June. The details of the survivors' stay there remain obscure, but splinter-group communists came to their aid. Adherents of such a group had followed Moisés Guevara from the mining area less than a year earlier to join the guerrillas, and those who now helped the survivors could well have been family and friends of Guevara's volunteers. Whoever assisted them in Catavi provided them with new clothes and footwear, supplied them with knapsacks full of food, cigarettes, and even whiskey, and gave them maps and a new radio. They also acquired an additional Bolivian guide.[48]

After leaving Catavi, they were soon moving through passes at some 15,000 feet toward the Chilean border. They had almost reached it eight days later when they were discovered. A salesman on a business trip somehow had seen them and their weapons and notified the authorities in a nearby village. They in turn notified La Paz at once. Smugglers of all kinds of commodities roamed the border area but not smugglers with rifles. This group clearly was different.

Two planeloads of paratroopers took off immediately for the frontier, but by an enormous stroke of luck for the guerrillas, torrential rains began that day and continued for several more. Droning through the foul weather, the aircraft made successive but useless efforts to drop the troops. By the time the rains stopped, the guerrillas—three Cubans and two Bolivian guides—had crossed the border. The two Bolivian guerrillas who had escaped from the Churo ravine and survived the subsequent battles with the army remained in Bolivia in hiding. (Both were subsequently killed in shoot-outs with police in La Paz, Inti Paredo in September 1969 and David Adriázola [Darío] in December 1969 following an attack on the national brewery.)[49]

At the border town of Sabaya, the fugitives hid their weapons and told a Chilean customs official that they had no documents because they were smugglers returning from Bolivia. They wondered if $200 might make that all right. No, it would not, the official said. Four hundred dollars, however, might do the job. By then, February 21, they had traversed a distance that, had they flown, would have been approximately 400 miles. They had walked across some of the most rugged terrain in the world while trying most of the way to avoid even well-worn paths. The Chilean government at first refused to let the fugitives make any public statement but then relented and permitted them to hold a press conference. There, Pombo declared that "the communists did not support us, and that is why the guerrilla movement failed in Bolivia." It was the first time that point was authoritatively addressed to the noncommunist world.

In accordance with an agreement with Bolivia, the Chileans denied the group asylum but did permit it to leave safely, infuriating Bolivian officials. With the help of leftist statesman Salvador Allende, later Chile's president, the group made arrangements to fly to Havana, going the longest way possible. In Allende's company, they flew to Easter Island and then Tahiti, where Allende turned them over to French authorities. Next, they went to Sydney, Singapore, Colombo, Athens, and finally Prague. From there, they flew in a Soviet aircraft to Havana, arriving March 6, 13 days after they left Santiago. They explained this exotic routing as a way of avoiding Bolivian authorities who had offered $10,000 for each of them, dead or alive; also, because the Cubans had entered Bolivia on false passports from other countries in the hemisphere, they felt it best to avoid Latin American customs officials.[50]

Scrambling for the Diary

Guevara's literary remains created as much turmoil as his physical ones, causing the declaration of a state of emergency in Bolivia and nearly bringing down the government. The diary found in his rucksack received enormous publicity, especially because the Bolivians used parts of it at once as evidence in the trials of Debray and Bustos, making it clear that they were more than journalists covering a story.

The day the world learned the diary existed, October 11, Debray changed his defense. Sobbing over Guevara's death, he told a group of law students that he would demand that the court do him "the honor" of considering him "politically and morally" responsible for the acts being judged. (He, like Bustos, was being charged with murder, robbery, and treason by dint of being active in the guerrilla band.) He repeated, however, that in fact he left the guerrilla zone unarmed, adding that, despite his request to join the rebels, Guevara believed that he would be more useful on the outside. He was sorry, he said, that he left, but he pointed out that he had not fired a single shot.[51]

By mid-November, however, under the impact of large amounts of the diary and other documents read at his trial, Debray confessed to more direct involvement with the insurgency: He said he had been a "liaison agent." The U.S. embassy told Washington that the diary implicated Debray as a courier for the guerrillas, delivering funds and undertaking a mission on their behalf, and provided the "most incriminating evidence" against him. The trial ended with convictions a few days later.[52]

Almost as soon as the diary's existence became known, La Paz saw a flurry of publishers' representatives falling over each other to make generous offers for the right to publish it. Ovando reportedly said the regime would sell it to the highest bidder, and the notion quickly became widespread that it would use the funds to help the families of soldiers killed or wounded by the guerrillas, although the government never said officially that it would. Juan de Onis, sent by the *New York Times* to assess it in publishing terms, said he and other potential buyers received reluctant permission from the Bolivian high command to view it in a special room but only after they had sworn to remain silent about its contents until a deal was struck. The Bolivians guarded it, Onis remembers, "as though it were the Dead Sea Scrolls."[53]

Michèle Ray, despite her remark in *Ramparts* that she desisted in her effort to buy the rights, did not do so before she made a $400,000 offer, if Agence France Presse is to be believed. Magnum Photos, in a consortium that included the *New York Times*, offered at least $125,000 but lost interest when no book publisher would join the group, feeling that copyright guarantees were too questionable. Time-Life, Grove Press, and an international European-U.S. consortium were also reported to be bidding for the diary. According to Castro, McGraw-Hill tried for rights, dealing not with the Bolivians but with the Guevara family, who they felt to be the rightful heirs, but were turned down. New York publishers Stein and Day persisted and received rights from the Bolivians for Daniel James to edit not only the Guevara diary but also those of several other members of the band.

While this scramble for rights continued, however, much of the diary was being made public at the Debray and Bustos trials. Furthermore, it seemed increasingly likely that Havana might well have a real copy that it would publish and distribute free. Consequently, many publishers soon hesitated to pay large sums for rights.[54]

Their caution proved well founded. In July, Havana took several steps with the diary. It sent a copy to *Ramparts*, which published it in the July 1968 edition, devoting the entire magazine to it. Again, *Ramparts* made national news, and much of the diary received even wider distribution by being excerpted in news reports. The *New York Times*, for example, ran the story of the diary on page 1 and devoted an entire inside page to it, including numerous excerpts. In addition, *Ramparts* made an arrangement with Grosset and Dunlap to distribute it in book form through its Bantam Books subsidiary. The *Ramparts*/Bantam version, obviously translated in white heat, is at times utterly perplexing, but happily later printings include the original Spanish. Meanwhile, on July 1, 1968, the Cuban Book Institute began distributing a book version free of charge, and two Cuban magazines, *Verde Olivo* and *Bohemia*, published the diary. In all, Havana made hundreds of thousands of copies available, all free.[55]

The diary soon became as prominent in the world of international intrigue as in the world of publishing. Back in October, the diary had found its way to Castro almost immediately, along with additional documents from the other guerrillas and photos of the dead Guevara. Thus, Castro was able to confirm the death of his former comrade as early as October 15, less than a week after his execution. Officials in La Paz remained surprisingly quiet about this development for several months, until Havana announced that it planned to publish the diary, eliciting sneers of disbelief from La Paz and beginning a spat between Castro and Barrientos. Barrientos called the Cuban diary "fictitious," created to "lift the morale of a people who have been subjected to so much want for such a long time." Castro replied in a typically interminable statement on radio and TV saying, among much else, that Bolivian leaders, guided by Yankee imperialism, "lie when they assert that no copy of Che's diary has come out of Bolivia." Once during the exchange, Castro announced that he would trade 100 political prisoners for Guevara's body; Barrientos scoffed, and after several more volleys from each capital, the dialogue ended with Radio Havana calling Barrientos a "gorilla," the Pan–Latin American term of disdain for a military figure who seizes political power.[56]

But in La Paz, beneath the bluster lurked a dreadful suspicion that someone, somehow, had slipped a copy of the diary to Castro. With Cuba flooded with copies and an edition even brought out in La Paz itself that quickly sold 100,000 copies, Bolivian authorities finally admitted that Castro had the authentic version. But who sent it? There were fingers pointing in many directions, some, of course, toward the CIA, where, according to one theory, a double agent did the deed. That proved to be very much on the mark.

Barrientos proclaimed emphatically that no Bolivian military figure had sent the diary to Castro, and Ovando quickly announced that a special court would investigate the matter. Meanwhile, opposition parliamentarians clamored for an investigation and punishment, saying, "Even if there were no fraud, deals, or bribes . . . it is clear that there was negligence or carelessness . . . the more so if, as has been declared, photostatic copies were supplied to . . . the Central Intelligence Agency."[57]

Bolivian Minister, CIA Agent, Castro Sympathizer

The mystery became clear on July 19, when an astonished La Paz awoke to discover that Antonio Arguedas, the minister of government, one of the most sensitive posts in Bolivia, had fled to Chile the day before and from there announced that he had sent Guevara's diary to Castro. Arguedas's post gave him responsibility for many intelligence and internal-security operations. As one analyst described it, "there is no prime minister in Bolivia, but the Interior minister or *ministro de gobierno* is indeed a virtual prime minister on internal matters."[58] The CIA had arranged with Arguedas to bring several Cuban-exile agents into his ministry to assist it with its intelligence efforts during the insurgency—"to put some professionalism" into them, as one former CIA officer put it. One of them, code-named Gabriel García García, served as Arguedas's personal intelligence adviser and once interviewed Debray, although Garcia then used the code name Marco González.[59]

Suddenly, Arguedas, who had long cooperated with the CIA, had been involved in the Saint John's Day massacre of the miners, had directed the arrest of Loyola Guzmán, and had mopped up what remained of Guevara's La Paz network, was now talking from self-imposed exile in a revolutionary idiom befitting Castro or Guevara. Why? Reportedly,

Barrientos had learned who sent the diary, and Arguedas fled just before being apprehended. Thus began an extraordinary episode in which Arguedas's sympathies and motives became utterly blurred, mostly by his own conflicting statements made in continual press interviews over the period of one month and by what appeared to be neurotic behavior. These events have been the subject of much comment, with the best overall description coming from Leo Sauvage.[60] Consequently, only a bare outline will suffice here.

Suggestions quickly arose that Arguedas was a CIA agent, which he was, although he hotly denied it; meanwhile, the CIA tried desperately to get him under some kind of control. From Santiago, he flew to London in the company of a CIA agent and lodged at a safe house there, as he did elsewhere on the trip. After six days, he left London and, declining an offer from Castro for asylum in Cuba, flew to New York for a brief stay and then to Lima. Along the way, he proclaimed more than once his intention to return to La Paz to face trial, which he did, arriving in the city on August 17. He was taken into custody at once but permitted to hold a press conference, which proved sensational.[61]

Earlier denials of being a CIA agent were false, Arguedas said, and he then outlined his recruitment by that agency. Because he had once been a communist, he said, he was approached by the U.S. air attaché, the flamboyant Colonel Edward Fox, in 1964 and was told that if he did not leave the government, U.S. aid would come to a halt. He left his post, but Fox and CIA station chief Larry Sternfield arranged for him to get it back if he cooperated with the CIA, he claimed. After several days of careful interrogation in Lima, the deal was made, said Arguedas, and he became a CIA spy in Barrientos's government. Why then did he send the diary to Cuba? Answer: to help destroy "the imperialist entanglement into which Bolivia had fallen."[62]

Fox, who had long known the Bolivian president personally (a fellow embassy officer called him "our secret weapon with Barrientos"), denies that he told Arguedas to leave his post but affirms that he urged Barrientos to fire him. Furthermore, according to knowledgeable embassy sources, Arguedas told the truth about being recruited by the CIA and being taken to Lima, which the station used as a safe haven for operations relating to Bolivia.

Still, the public does not yet know why Arguedas sent the diary to Castro. His answer, to help Bolivia escape imperialist tentacles, is the response of someone who never read the diary, and perhaps he never had. That document is not a ringing call to arms and rebellion, not the "Marseillaise," nor was it ever intended to be. It is the personal story of everyday effort, struggle, and to a great extent disappointment, written by an addicted diarist, who habitually produced such documents during the major epochs of his life. In fact, because it could so easily dampen the ardor of incipient revolutionaries, Sauvage suggests that Arguedas sent it to Castro at the CIA's instigation. He speculates that the agency hoped Castro would be foolish enough to publish it, thereby stamping it as authentic and at the same time discouraging rebellion and stabilizing the hemisphere—an interesting but questionable thesis.[63]

Later, Arguedas told a Mexican journalist that he sent Castro the diary to thwart the CIA, which he believed intended to gain exclusive rights to it, alter it in ways that would incriminate persons it opposed, and then publish it. Before dismissing this rationale as another case of Arguedas's rhetoric, we should note that the Chilean office of Havana's news service, Prensa Latina, put out a story on October 26 to the same effect. It said "CIA technicians" were working in "specially constructed laboratories in the U.S. Embassy" to falsify the document. The CIA's purpose, according to Prensa Latina, was to suppress popular movements in Latin American countries, especially Chile, by inserting names of people the agency wanted to crack down on.

The story was written originally for the Communist Party daily, *El Siglo*, in the days immediately after Guevara's death, before Castro announced that he had the diary. The truth of the story, which is more than doubtful, is not important here. The point is, it must have represented a real communist fear. In that case, Arguedas, by sending photocopies of the handwritten diary pages to Castro, was keeping the CIA honest. In fact, with copies of the diary written in Guevara's hand now in Washington, La Paz, and Havana, nobody could tamper with the contents without someone else blowing the whistle. Furthermore, with the diary in hand, Castro could see who really was named in it and send warnings, if necessary, to incriminated collaborators throughout the hemisphere.[64]

Even those CIA agents who were very close to Arguedas remain uncertain about the full scope of his espionage commitments. One states that "he probably was everybody's agent," while another maintains that he certainly was not serving Castro until he sent the diary. One agent described him very plausibly as a personality in "turmoil," a leftist who was loyal to Barrientos, the man who promoted him from warrant officer to minister. But at the same time, he said, Arguedas suffered deeply as he followed orders to cooperate closely with the U.S. government and especially the CIA, the bête noire of leftists around the world, in destroying an insurgency led by one of the greatest heroes of the international left.[65] It stretches the imagination to think of the anguish a man who had once handed out communist literature on the streets of La Paz must have suffered when he offered to provide the La Paz station chief with one of Guevara's fingers for identification purposes, as one agent claims he did. Furthermore, as Arguedas cooperated with the U.S. embassy, he saw clearly the enormous influence of its government in his country. Consequently, some people in the CIA see Arguedas's actions with the diary much as he himself describes them—as making amends with his own leftist conscience.

There is an interesting sidebar to the diary episode. When Rodríguez copied the diary, he took other original materials from Guevara's rucksack, including three specially coded "accommodator addresses," where the recipients would recognize mail that should go to Havana and then deliver it to the local Cuban embassy for relay. He delivered these and other documents along with the copy of the diary to the CIA station in La Paz, which in turn gave copies of all of it to Arguedas. It was, says Rodríguez, one of these coded addresses that Arguedas used to send the diary to Castro.[66]

The episode destabilized Bolivia very considerably. The opposition, especially the Socialist Falange, upon discovering that there had apparently been a Castroite in Barrientos's government, had a field day, some suggesting that even the president himself might be tainted. His opponents whipped up violent demonstrations in La Paz and other cities, in which two police officers died and five other persons were wounded. Barrientos retaliated by arresting more than 50 political opponents, but the issue troubled even his supporters in the Social Democratic Party, including his vice president, Luiz Adolfo Siles Salinas. As a result of the turmoil, Barrientos closed Congress and declared a state of emergency. Then, a week after Arguedas fled, when his cabinet resigned in protest, Barrientos named an all-military replacement, including many close friends.

Naturally, Washington watched the situation carefully, and on August 2 President Johnson received a summary from Bowdler saying Barrientos faced "the most serious political crisis of his two years in office," pointing out that the diary was furnished to Castro "by someone in Bolivia." But even two weeks after Arguedas's confession, the White

House remained unconvinced that he was the culprit and not a "scape-goat for his old friend Barrientos in order to take the heat off the restive armed forces," as Bowdler put it. Bowdler, in fact, believed someone in the military sent the diary because it was kept under "lock and key" by the army.[67]

The United States could do little, Bowdler told Johnson, but give Barrientos moral support, which it was doing, and he added, "It is definitely in our interest that he remain in power, because it is doubtful that anyone else could make as good a showing in managing that difficult country." Meanwhile, Henderson had made it clear to Barrientos that the United States hoped he could complete his constitutional term. Then, assuming the nannyish mode he often used with Bolivian officials, he admonished the president to allow the new congress to convene on schedule and to return quickly to a civilian cabinet. Those acts, Henderson said, would help him last out his term.

By August 4, Barrientos agreed to summon the new congress as scheduled, and the crisis abated.[68] Soon afterward, Arguedas faced trial and defended himself admirably, arguing that since his copy of the diary had come from a CIA agent, it could not be considered a Bolivian state secret and so he could not be guilty of treason. He also pointed out that Bolivian military officials had already stated that the diary had no military significance. On Christmas Day 1968, he was freed on bail of about $750. But after dynamite damaged his house and a machine-gun burst from a passing automobile wounded him on the street, he asked for a passport to leave Bolivia. Denied his request by the new minister of government, he took asylum in the Mexican embassy and in 1970 moved to Mexico.[69]

"You Are Killing a Man"

With the end of the Arguedas affair, even the aftershocks of Guevara's insurgency all but disappeared. His dream of hemispheric revolution, once an inspiration for so many in the Latin American left, faded rapidly in the face of the Bolivian disaster. By the late 1990s, neither Havana nor any other force had since frightened the continent with the threat of widespread insurrection. (Indeed, even in the case of Guevara in Bolivia, that threat was largely a chimera, as we now know.)

Various quotes have been attributed to Guevara after his capture. One that has been widely publicized has him saying to his captors, "Don't shoot. I am Che Guevara and I am worth more to you alive than dead." There is no way to know whether or not he actually said this. In that extreme situation, one might say something highly uncharacteristic, but certainly that statement seems odd coming from a man who courted danger and death all of his life as though seeking to die, whose disregard for his own safety worried even Castro, who himself lived so dangerously for so long that it is remarkable that he has survived. Furthermore, the quote implies that Guevara would collaborate with his enemies in order to live, again highly uncharacteristic, and in fact the opposite of what he did. His encounters with military officers after his capture were hostile, and when Rodríguez said he wanted to talk to him, Guevara replied, "Nobody interrogates me."[70] Judging from the records, nobody did.

There is, however, one quote we can believe because it comes from the man who executed him, an enemy with little to gain by concocting the words. The man is Sergeant Mario Terán. Guevara was standing. He knew why Terán had entered the room. Terán told him to sit down, but he said, "No, I will remain standing for this." Then he looked at Terán and said, "Know this now, you are killing a man."[71]

Guevara had lost and lost badly, but he had not only aspired to great things but also performed acts of high consequence and developed enormous influence in the world. Killing him certainly was not to be undertaken casually. But, self-deprecating as he was, he may well have meant something quite different from that. Death had been dealt quickly and reflexively in the Bolivian insurgency as in all wars. Surely it was now worth a moment's pause to consider what it meant. Guevara, with his insistence that the new world and the "new socialist man" could only be born in the fires of revolution, was far from a pacifist. But he may have been saying to Terán that many of the acts required by revolution and counterrevolution should from time to time be recognized as the desperate measures they are and that killing another human being should be understood clearly as an act of great moment.

Memories and Legacies

At the end of Guevara's story in Bolivia, one cannot help but ask how that campaign could have ended so disastrously for so experienced a guerrilla captain. The answer has emerged in fragments throughout this narrative, but now it will be useful to pull those separate strands together.

Castro felt he needed another revolutionary victory in addition to the overthrow of Batista if he was to achieve a leadership position among communists in the Third World. That success would also establish the validity of the Cuban view of revolution, which held that insurgencies needed to be undertaken at once, without waiting indefinitely for proper conditions. Guevara and the Cubans not only had challenged the orthodox communists' attitude toward revolution for nearly a decade but also in the process had incurred widespread hostility.

The Congo expedition might have provided Cuba with the revolutionary success it sought, but it had clearly failed. When it did, Havana returned its focus to its home turf. The Cubans had long made efforts throughout Latin America to create a sustainable revolution, doing so with relatively minor investments of men and matériel—training guerrillas from abroad, sending arms overseas, dispatching advisers to nascent rebellions. Nothing had prevailed. Revolutions had been contained and snuffed out by local governments with U.S. assistance, and Castro's efforts seemed, if anything, to prove that the orthodox communists were right: The successful revolutionary did indeed need to prepare the ground carefully and then await the propitious moment. Havana's impetuosity had led only to defeat.

To achieve the success it wanted, Cuba needed to escalate its effort in its hemisphere, and that was where Guevara and his corps of some 16 experienced Cuban guerrillas entered the picture.[1] They would follow the model of the Sierra Maestra, which Guevara had cast into a theory of revolution in his manual of guerrilla warfare. Above all, they would control the operation and not simply offer help from the sidelines as Cuba had often done in the past.

Bolivia was chosen first to be a supply depot for revolutions in other areas but then to be a *foco* of revolution itself in the hope that rebellion would spread from there, almost the center of the continent, to adjacent countries. Like its Cuban predecessor, this revolution would start in the mountains, and the leader there—Guevara in this case—would have total command, including control over any urban support systems.

The small size of the initial group of dedicated revolutionaries seemed not to present a problem; it was about the same size as the initial group that reached the Sierra Maestra after the disastrous battle at Alegría de Pío. Before long, recruits had begun to stream to the Cuban mountain stronghold, and eventually the rebels prevailed. Why should Havana assume that volunteers would not also be eager to enlist in Bolivia, where the standard of living was among the lowest in the world and a U.S.-supported military government held power just as one had in Cuba in the late 1950s? Guevara had written, after all, that if it persisted even a small group of dedicated revolutionaries could overcome great opposition.[2]

The role of the United States, often mentioned in accounting for Guevara's defeat, was, of course, significant. But considering what Cuba's leaders knew of U.S. military and paramilitary involvement in the hemisphere, especially after the Guatemalan invasion in 1954 and the subsequent civil war in Cuba, not to mention the Bay of Pigs, they could not have been surprised at U.S. aid to the Bolivian armed forces. Guevara makes clear in his diary that he anticipated that Bolivia would receive even greater armed assistance from the United States than was provided. Consequently, help from Washington to the Bolivian government must be discounted as an unexpected factor in Cuban calculations.

The Cubans, however, clearly ignored the force of nationalism and of local sentiment in Bolivia, just as they had ignored the troublesome effects of tribalism in the Congo. What little population there was in the guerrilla area was politically apathetic and hostile toward strangers, while much of the rest of the campesino population supported the Bolivian government. Miners appeared to be sympathetic, but few ever reached Guevara, and many who did caused more harm than good by deserting and betraying his band.

In short, the Cubans completely miscalculated the sentiment of the population they depended upon. In Cuba in the 1950s, the population was ready for revolution and flocked to the aid of a Cuban rebel force. That support must have been paramount in misleading Guevara and the others who planned the Bolivian campaign, causing them to overlook the fact that much of the population in Bolivia had no desire for a revolution and certainly not one led by foreigners.

The greatest miscalculation of all, however, was to ignore the opposition of the orthodox communists to what Guevara was trying to do. Moscow had long made clear its concern over Cuba's revolutionary adventures, and throughout Guevara's war in Bolivia, it neither helped him directly nor pushed the Bolivian Communist Party to do so. That party, meanwhile, was so opposed to the undertaking that it not only watched with folded arms as Guevara was eliminated but also actually aided his enemies by impeding recruitment, the one thing he needed desperately and an area in which it could have helped.

The Cubans not only disregarded communist antipathy to their policy of revolution but also completely misunderstood the degree of nationalism in Latin America, even among communists. The Bolivian Communist Party quickly made very clear that a revolution in Bolivia led by an Argentine with Cuban lieutenants, with the party playing only a supporting role, was something they would not even contemplate. Unfortunately for Guevara, that was not clarified until he and his corps had established themselves in Bolivia.

The attitude of the main Communist Party became obvious to Guevara when Monje visited him in his camp in Ñancahuazú, and here again there was more than an echo of the Sierra Maestra campaign. Once more, the issue of the rural guerrilla versus the city operative lurked in the background. Certainly Guevara, who had come all this way to score a badly needed victory for Cuba, was not going to turn the whole business over to a local Communist Party chief; in addition, he was not about to abandon a sacred Cuban principle of revolution, one formulated in the Sierra Maestra and promulgated in his writing: The leadership of the revolution emanated from the guerrilla force in the hinterland, not from the communists or any other group in the city.[3] Furthermore, according to the Cuban scheme of things, when the revolution was won, leadership remained with the guerrilla chiefs, something Monje and his Communist Party colleagues must have been aware of. Where would that leave them after the victory?

Unfortunately for Guevara, these very basic questions of leadership, cooperation, and command remained unanswered until it was too late to resolve the differences they raised. Few things did him as much damage as that omission. In short, Guevara's campaign in Bolivia was a desperate throw of the dice on Cuba's part that suffered mainly from a shallow understanding of the political scene in Bolivia and, more surprising, in the international communist community.

In many ways, the very success of the Sierra Maestra came to haunt Guevara in Bolivia, teaching him all of the wrong lessons, many via his own manual. In Bolivia, the insurgents did not enjoy popular approval, did not attract streams of recruits, did not have urban support, and could not sidetrack the Communist Party with impunity, all of which was contrary to their experience in Cuba in the 1950s.

The U.S. Response: The Importance of Restraint

The U.S. government had developed enormous resources to combat insurgencies by 1967. By bringing all of them into play, including economic assistance, military aid, counterinsurgency training, and an extensive intelligence and communications network, it checked Cuba's drive for revolution in the Americas, especially with the defeat of Guevara.

One of the U.S. government's principal achievements in Bolivia, however, was to use its resources with restraint. The State Department and Southern Command made it clear almost the moment the insurgency was discovered that U.S. officials, including soldiers, must resist the temptation to enter the combat zone; without them there, Guevara's hopes to make Bolivia another Vietnam became increasingly vain.

Major credit for moderating the U.S. response, however, must go to Ambassador Douglas Henderson, although it was never accorded to him by Washington, just as the story of Guevara's defeat in Bolivia is rarely interpreted in terms of successful U.S. diplomacy. Henderson's refusal to be gulled by panicky or opportunistic Bolivian officials who pushed for increased firepower while disdaining patient Green Beret training helped assure a low-level but effective response to the insurgency.

Nevertheless, for months after he left Bolivia, the State Department gave Henderson only temporary jobs in Washington and at times no job at all. He "walked the corridors," as that condition is described in the State Department. Eventually, the department named him to a subambassadorial post at the OAS, where he continued until he retired in 1974.

Certainly a seasoned bureaucrat could comb through Henderson's career and with hindsight point out where he went wrong, making mistakes a man cleverer in the ways of the system would never have made. For example, a career officer who was willing to tell Robert Kennedy, albeit during the Johnson administration, that one of his major ideas was foolish and that he did not intend to comply with it was not likely to skyrocket. Furthermore, at a time when the Pentagon had unparalleled influence in Washington, Henderson developed an antimilitary image, which he did little to change.

Brian Moser's film, seen in early December 1967 in Great Britain, also harmed Henderson, who had agreed to an interview. Hardly a film Washington could like, it portrayed the Bolivians as mean and ridiculous, Debray as noble, and the Green Berets as oafish, and it correctly identified a CIA agent. Furthermore, in the midst of the strife it portrayed, it opened the Henderson interview with footage of him not quite fiddling like Nero but playing croquet. It was viewed in the White House and apparently made President Johnson furious. Henderson believes, surely correctly, that it had a serious adverse effect on his career.[4]

Unfortunately, Washington officialdom never recognized that Henderson was a major factor, although far from the only one, in preventing Guevara's dream of creating another Vietnam in the center of South America from coming true. To appreciate the significance of that contribution to American diplomacy, we need to remember President Kennedy's statement on November 18, 1963, that the United States needed to "use every resource at [its] command to prevent the establishment of another Cuba in this hemisphere."[5] There is no reason to believe succeeding presidents felt any differently. Richard Helms noted how strongly official Washington felt about Castro's Cuba and how determined it was to do whatever was needed to stop the insurgency in Bolivia; as Kennedy pointed out, the U.S. government viewed Cuba as an incursion of the Soviet Union into the Western Hemisphere and therefore, although he did not say so directly, a violation of the Monroe Doctrine. Consequently, the Guevara insurgency seemed like "heresy" in Washington, to use Helms's word.[6]

Guevara knew that the United States by 1967 was paying a large price at home and abroad for its involvement in Vietnam, and he and Castro believed that the way to advance world communism was to enmesh the United States at that moment in a major battle in South America. Conversely, it was very much in the interest of U.S. policy to keep the battle in Bolivia as small as possible, despite Washington's enormous concern and willingness to do what needed to be done to prevent another Cuba. The trick was to prevent another Cuba without creating anything like another Vietnam. That was Henderson's achievement.

In retrospect, it seems clear that Guevara himself never had a chance of making the Bolivian insurrection much of a military event, much less another Vietnam. Aided by an inept American ambassador, however, Guevara might have brought about a repetition of the 1965 Dominican Republic crisis, where American troops went barging ashore to settle a local rebellion. Had Henderson become as nervous as the Bolivians had, U.S. troops could have gone to Bolivia despite Washington's reluctance, as Guevara's diary makes clear he hoped they would. In assessing Henderson, Washington focused on the minor irritations he caused it and overlooked the real benefit it gained from his ambassadorship, in part because his principal contribution was not a major event but rather a major nonevent. That is much harder to see.

The End of an Era in Bolivia

For Bolivia, the revolution of 1952—or at least that key element, civilian constitutional rule—had ended. Perhaps it died when Paz Estenssoro tried to extend his term or maybe when Barrientos and the rest of the military took over the government in 1964. Barrientos won a fair election in 1966 and served with a civilian vice president, Siles, who took over in the months following Barrientos's death in 1969. Nevertheless, the democratic ethos had been violated and old habits began to reassert themselves. By 1970, few people doubted that General Ovando would assume the presidency, almost as though being head of the armed forces made it his by right. And, indeed, in a bloodless coup d'état that September, he took the government away from Siles, launching a long period of political intrigue and military rule far beyond the scope of this book.

Reflections on Intelligence

The story of the U.S. relationship to Guevara can make a small contribution to the debate in the post–Cold War era about the role of intelligence generally and the CIA specifically. The agency's Directorate of Operations has received much criticism, some even from current and former CIA officials who in the early 1990s castigated it publicly, claiming, among other things, that covert operations were an inappropriate activity.[7] Some of the agency's most memorable troubles occurred in relation to Cuba. The sabotage operations called Mongoose had little to recommend them, and the CIA suffered its most humiliating defeat ever with the Bay of Pigs disaster. Whether or not the agency should undertake "operations" remains an open question, but there is nothing in its role in U.S.-Cuban affairs in the 1950s and 1960s to recommend that it do so.

But "operations" calls for definition, and the CIA's work in Bolivia surely lies somewhere between paramilitary activity and intelligence gathering. Whether such action is acceptable or not to those who would remove the CIA from operations, the agency performed masterfully in creating a useful intelligence system for the Bolivian armed forces. Unfortunately, some of the professionalism of that operation was marred by the Cuban-exile agent in Vallegrande who did not know when it was time to go home and whose presence launched the notion that the CIA played a major role in Guevara's execution. The operation was marred again when the CIA lost control of its accomplice, Antonio Arguedas, who traveled around the world telling embarrassing and on the whole exaggerated tales about the CIA's manipulation of the Bolivian government.

In addition, the agency suffered a surprising lapse in its primary mission, that is, helping to inform the president of international events related to U.S. security. One of its agents was at the site of Guevara's execution and says that he reported it to CIA headquarters that day. Yet the communications of both the U.S. embassy in La Paz and the White House make it clear that they were left groping for two days as they tried to piece together what really had happened to Guevara. It was only on October 11 that Helms informed the White House that the Bolivians had executed him, something agency headquarters had known since October 9, the day it happened. Perhaps, suggests one agent, the delay stemmed from embarrassment at announcing Guevara's death a second time.

In the realm of analysis, as distinct from operations, the picture is mixed, especially compared with INR. The comparison is relevant because some commentators in the 1990s have suggested that the CIA's intelligence-gathering duties should be given to the State Department. Senator Daniel Moynihan, in fact, introduced legislation to this effect in 1991.[8] The CIA did take longer than INR to recognize Cuban efforts to assist and participate in the Congo insurgency, remaining unconvinced until well after it had begun. The agency was also greatly misled by Guevara's stunning Samaipata raid, as was the media. INR, on the other hand, did not let the raid alter its accurate analysis of Guevara as a spent force that by then posed little threat to Bolivia or anyone else.

But INR's record is not perfect either. In a generally accurate analysis of the situation between the government and the miners, it predicted that Barrientos would avoid violence. Moreover, it did so on the very eve of the army's bloody Saint John's Day occupation, which has become legendary even in the long story of violence between government and miners in Bolivia. Nevertheless, although the CIA poured in masses of useful information about Guevara throughout his revolutionary career, the INR in its more limited output, at least concerning the major events in our story, was highly accurate in its major assessments, more so than the CIA.

Guevara's Memory

On October 21, 1967, twelve days after his death, an estimated 50,000–55,000 Americans stood silently before the Lincoln Memorial in Washington, D.C., their heads bowed in silent memory of Che Guevara. By taking part in a massive peace rally and a march to the Pentagon that followed, they hoped to hasten an end to the war in Vietnam. Almost all of them young people, sharing varying degrees of rage against the policies of the U.S. government, they easily agreed with the implicit suggestion by one of the demonstration's leaders that Guevara was a kindred spirit, and they stood silently in his homage.

To many Americans, like many others throughout the world, Che Guevara had become an icon of revolution. Millions in the West, certainly in the United States, had come to believe that the condition of their society and their government called for revolution or something close to it. Not only was Guevara a dedicated enemy of everything they considered wrong with the United States—the Pentagon, the CIA, the policies he and they believed exploited minorities at home and less-developed nations abroad—he was also an itinerant revolutionary, infinitely appealing to a country that harbors a constant admiration, at least in part of its heart, for the unfettered rebel. And rarely did wanderlust and rebellion have stronger appeal in the United States than in the late 1960s, particularly among the country's youth.

Guevara was also young, 39 when he died, lending him enormous appeal in an age that not only celebrated youth (nothing unusual in that) but also considered maturity an evil that had helped lead the country to a state of moral decay. In many ways, Guevara was a Lord Byron of the twentieth century, an intelligent, highly literate revolutionary fighting far from home. Like Byron, he was physically attractive, in an epoch when, peculiarly enough, bodily beauty often became linked with political virtue. A Cuban photographer, Alberto Diaz Gutierra (known as Korda), defined Guevara for youths throughout the world with one of those rare, great photographs that have done so much to characterize this century. His famous picture of Guevara in his guerrilla major's beret, discovered and published by Italian publisher and revolutionary Giangiacomo Feltrinelli, portrayed Guevara for all time exuding youth, sensitivity, and revolutionary purpose. In the late 1960s, few dormitories in American universities were without it.[9]

Guevara also fit the age in another way. Like many before it, that age looked forward but also back to times when things were simpler, less corrupted, nobler. This search led young people time and again to the Arthurian legends. The effects could be seen in their clothing, in the popular poster art of the time, in the renewed interest in Glastonbury's lore, to say nothing of America's own embrace of the Camelot myth to fit the Kennedy administration. Amid this hunger for that legendary moment, no one brought the Round Table to the twentieth century like Guevara, not only as young and handsome as any Launcelot or Gawain but also embracing with total selflessness a life of recurring hardship in foreign lands, struggling to destroy the evil he perceived as he followed a continuing quest for his own kind of grail: a Marxist justice for the world's dispossessed and downtrodden.

Had the young rebels of America's counterculture ever known Guevara, the bloom on the romance surely would have faded. A powerful hedonist streak ran through much of the American movement. "If it feels good, do it" was one of its mottoes, and it believed sincerely in the slogan—created in France—"It is prohibited to prohibit." Nothing could have been further from Guevara's views, dedicated as he was to rigorous personal discipline, which often made him seem dour, even in the eyes of admiring colleagues. The duty of a revolutionary was to create revolution. How it felt had little to do with anything; for the most part, it would probably hurt, and the final reward could easily be violent death. The only thing that would feel good would be the satisfaction of serving the cause. Furthermore, the fruit of the final victory would be a highly disciplined, powerful, centralized state that in fact would prohibit a very great deal.

In ironic contrast to the homage paid to Guevara in the U.S. capital, his death went almost unnoticed in Moscow, where the only public demonstration was a sad little rally by a handful of Latin American students from the city's Patrice Lumumba University in front of the U.S. embassy.[10]

Nor did the communist media soften its views about Guevara because of his death. In the Soviet Union, it relayed many Latin American communists' disdain for his "adventurism," while in China, the media generally took the same line, though it spoke about him less. The New China News Agency ran large excerpts of an article from a Bolivian communist publication warning that armed struggle without mass support leads to defeat, adding that the party controls the gun, not the gun the party. Dramatic, self-sacrificing heroism, the article said—a clear reference to Guevara's Bolivian campaign—was insufficient to win an armed struggle.

On November 3, less than a month after Guevara's death, Soviet Communist Party secretary general Leonid Brezhnev, clearly targeting Cuba's revolutionary theories and Guevara's failure, said a socialist revolution should be undertaken only where the necessary objective conditions existed and should be led only by a Marxist vanguard that had mastered all forms of revolutionary struggle. It could not, he claimed, be "a conspiracy of heroes."[11] Orthodox parties throughout Latin America echoed these sentiments: Jorge Kolle of Bolivia said revolution must be an "essentially national phenomenon"; Rodolfo Ghioldi of Argentina stated that it is impossible "to supply revolution . . . from beyond the frontier," and so on.[12]

The world of communist orthodoxy had been offered a perfect opportunity to hack away at the despised mystique of the Sierra Maestra, and it did not intend to miss it. The Soviets especially "were busy running an empire," as Helms put it. While they intended to maintain a base in Cuba, they also intended, if at all possible, to keep Castro in hand, which would certainly be easier after the failure in Bolivia.[13]

The Marxist ideals in which Guevara had such a profound belief were nearly swept off the world scene in 1989 when the Soviet Union and its hegemony in Eastern Europe began to disintegrate. China remained communist but with a powerful free-enterprise dimension to its economy that would have appalled Guevara. Cuba generally kept the faith under Castro's rule, but having lost Soviet support, even it began encouraging market capitalism and foreign investment. In much of Latin America, despite considerable improvements, many of the problems that distressed Guevara remain—extreme poverty, dreadful living conditions, lack of education, enormously inequitable income distribution. Violence has occurred in a number of places, sometimes with revolutionary intent but often mixed heavily with banditry and drug trafficking.

What does Guevara's memory offer the world today? Perhaps primarily his personal example, his Arthurian qualities, that remarkable determination to struggle and sacrifice for a set of beliefs. In an age when license and personal advantage continually dominate other considerations in private and public life, Guevara's disdain for any reward but the victory of his ideals, his insistence upon discipline, especially for himself, his obliviousness to discomfort and danger in the pursuit of what he believed to be right should surely be inspiring regardless of how one evaluates the philosophy that impelled him.

Appendix: Chronology

July 7, 1953	Guevara leaves Argentina on his second long trip through Latin America.
June 18–29, 1954	A CIA-backed force overthrows Guatemala's leftist government while Guevara is there. He tries vainly to stimulate resistance, then flees to Mexico.
ca. July 10, 1955	Guevara meets Fidel Castro in Mexico City.
November 25, 1956	Guevara sails with Castro's force to invade Cuba.
January 1, 1959	Cuban dictator Fulgencio Batista flees the country. Castro assumes control.
April 17–20, 1961	A CIA-backed Cuban-exile attempt to invade Cuba at the Bay of Pigs fails disastrously.
April 22, 1961	President Kennedy asks retired general Maxwell Taylor to analyze the failure at the Bay of Pigs. New U.S. approaches to "limited warfare" result.
November 4, 1964	A military junta takes over the Bolivian government, turning out the party that had ruled since the 1952 revolution.
November 20, 1964	Douglas Henderson becomes U.S. ambassador to Bolivia.
November 22–29, 1964	Latin American communist parties meet in Havana at the Kremlin's instigation in part to limit uninvited Cuban interference in their countries.
December 9, 1964– March 14, 1965	Guevara makes his last diplomatic trip, starting at the United Nations, then winding through Africa with a side trip to China.

March 1965	By the end of the month, observers in Havana notice Guevara's peculiar absence from public view. He is never seen publicly again.
ca. April 24, 1965	Guevara arrives in the Congo to head a Cuban force assisting a rebellion there.
April 28, 1965	U.S. troops land in the Dominican Republic, helping end a rebellion there. Ralph Shelton, who will lead the Green Beret team in Bolivia, serves with the U.S. force. Top CIA officials believe Guevara dies there at that time.
ca. November 22, 1965	Guevara leaves the Congo and spends the next eight months first in Dar-es-Salaam, then in Prague.
July 1966	Guevara's advance team, later including Frenchman Régis Debray, arrives in Bolivia to lay the groundwork for the insurgency there.
ca. July 21, 1966	Guevara arrives in Cuba to prepare for the Bolivian insurgency.
August 6, 1966	Air force general René Barrientos, winner of the Bolivian presidential elections, is inaugurated.
November 3, 1966	Guevara arrives in Bolivia.
December 31, 1966	Mario Monje, Bolivian Communist Party chief, and Guevara have a showdown over who will lead the insurgency. Guevara prevails but loses the party's support.
January 19, 1967	Bolivian authorities discover the band's camp and think the guerrillas are drug smugglers.
March 15, 1967	Bolivian deserters reveal that the band is a revolutionary force with a Cuban contingent, but Guevara's leadership remains in doubt.
March 16, 1967	Barrientos and his military chiefs first call for U.S. aid, eventually straining relations with the U.S. government, which soon finds the requests excessive.
March 20, 1967	One of Guevara's men reports that he has killed a Bolivian soldier.
March 23, 1967	The first ambush of an army patrol shocks the Bolivian government and begins the fighting.
ca. March 26, 1967	A key Guevara undercover agent, Tania, is exposed when Bolivian authorities find incriminating documents in her jeep.
March 31, 1967	Washington prohibits any U.S. personnel from entering the guerrilla area.

April 17, 1967	Guevara splits his band in two, he assumes temporarily, but can never relocate the other column led by Joaquín.
April 20, 1967	Soldiers capture Debray, Argentine revolutionary Ciro Roberto Bustos, and writer George Andrew Roth as they leave the guerrilla band.
April 29, 1967	A 17-man Green Beret team, originally scheduled to arrive in 1968, arrives to train the Bolivian 2nd Ranger Battalion created to counter the insurgency.
May 6, 1967	U.S. General William Tope reports on Bolivian military needs, stressing intelligence. U.S. intelligence advisers soon include Cuban exiles, two of whom may enter the combat area.
ca. June 30, 1967	Debray reveals Guevara's presence in Bolivia. Barrientos and some U.S. officials, however, remain unconvinced.
July 7, 1967	Guevara's guerrillas, although now constantly on the run, stage a stunning victory at Samaipata, leading most observers to conclude that they are growing continually stronger.
July 8, 1967	Roth is freed.
ca. July 10, 1967	Bustos says Guevara leads the guerrillas. He also incriminates Debray and draws portraits of the insurgents and maps of the Ñancahuazú camp.
August 1, 1967	The Latin American Solidarity Organization (LASO) meets in Havana and reaffirms the Cuban view that revolutionaries should make revolution, not wait for propitious conditions.
ca. August 6, 1967	Bolivian soldiers begin uncovering guerrilla equipment and documents that establish Guevara's presence and incriminate his urban collaborators.
August 31, 1967	A Bolivian farmer betrays Joaquín's column, leading it into an ambush. Of two survivors, one is killed soon after and the other turns CIA informant.
September 25, 1967	The 2nd Ranger Battalion finishes its training and enters combat. By now Guevara's force is squeezed between at least 1,500 soldiers in two divisions.
October 8, 1967	Guevara is wounded and captured when soldiers of the 2nd Ranger Battalion encounter his band near La Higuera.
October 8, 1967	CIA agent Félix Rodríguez copies documents in Guevara's knapsack, including his diary, which

	recounts his experiences in Bolivia. The Bolivian government receives a copy from the CIA and hopes to sell publishing rights to it.
October 9, 1967	Guevara is executed at the order of the Bolivian high command.
October 15, 1967	Castro acknowledges Guevara's death, declares three days of national mourning, and proclaims October 8 an annual holiday in Guevara's honor.
November 17, 1967	Debray and Bustos are sentenced to 30 years of imprisonment, commuted to 3 years.
February 21, 1968	Three Cuban survivors of Guevara's band reach Chile and go on to Cuba. Two Bolivian survivors remain in Bolivia but die in shoot-outs with the police in 1969.
July 19, 1968	Bolivian minister Antonio Arguedas creates a government crisis by revealing, and renouncing, his CIA links and admitting that he sent Guevara's diary to Castro, who made it widely available.
April 27, 1969	Barrientos dies in a helicopter crash in Oruro Province; Vice President Luis Adolfo Siles becomes president.
September 26, 1969	General Alfredo Ovando, Bolivian chief of staff, overthrows Siles and assumes the presidency, launching an era of political intrigue and military rule.
July 4, 1997	A handless skeleton, almost certainly Guevara's, is found in a communal grave in Vallegrande and scon sent to Cuba to be interred at Santa Clara, scene of his greatest victory in the Cuban revolution.

Notes

ABBREVIATIONS

The following abbreviations are used throughout the notes.

FAOHP   Foreign Affairs Oral History Program, National Foreign Affairs Training Center, Washington, D.C.
FBIS   Foreign Broadcast Information Service
FRUS   U.S. Department of State, *Foreign Relations of the United States* (Washington, D.C., 1942–60).
JFK Libr.   John Fitzgerald Kennedy Library, Boston, Mass.
LBJ Libr.   Lyndon Baines Johnson Library, Austin, Tex.
NARA   National Archives and Records Administration, Washington, D.C.
NSA   National Security Archive, Washington, D.C.
NSF   National Security File

INTRODUCTION

1. See, for example, "Secret Lives: Che Guevara," Dec. 21, 1995, Channel 4 (U.K.), and the U.S. version, "Che Guevara," Aug. 22, 1966, Discovery Channel. See also "The Revised Che Guevara," *New York Times*, Week in Review section, Nov. 26, 1995. For an earlier version of these views, see "In Search of the Real Che Guevara," Nov. 16, 1971, BBC-TV. On the other hand, the latest and best Guevara biography to date Anderson's *Che Guevara*, published in 1997, helps correct these misconceptions.

2. See Llovio-Menéndez, *Insider*, pp. 118–19, for a comparatively recent example. Llovio-Menéndez sees Guevara as going into self-imposed exile because he believed he was a "stumbling block" to better Cuban-Soviet relations.

3. "In Search of the Real Che Guevara," BBC-TV, for example, portrays his trip in these terms.

4. Llovio-Menéndez, *Insider*, pp. 111–19.

5. See "The Revised Che Guevara," for example.

6. For the identities of the Cubans who served with Guevara in Bolivia, see Mallin, *Che Guevara on Revolution*, pp. 229–31.

7. "World in Action," Dec. 7, 1967, Granada TV (U.K.).

CHAPTER ONE

1. Rodríguez and Weisman, *Shadow Warrior*, pp. 9–11. The authors deal with the Guevara episode in the prologue and in Chapters 10 and 11.

2. Félix Rodríguez and several embassy officers have confirmed this in interviews with the author.

3. Rodríguez makes this claim in *Shadow Warrior*. Gary Prado Salmón, leader of the company that captured Guevara, however, denies it hotly in *The Defeat of Che Guevara*, pp. 181–83. See below, Chapter 6.

4. Author's interviews with Henderson, FAOHP, Sept. 22, 1990, and NSA, Jan. 12, 1992 (tape).

5. Author's interview with Henderson, FAOHP, Sept. 22, 1990, pp. 11, 12, 20, 26, 27; JFK Libr., Henderson oral history, Aug. 30, 1978, pp. 136–38.

6. My principal sources on Guevara's life before he went to Cuba are Guevara, *The Motorcycle Diaries*, Guevara Lynch, *Mi hijo El Che* and *Aquí va un soldado de América*; author's interviews with Dolores Moyano Martin, a childhood friend of Guevara's, Oct. 17, 1991, Mar. 17, 1992; Moyano Martin, "A Memoir of the Young Guevara," and "From El Cid to El Che"; *Ernesto*, by his first wife, Hilda Gadea; *Con El Che por Sudamérica*, by his traveling companion, Alberto Granado; *My Friend Che*, by another traveling companion, Ricardo Rojo; Richard Harris's *The Death of a Revolutionary*; Daniel James's *Ché Guevara*; and Jon Lee Anderson's *Che Guevara*.

7. The flagship study of U.S.-Guatemalan relations from 1944 until 1954, when the U.S. government created a surrogate force to overthrow the regime, is surely Gleijeses, *Shattered Hope*, which relies heavily on declassified American documents and extensive interviews with American and Guatemalan participants. Besides his careful scholarship and good writing, Gleijeses refreshingly avoids the polemics that creep into so much of the discussion of this subject. Other useful studies using declassified documents include Schlesinger and Kinzer, *Bitter Fruit*; Immerman, *The CIA in Guatemala*; and Cook, *The Declas-*

sified Eisenhower. Blaiser, *The Hovering Giant,* published before many of the documents were declassified, is nevertheless a valuable and interesting study of the revolutions in Mexico, Guatemala, Bolivia, and Cuba and of the U.S. reaction to them. President Eisenhower gives his view of the episode in *Mandate for Change,* pp. 420–27, presenting U.S. government involvement as limited to the supply of two airplanes to the invaders. CIA chief Allen Dulles says only that "support from outside was given to loyal anti-Communist elements" in *The Craft of Intelligence,* p. 224; see also pp. 122, 221, 234.

8. *Cambridge Biographical Dictionary* (1990).

9. For Guevara's account of launching the expeditions, see Mallin, *"Che" Guevara on Revolution,* p. 51. Szulc also gives a detailed account in *Fidel,* pp. 367–68.

10. Guevara Lynch, *Aquí va un soldado de América,* pp. 137, 150.

11. I am greatly indebted to Szulc, *Fidel,* for details of the *Granma*'s voyage and the subsequent civil war in Cuba. I have also used Guevara's own account of these events, which can be found in several English-language collections of his writings. A comprehensive edition of his war memoirs is Gerassi, *Venceremos!,* but other very useful works are Deutschmann, *Che Guevara and the Cuban Revolution,* and Mallin, *"Che" Guevara on Revolution.* Guevara's best description of the boat trip can be found in the Deutschmann and Mallin collections.

Guevara wrote his recollections of the war as articles for various periodicals, including *O Cruzeiro,* a Brazilian weekly magazine; *Revolución,* the daily newspaper of the July 26 Movement; and *Verde Olivo,* a weekly magazine of the Cuban revolutionary armed forces. The various collections of his writings have used different articles by Guevara on the war, many originally published in Havana in 1963 under the title *Pasajes de la guerra revolucionaria* and translated by the Cuban government in 1967 as *Episodes of the Revolutionary War.* Note, however, that some English editions of *Pasajes* are entitled *Reminiscences of the Revolutionary War.* Waters has edited an excellent edition of Guevara's wartime writing, *Episodes of the Cuban Revolutionary War, 1956–58,* published in 1996, including correspondence, maps, campaign diagrams, and other useful information. Unless otherwise noted, I have used Guevara's description of the trip from Mexico and the war in *O Cruzeiro,* presented in English by Mallin, *"Che" Guevara on Revolution.*

12. Guevara, *Episodes of the Revolutionary War,* pp. 13–14. He described being wounded most vividly in a letter to Gadea. See Gadea, *Ernesto,* p. 168.

13. Geyer, in *Guerrilla Prince,* p. 162, says there were "probably around eighteen" survivors but suggests that Castro has fostered the myth that there were 12 for its apostolic resonance. Castro's former colleague, Carlos Franqui, in *Family Portrait with Fidel,* p. 13, shares this view.

14. Author's interviews with Ramón Bonachea, Apr. 10, 1992, and Huber Matos, Apr. 14, 1992.

15. For Guevara's account of the campaign, see Mallin, *"Che" Guevara on Revolution*, pp. 58–65.

16. Author's interview with Nasário, Apr. 10, 1992.

17. For events on the last days of the revolution, see *FRUS*, 1958–60, 6:251–333; Tetlow, *Eye on Cuba*, pp. 10–18; Phillips, *Cuba*, pp. 396–402; Szulc, *Fidel*, pp. 552–59; Mallin, *"Che" Guevara on Revolution*, pp. 65–66; Smith, *The Closest of Enemies*, p. 39; Franqui, *Family Portrait*, pp. 3–7; Smith, *The Fourth Floor*, pp. 200–203.

18. Smith, *The Closest of Enemies*, p. 16; *FRUS*, 1955–57, 6:840; Szulc, *Fidel*, pp. 402–3; Mallin, *"Che" Guevara on Revolution*, p. 54.

19. Szulc, *Fidel*, pp. 455–59; Smith, *The Closest of Enemies*, pp. 17, 32.

20. Mallin, *"Che" Guevara on Revolution*, p. 31; CIA, Teletyped Information Report. Mar. 26, 1958, "Cuban Revolutionary Activity—Plans for a General Strike." Despite its title, this document reports on plans for other strikes also.

21. For U.S. government reporting and views on this relationship, see LBJ Libr., NSF, Country File: Cuba, vol. 4, box 19, INR Reports folder, docs. 6–15b, 21, p. 7, and Subversion folder, vol. 1, pt. 1, doc. 6; William G. Bowdler file, vol. 3, box 19; CIA Directorate of Intelligence, Special Report Weekly Review, "Cuban Subversive Activities in Latin America: 1959–1968," p. 3.

22. There are several English editions, one published by Praeger, another by Monthly Review Press, and one by the University of Nebraska Press, all in 1961. In 1985 Nebraska issued the book again, this time adding case studies of guerrilla activities in the Western Hemisphere, edited by Brian Loveman and Thomas M. Davis, Jr. After *Guerrilla Warfare*, Guevara published his essay, "Guerrilla Warfare: A Method," which is far more a political treatise on the need for such combat, especially in Latin America, than a manual (see Mallin, *"Che" Guevara on Revolution*, pp. 87–102). In addition, he wrote an introduction to the Cuban edition of Vietnamese guerrilla leader Vo Nguyên Giap's book, *People's War, People's Army*, stressing the role of the guerrilla army and the Communist Party in achieving "national liberation" (Mallin, *"Che" Guevara on Revolution*, pp. 101–9).

23. *FRUS*, 1958–60, 6:33, 60, 71; Eisenhower, *Waging Peace*, p. 520; Anderson, *Che Guevara*, pp. 329–30.

24. *FRUS*, 1958–60, 6:117–57; Szulc, *Fidel*, pp. 448–50; Paterson, *Contesting Castro*, pp. 160–72.

25. Author's interview with an anonymous authoritative CIA source, Dec. 5, 1991.

26. Author's interview with Stevenson, who in 1958 was head of the Middle American Branch of INR, May 15, 1995. See also Stevenson oral history, FAOHP, Sept. 19, 1989, pp. 15–17. Paterson in *Contesting Castro*, p. 15, says that the FBI had a file on Castro since 1955, but the State Department officers were unaware of it, nor does the FBI appear to have shared it with the CIA.

27. CIA, Information Report, CS 3/406,916, July 28, 1959. Other samples are Information Reports, TDCS 3/350,959, Apr. 3, 1958; CS 3/351,466, Apr. 15, 1958; CS 3/350,670, Apr. 2, 1958; TDCS 3/340,835, Jan. 6, 1958; CO B-3,098,099, Feb. 13, 1958; and CO B-3,094,401, Dec. 17, 1957. The contents of all of these reports are unevaluated and considered "tentative."

28. Minà, *An Encounter with Fidel*, p. 218.

29. CIA, Information Report, CO B-3,098,099, Feb. 13, 1958.

30. *FRUS*, 1958–60, 5:396.

31. NARA, RG 287, Y4.J89/2:C73/27/pt 8, Senate Internal Security Sub-committee hearings, testimony of Alfredo Manuel Rojo Boche, and pt. 22, Senate Internal Security Subcommittee hearings, testimony of Antonio Teira Alfonso, Feb. 24, 1971; Y4.F76/1:C73/6, Hearings before the House Subcommittee on Inter-American Affairs, Feb. and Mar. 1965. See also LBJ Libr., NSF, Country File: Cuba, Subversion folder, vol. 1. pt. 1, doc. 6c. Regarding the invasion of the Dominican Republic, see *FRUS*, 1958–60, 5:322–33, 391–92, 6:558; Geyer, *Guerrilla Prince*, pp. 222–23; Phillips, *Cuba*, p. 99.

32. NARA, RG 287, Y4.J89/2:C73/27/pt. 14, Senate Internal Security Sub-committee hearing, "Communist Threat to U.S. through the Caribbean," Juan Orta Cordova testimony, Mar. 31, 1965; CIA, Office of Current Intelligence, Special Report, OCI no. 0316/64A, "Cuban Training and Support for African Nationalists," Jan. 31, 1964.

33. NARA, RG 287, Y4.F76/1:C73/6, Hearings before the House Subcommittee on Inter-American Affairs, Feb. and Mar. 1965, p. 119.

34. NARA, RG 287, Y4.J89/2:C73/27/pt. 14, Senate Internal Security Sub-committee hearing, "Communist Threat to U.S. through the Caribbean," Orta testimony, Mar. 31, 1965; Phillips, *Cuba*, p. 92.

35. NARA, RG 287, Y4.J89/2:C73/27/pt. 4, Senate Internal Security Sub-committee hearings, Sept. 27, 1971. See also pt. 14, Orta testimony, Mar. 31, 1965.

36. LBJ Libr., NSF, Country File: Cuba, Subversion folder, vol. 1, pt. 1, docs. 72, 72a, and CIA Daily and Weekly Summaries folder, vol. 2, doc. 6c, p. 4.

37. LBJ Libr., NSF, INR Reports folder, doc. 22, p. 3, and Subversion folder, vol. 1, pt. 1, docs. 72, 72a.

38. LBJ Libr., NSF, Meetings folder. The entire folder, which is heavily censored, concerns this issue, but see especially docs. 42, 39, 18, 10.

39. Richard Reeves devotes the better part of chapters 5–8 of *President Kennedy* to the Bay of Pigs episode, and Piero Gleijeses has a long and authoritative article regarding its policymaking aspects in the February 1995 *Journal of Latin American Studies*. Lucien S. Vandenbroucke, "Confessions of Allen Dulles," using Allen Dulles's papers, explores the CIA's hidden expectations. Vandenbroucke's book, *Perilous Options*, dedicates two chapters to the policy formulation and execution of the attack. Another good and relatively recent

study is Trumbull Higgins's *The Perfect Failure*. In the 1960s, Karl E. Meyer and Tad Szulc wrote a very thorough study, *The Cuban Invasion*, as did Haynes Johnson in *The Bay of Pigs*. Peter H. Wyden's *Bay of Pigs* is a lively review of the events, as is former CIA agent E. Howard Hunt's first-person account, *Give Us This Day*. Albert C. Persons, one of the U.S. pilots who supported the invaders, gives a personal account in *Bay of Pigs*, and Arthur Schlesinger, Jr., a key Kennedy adviser, gives a White House view in *A Thousand Days*, chap. 10. Theodore Draper's *Castro's Revolution*, pp. 59–113; Wayne S. Smith's *The Closest of Enemies*, pp. 62–74; and Szulc's *Fidel*, pp. 539–61, all provide useful accounts. Kennedy's secretary of state, Dean Rusk, addresses these events in *As I Saw It*, pp. 207–17, criticizing himself sternly for not opposing the scheme more forcefully.

40. See, for example, Greene, *The Guerrilla and How to Fight Him*, p. 59.

41. Guevara, "Guerrilla Warfare: A Method," in Mallin, *"Che" Guevara and Revolution*, pp. 87–102.

42. Several of the great guerrilla captains of the period wrote on the subject. Besides Guevara's *Guerrilla Warfare*, see Mao Tse-Tung, *On Guerrilla Warfare*, and Vo Nguyên Giap, *People's War, People's Army*. On the other side, Maxwell D. Taylor published his extremely influential *The Uncertain Trumpet* in 1959. In addition, many studies appeared in the early 1960s, including Leighton and Sanders, *Insurgency and Counterinsurgency*; Paret and Shy, *Guerrillas in the 1960s*; *Studies in Guerrilla Warfare* by the U.S. Naval Institute; Valeriano and Bohannan, *Counter-Guerrilla Operations*; Thayer, *Guerrilla*; Ney, *Notes on Guerrilla War*; Osanka, *Modern Guerrilla Warfare*; Greene, *The Guerrilla and How to Fight Him*; and, in mid-decade, the very important *Defeating Communist Insurgency* by Robert G. K. Thompson.

Works on the subject in later decades include Thompson's *Revolutionary War in World Strategy* and *War in Peace*, edited with John Keegan. Other significant works are Blaufarb's *The Counterinsurgency Era* and *Who Will Win?*, written with George K. Tanham; Fauriol, *Latin American Insurgencies*; Beckett, *The Roots of Counter-Insurgency*; Allen, *The Savage Wars of Peace*, which reflects British post–World War II experience; Sturgill, *Low-Intensity Conflict in American History*, and his largely statistical *Military History of the Third World since 1945*; and finally Mockaitis, *British Counterinsurgency in the Post-Imperial Era*.

43. JFK Libr., NSF, Country: Cuba, Subject: Taylor Report (Paramilitary Study Group Report), boxes 61A, B. The study consists of three parts: a 54-page report to the president, minutes of the study group's 21 meetings and 54 interviews, and 304 pages of documents and maps used in the report. Some of the study remains censored. Parts 1 and 2 have been published, except for the censored material, as Aguilar, *Operation Zapata*. (Zapata is the name of the peninsula where the Bay of Pigs is located.) JFK Libr., Taylor oral history, Apr. 12, 26, June 21, 1964.

44. JFK Libr., Taylor oral history, Apr. 12, 26, June 21, 1964, pp. 9, 10.

45. Taylor, *Responsibility and Response*, p. 69.

46. CIA, Jack B. Pfeiffer, "The Taylor Committee Investigation of the Bay of Pigs," Nov. 9, 1984. Although written as an unclassified document, parts of it were blacked out before being released through the Freedom of Information Act, even including Pfeiffer's title, chief historian.

47. JFK Libr., NSF, JFK, Meetings and Memos, boxes 328–30, Memo, Taylor to Bundy, June 26, 1961, plus attachments, and NSAM 55.

48. Taylor served as chairman of the Joint Chiefs of staff until 1964, when President Johnson named him ambassador to South Vietnam. He resigned in 1966 but continued as a special adviser to Johnson.

49. Szulc, *Fidel*, p. 542.

50. Massive documentation of this counterinsurgency effort is housed in JFK Libr., NSF, JFK, Meetings and Memos, box 319, Special Group (C1), Military Organization and Accomplishments, July 1962 and July 1962–Nov. 1963, and Meetings, 1961–63, boxes 326–27, Staff Memoranda, Maxwell Taylor, Sept.–Dec. 1961, Walt W. Rostow, Guerrilla and Unconventional Warfare, July 1–15, 1961, and Aug. 1–14, 1961, boxes 328–30, NSAM 44, 49, 56, and replies, and boxes 335A–37, NSAM 163; Departments and Agencies, boxes 275–83, White House General, 1961–62, and Dept. of Defense (B), Joint Chiefs of Staff, vol. 1, Inter-American Defense Board, Aug. 23, 1961. Regarding Central American security ministers' meetings, see LBJ Libr., NSF, Country File: Cuba, Subversion folder, vol. 1, pt. 1, docs. 40–51, 68.

51. JFK Libr., NSF, JFK, boxes 328–30, NSAM 2, Development of Counter-Guerrilla Forces and McNamara's response.

52. *FRUS*, 1958–60, 6:542, 560, 589; CIA, FBIS g 1, Cuba, Sept. 9, 1959, "Guevara Home from Tour Meets Press," Prensa Latina.

53. CIA, Press Review #252, Nov. 1, 1960, and Current Intelligence Weekly Summaries, Jan. 12 and 26, 1961; *FRUS*, 1958–60, 6:1187.

54. CIA, FBIS 81, "Cuban-Soviet Talks," Havana Domestic Spanish, Nov. 18, 1964; FBIS DR#236, Dec. 4, 1964, "Guevara Reviews Cuban Industrial Development," TASS International in English; Office of Central Reference, Biographic Register, Cuba, Ernesto "Che" Guevara de la Serna, Minister of Industries, Dec. 1964; LBJ Libr., NSF, Country File: Cuba, INR Reports, doc. 21. See also Guevara, "The Cuban Economy," p. 589.

55. Benemelis, *Castro*, p. 59. Embassy and CIA reports on Guevara's activities throughout the Africa trip can be found in the LBJ Libr., NSF, Country File: Cuba, Personalities folder, box 20.

56. For a very useful chronology of Guevara's travels on this trip and throughout his life, see Deutschmann, *Che Guevara and the Cuban Revolution*, pp. 11–18.

57. The text of Guevara's U.N. speech and subsequent debate with other

Latin American delegates can be seen in a collection of his and Castro's speeches entitled *To Speak the Truth*, pp. 121, 153.

58. LBJ Libr., NSF, Country File: Cuba, Personalities folder, box 20, doc. 42.

59. Ibid., docs. 18, 42.

60. Ibid., doc. 56.

61. CIA, FBIS DR #40 (M.E., Africa, W.E.), Mar. 2, 1965, "Che Guevara's Speech before Afro-Asian Seminar," Prensa Latina in Spanish and "Interview with AFP," Paris AFP in English.

62. Durch, "The Cuban Military in Africa and the Middle East."

63. CIA, FBIS, DR #19 (M.E., Africa, W.E.), Jan. 29, 1965, "Gbenye Arrives in Algiers, Met by Ben Bella," Paris AFP in French; Crowder, *The Cambridge History of Africa*, 8:722–31.

64. LBJ Libr., NSF, Country File: Cuba, Personalities folder, box 20, doc. 18.

65. CIA, FBIS, DR #55, Mar. 23, 1965, "Guevara Interview with Weekly Liberation," and DR #54, Mar. 22, 1965, "Interview with Che Guevara in Jeune Afrique," both based on Algeria correspondent's dispatch in Spanish to Prensa Latina, Havana.

66. CIA, FBIS 64, Jan. 22, 1965, "Guevara Statement," Prensa Latina, Havana, in Spanish.

67. CIA, FBIS, DR #55, Mar. 23, 1965, "Guevara Interview," and DR #54, Mar. 22, 1965, "Interview with Che Guevara."

68. LBJ Libr., NSF, Country File, Cuba, CIA Daily and Weekly Summaries, vol. 1, box 36, Dec. 1964–Feb. 1965, weekly summary, Dec. 30, 1964, p. 10.

69. LBJ Libr., NSF, Country File: Cuba, INR Reports, doc. 7. For an INR overview of "Cuba and Africa," see also doc. 8.

70. LBJ Libr., NSF, Country File: Cuba, Intelligence, vol. 1, doc. 25; CIA Daily and Weekly Summaries, vol. 2, doc. 6c, weekly summary #3, Feb. 3, 1965, p. 9.

71. LBJ Libr., NSF, Country File: Cuba, Intelligence, doc. 25; Personalities folder, box 20, doc 52; and CIA weekly summary #3, Feb. 3, 1965.

72. Benemelis, *Castro*, p. 85.

73. CIA, Biographic Sketch, "Cuba—Ernesto Guevara de la Serna," Apr. 1967.

74. CIA, FBIS, "Guevara Rumor," June 11, 1965, London Reuters in English; Current Intelligence Digest, Notes, Cuba, June 24, 1965; FDD 6613, June 30, 1965, "Cuban Foreign Trade Minister Comments on Guevara Disappearance"; FBIS 56 and 07, Aug. 21 and 23, 1965, "For Your Information F/E/X" and "Guzman Title," Havana Domestic Service in Spanish and Havana correspondent's dispatch in Russian to TASS Moscow, respectively. (FBIS linked these two reports.)

75. CIA, Information Report No. 00-K-323/08041-65, May 6, 1965, and No. 00-B-321/06571-67, Mar. 14, 1967.

76. CIA, Information Report No. CS DB-312/01029-65, Apr. 26, 1965, No. CSOB-312/01072-65, Apr. 28, 1965, and No. 00-K-323/08041-65, May 6, 1965; *Verde Olivo*, Apr. 11 and 25, 1965.

77. CIA, FBIS 35, 09, 10, June 17, 1965, Castro speech.

78. CIA, FBIS, DR #233, Dec. 3, 1965, "Castro Speaks to Graduating School Teachers," Havana Domestic Radio and Television Services in Spanish.

79. CIA, FBIS, DR #76, Apr. 20, 1966, Cuba, "Castro Interview with West German Magazine."

80. CIA, Intelligence Information Cable, TDCS DB-315/03208-65, Cuba, September 28, 1965, "Castro's Statement on Freedom of 'Exodus' from Cuba" (despite this title, it also contains his promise to read a document about Guevara). For the translation of the speech in which Castro read Guevara's letter, I have used FBIS, DR #191, Oct. 4, 1965, "Castro Refers to Guevara, etc.," Havana Domestic Radio and Television Services in Spanish.

81. CIA, GUO, 2053, June 29, 1966, "Ernesto 'Che' Guevara is Cuba's Gift to the Revolution," by Michele Firk, trans. from *Jeune Afrique*, June 5, 1966, by the U.S. Department of Commerce.

82. Jorge Castañeda, for example, in an interview for "Secret Lives: Che Guevara," Dec. 21, 1995, Channel 4 (U.K.), also shown Aug. 22, 1996, on the Discovery Channel, entitled "Che Guevara." These two shows were substantially different, but the Castañeda interview appeared on both.

83. Castro told a journalist "about 100" Cubans went with Guevara. See Castro's *Che*, p. 118. Juan Benemelis, then a Cuban official involved with African affairs, puts the figure at 200 in his *Castro*, pp. 169, 181. Congolese military officers put the number at about 160, which the U.S. defense attaché thought inflated. See LBJ Libr., NSF, Country File: Congo, vol. 11, Cables, doc. 8.

84. CIA, FBIS, DR #194, Oct. 7, 1965, Argentina, "Che Guevara Letter Believed Fictitious," Lima AFP in Spanish; Current Intelligence Digest, Oct. 4, 1965, "'Che' Guevara Dropped from Communist Party Hierarchy"; FDD 7002, Dec. 16, 1965, "Che Guevara" (a collection of four articles speculating on Guevara's fate and the reasons Castro read the letter).

85. CIA, FBIS 16, Jan. 3, 1967, "Moscow Report on Castro Speech," Moscow TASS International Service in Russian; FBIS, Survey of Communist Bloc Broadcasts (Dec. 22, 1966–Jan. 5, 1967) and Jan. 6, 1967, Cuba, "Predicts Guevara Will Appear 'Where Imperialism Least Expects'"; FBIS, DR #24, Feb. 3, 1967, Cuba, "News about 'Che' in November, Report Says," Santiago, Chile, correspondent's dispatch in Spanish to Prensa Latina, Havana; FPIR 0151/67, Feb. 13, 1957, Cuba, "Writer Reports Castro Will Give News of Guevara in November."

86. CIA, Memo, "Major Ernesto Guevara de la Serna, Minister of Industries and Member of the Secretariat of the PURS National Directorate," June 1, 1965, p. 12.

87. CIA, Information Report No. 00-K-323/08041-65, May 6, 1965, for example.

88. CIA, FDD 6692, Political Activities of Leading Personalities, "Guevara Is in Quarantine," *El Siglo*, Bogota, July 21, 1965 (quoting *L'Express*); regarding incentives, see FPIR 0238/67, Mar. 9, 1967, "Peruvian Writer Views Cuba Sympathetically after Recent Visit."

89. For examples of the conflict with Castro speculation, see CIA, Information Report No. 00-K-323/11350-65, June 29, 1965, and JPRS 31338, June 30, 1965, Political, "Guevara's Disappearance Linked with Moscow-Peking Feud."

90. Author's interview with Helms, June 16, 1995.

91. Smith's comment to author, Mar. 7, 1996.

92. "In Search of the Real Che Guevara," Nov. 16, 1971, BBC-TV.

93. CIA, Information from Foreign Documents or Radio Broadcasts, Report CR-W-333/00049-65, distributed Nov. 22, 1965; FBIS, DR #76, Apr. 20, 1966.

94. CIA, FBIS, DR #147, Aug. 2, 1965, Uruguay (also stamped "Cuba"), "Marcha Articles Speculate on Che Guevara," Montevideo correspondent's dispatch in Spanish to Prensa Latina, Havana; FBIS, DR #161, Aug. 20, 1965, Cuba, "Havana Reads Guevara's Warfare Manual," Havana in Creole to Haiti; FBIS, DR #186, Sept. 27, 1965, "Rodriguez Refers to Che Guevara in Speech," Havana in Spanish to the Americas; FBIS, DR #205, Oct. 20, 22, 1965, "'Followers of Camilo and Che' Group to Form," Havana in English to Europe; Current Intelligence Digest, Dec. 1, 1965, "Guevara Continues to Receive Heavy Publicity in Cuba"; CIA, Information Report No. 00-K-323/12254-66, Aug. 3, 1966, "Che Guevara's Picture Given Prominence"; author's interview with Enrique Garcia, regarding current treatment in schools, Apr. 12, 1992.

95. CIA, FBIS, DR #211, Nov. 1, 1965, "Father Denies Che Guevara Death," Montevideo correspondent's dispatch in Spanish to Prensa Latina, Havana.

96. I have collected these stories from the files of the DIA and from the CIA's FBIS and other media-review services. The documents can be consulted at the NSA, where I have deposited them under the title "Guevara Disappearance—Rumors."

97. CIA, FBIS 07, Oct. 9, 1965, "Guevara Where Abouts [*sic*]," Montevideo Reuters in Spanish; FBIS, DR #204, Oct. 21, 1965, Montevideo correspondent to Prensa Latina, Havana; FBIS 82, Aug. 10, 1966, "Guevara Whereabouts," Buenos Aires correspondent dispatch in English to Reuters; FBIS, DR #70, Apr. 11, 1967, "Search for Guevara," Montevideo Prensa Latina in Spanish to Prensa Latina, Havana; for a good example of the official denial of Guevara's presence, see FPIR 0278/67, Cuba, "Bogota, El Tiempo, 7 Mar 67."

98. Author's interviews with Henderson, FAOHP, Sept. 22, 1990, p. 19, and Helms, June 16, 1995.

99. CIA, Information Report No. 00-K-323/09044-65, May 24, 1965; author's interview with anonymous U.S. official, Nov. 3, 1990.

100. CIA, FBIS 03, Apr. 17, 1967, "Guevara Document," Prensa Latina, Havana, in Spanish.

101. CIA, FBIS, DR #374, Cuba, Apr. 17, 1967, "'Che' Guevara Calls for World Revolutions," Prensa Latina, Havana (English text of the article; English translations are also published in various places, including Deutschmann, *Che Guevara and the Cuban Revolution,* p. 347); CIA, FPIR 0506/67, Cuba, May 23, 1967, Mexico City, *Siempre,* "Mexican Leftist Magazine Publishes Attack on Guevara's Message"; Guevara, *The Diary of Che Guevara* (hereafter, Guevara's diary), July 24, 1967.

102. CIA, JPRS, Sum. #41,379, June 14, 1967, Political, "An Appeal for War against the Imperialists" (translation of the *Bohemia* article).

103. JPRS Sum. # 41,379, June 14, 1967, Political, "An Appeal for War against the Imperialists"; FBIS 55, Cuba, Apr. 28? (date blurred), 1967, "Castro Speech." I have given these and other documents regarding Guevara's speech to the NSA, under the heading "Tricontinental Article." The number of Green Berets comes from the author's interview with team members, including its leader, Major Ralph Shelton, on May 31, 1991, and from a memorandum of understanding with the Bolivian government regarding the team. For the memorandum, see General William Tope's report of his trip to Bolivia in April 1967, now filed with the NSA.

104. Benemelis, *Castro,* p. 85 and chap. 9.

105. For background on these events, see Moore, *Castro, the Blacks, and Africa,* chaps. 14, 15, and Benemelis, *Castro,* pp. 59–183. See Minà, *An Encounter with Fidel,* pp. 223–24, for Castro's account.

106. Minà, *An Encounter with Fidel,* p. 224; Benemelis, *Castro,* p. 202, quoting Gabriel Garcia Márquez, *Operación Carlota*; Anderson, *Che Guevara,* pp. 672, 676, 682.

107. Minà, *An Encounter with Fidel,* p. 224.

108. Waters, *The Bolivian Diary,* p. 43; Mallin, *"Che" Guevara on Revolution,* p. 35. It remains unclear whether Guevara entered as a businessman, as James, for example, says in *The Complete Bolivian Diaries,* p. 11; as an OAS official, as Waters says, for example, *The Bolivian Diary,* p. 80, n. 8; or as a businessman on an OAS mission as Anderson states in *"Che" Guevara* p. 701, which seems likely. As Mallin points out, two Uruguayan passports with different names, known to be his, were found later, but it is unclear which, if either, he used to enter Bolivia on this occasion. According to González and Sanchez Salazar, *The Great Rebel,* pp. 55–56, neither passport bears an entry stamp for this trip.

CHAPTER TWO

1. Guevara's diary, Mar. 23, 1967; telegram, American embassy, La Paz (hereafter, La Paz) to State, #025223, Mar. 25, 1967. (Unless otherwise indi-

cated, telegrams and military documents cited can be consulted at the NSA.) *Ramparts* magazine first published Guevara's Bolivian diary in English, though it is a hasty and sometimes inscrutable translation. Later printings, however, have the benefit of including the original Spanish. Daniel James also translated the diary in *The Complete Bolivian Diaries*, which is useful but not entirely satisfactory either. Carlos P. Hansen and Andrew Sinclair in *The Bolivian Diary of Ernesto "Che" Guevara* have produced a good and readable translation in very colloquial English.

In 1994, Mary-Alice Waters edited a very useful edition, *The Bolivian Diary*, which includes a series of maps accompanying the text. It also contains writings of members of Guevara's band, biographic sketches of them and other persons involved (some extremely tangentially, such as Bertrand Russell), communiqués issued by the group, and an excellent index, unlike many books concerning Guevara. A relentlessly leftist introduction will make more mature readers nostalgic for the 1960s.

Where I have quoted the diaries, I have consulted these translations and sometimes translated myself, using the *Ramparts* Spanish.

2. Author's interview with Grover, FAOHP, Nov. 2, 1990, p. 1; Guevara's diary, Mar. 23, 24, 1967; telegram, La Paz to State, #028586, Mar. 29, 1967.

3 United States Southern Command Military Assistance Plan, Bolivia, vol. 1, Narrative B, p. 5, subpara. a.

4. Ibid., Narrative A, p. 1, subpara. a.

5. Ibid., vol. 2, MAP Element Description.

6. Guevara's diary, Mar. 1967 summary.

7. Guevara's diary, Apr. 16, 1967. See also July 3, 7, 8, Sept. 21, 22, 24, 25, July–Sept. 1967 summaries.

8. Author's interview with Broderick, FAOHP, Oct. 8, 1990, p. 3.

9. Conversations with Charles Grover, chief political officer, U.S. embassy, La Paz, Feb. and Mar. 1996.

10. Author's interview with anonymous CIA official, June 10, 1995.

11. Airgram, La Paz to State, #A-329, Apr. 26, 1967, "Guerrilla Activity, April 20–24" (note the embassy's airgram puts the meeting with the leaders at the nearby town of Ayango, but Guevara says it occurred at Muyupampa); González and Sánchez Salazar, *The Great Rebel*, p. 160.

12. Guevara's diary, Apr. 19, 20, 1967; telegram, La Paz to State, #004437, Apr. 5, 1967; remarks of Grover, Mar. 1996, about the political situation.

13. Author's interviews with an anonymous CIA official, Apr. 15, 1992, and Henderson, FAOHP, Sept. 22, 1990, pp. 5–6.

14. Martinez Estevez, *Ñancahuazú*, p. 45 (an account in great detail of the Bolivian Army's response to Guevara's insurgency); Guevara's diary, Jan. 19, Mar. 9, 1967; Pombo's diary, Mar. 10, 1967; in James, *The Complete Bolivian*

Diaries; James, *Ché Guevara*, pp. 241–42; telegram, La Paz to State, #022736, Apr. 22, 1967.

15. *The Times* (London), Apr. 11, 1967, report of Murray Sayles, who visited the camp.

16. For the distribution of indigenous languages in Bolivia, see the *Atlas de Bolivia* by the Instituto Geográfico Militar, Barcelona, esp. map 211, "Mapa de Distribución de Lenguas y Etnias." See also Guevara's diary, Jan. 11, about learning Quechua.

17. Martinez, *Ñancahuazú*, pp. 45–46; Pombo's diary, in James, *Ché Guevara*, p. 302; González and Sánchez Salazar, *The Great Rebel*, p. 102. Martinez, who I am inclined to believe, dates the find March 17; González and Sánchez Salazar date it March 19 with no citations.

18. Martinez, *Ñancahuazú*, p. 46.

19. *The Times* (London), Apr. 11, 1967.

20. Telegram, La Paz to State, #017238, Mar. 16, 1967.

21. González and Sánchez Salazar, *The Great Rebel*, pp. 101–2.

22. Guevara's diary, Mar. 19, 20, 1967; telegram, La Paz to State, #018786, Mar. 18, 1967.

23. Telegram, La Paz to State, #017238, Mar. 16, 1967.

24. Ibid.

25. Ibid., #01801[?]. (one digit obscured), Mar. 17, 1967.

26. Ibid., #018757, Mar. 18, 1967.

27. Ibid., #018786, Mar. 18, 1967.

28. Ibid., #01998, Mar. 20, 1967.

29. Ibid., #31223, Mar. 21, 1967.

30. Author's interviews with Horras, Apr. 8, 1992, Henderson, Jan. 12, 1992, and Porter, Oct. 22, 1991; telegrams, State to La Paz, #166433, Mar. 31, 1967, and La Paz to State, #029870, Mar. 30, 1967, and #000510, Apr. 1, 1967.

31. Author's interviews with Henderson, Jan. 12, 1992, Horras, Apr. 8, 1992, and Grover, FAOHP, Nov. 2, 1990, p. 13.

32. Author's interviews with Henderson, Jan. 12, 1992, and Horras, Apr. 8, 1992.

33. Author's interviews with Henderson, FAOHP, Sept. 22, 1990, and Horras, Apr. 8, 1992.

34. The following 1967 cables refer to this episode: La Paz to State, #027274, Mar. 28; #000317, Mar. 31; #003844, Apr. 5; #017517, Apr. 18; State to La Paz, #166280, Mar. 31; #167140, Apr. 1; #170887, Apr. 7; #008100, Apr. 9; #173504 and #173276, Apr. 12.

35. Telegrams, La Paz to State, #025816, Mar. 27, 1967, and #028586, Mar. 29, 1967.

36. Telegrams, La Paz to State, #027354, Mar. 28, 1967; #008100, Apr. 9,

1967; #017517, Apr. 18, 1967; State to La Paz, #170887, Apr. 7, 1967; #173276, Apr. 10, 1967.

37. Telegram, State to La Paz, #188888, May 5, 1967.

38. Author's interviews with Grover, FAOHP, Nov. 2, 1990, p. 3, and Gott, Sept. 6, 1994.

39. Author's interviews with Henderson, FAOHP, Sept. 22, 1990, and Morris, FAOHP, Nov. 12, 1990, pp. 32–33; author's interview with Henderson, Jan. 12, 1992.

40. JFK Libr., Henderson Papers, box 43, "Travels of General O'Meara, Bolivia, 4/27/64–4/30/64," about number of military personnel.

41. Telegrams, State to La Paz, #160252, Mar. 22, 1967, and La Paz to State, #023019, Mar. 23, 1967.

42. Telegram, La Paz to State, #023019, Mar. 23, 1967; author's interview with Morris, FAOHP, Nov. 12, 1990, p. 26.

43. Author's interviews with Shelton, May 30, 31, 1991.

44. Telegram, La Paz to State, #025223, Mar. 25, 1967.

45. Author's interview with Broderick, FAOHP, Oct. 8, 1990, p. 2; telegram, La Paz to State, #028057, Mar. 28, 1967.

46. Telegram, La Paz to State, #028057, Mar. 28, 1967.

47. Telegrams, State to La Paz, #159467, Mar. 21, 1967, and La Paz to State, #028057, Mar. 28, 1967.

48. Author's interview with anonymous source, Nov. 2, 1990.

49. Biographic material concerning Henderson comes from two oral histories in the FAOHP archives, one done by the author on Sept. 22, 1990, and another by Richard Nethercut on Apr. 29, 1988; from an oral history in the JFK Libr. done by Sheldon Stern, Aug. 30, 1978; and from JFK Libr., Henderson Papers, box 1, Correspondence, 1942–1947, folder 1.

50. Author's interviews with Henderson, Jan. 12, 1992, and Broderick, FAOHP, Oct. 8, 1990, pp. 23–24.

51. Nethercut interview with Henderson, FAOHP, Apr. 29, 1988.

52. CIA, Directorate of Intelligence, Office of Current Intelligence, Intelligence Memorandum, "Instability in Latin America," OCI #1758/65, May 19, 1965.

CHAPTER THREE

1. Guevara's diary, Feb. and Mar. 1967.

2. Author's interview with Maidanik, Dec. 4, 1990.

3. LBJ Libr., NSF, Country File: Cuba, William G. Bowdler file, vol. 3, box 19.

4. LBJ Libr., NSF, Country File: Cuba, vol. 4, box 19, CIA, Directorate of In-

telligence, Intelligence Report, "Cuban Subversive Policy and the Bolivian Guerrilla Episode," May 1968, p. 45. Anderson, *Che Guevara*, p. 687, says Monje told him he went to Moscow in early 1966 but would not reveal why. Anderson assumes that he must have discussed Cuban plans for revolution in Bolivia.

5. CIA Intelligence Report, "Cuban Subversive Policy and the Bolivian Guerrilla Episode," May 1968, pp. 6, 11, 12.

6. Ibid., p. 11; INR Reports Folder, docs. 6–15b and 21, p. 7; Subversion folder, vol. 1, pt. 1, doc. 6; William G. Bowdler file, vol. 3, box 19, CIA Directorate of Intelligence, Special Report Weekly Review, "Cuban Subversive Activities in Latin America: 1959–1968," p. 3.

7. Author's interviews with Henderson, FAOHP, Sept. 22, 1990, p. 7, and Morris, FAOHP, Oct. 17, 1990, pp. 25–27; CIA Intelligence Report, "Cuban Subversive Policy and the Bolivian Guerrilla Episode," pp. 14, 17.

8. CIA Intelligence Report, "Cuban Subversive Policy and the Bolivian Guerrilla Episode," May 1968, pp. 26–34; CIA, JPRS Sum. #46,251, Aug. 22, 1968, Cuba file, Ernesto Guevara, Bolivia, "Castro Reneged on Promise of Nonintervention" (Monje's report to the Central Committee, submitted on July 15, 1968, and printed in the Bolivian newspaper *Presencia* on July 25); Debray, *Che's Guerrilla War*, pp. 27–39. See Waters, *The Bolivian Diary*, p. 421, for the account of Pombo, a member of the advance team. See also Anderson, *Che Guevara*, pp. 679–87, for a discussion of Cuban planning for a *faco* in Bolivia and of the Cubans' relations with Monje.

9. CIA, JPRS Sum. #46,251, Aug. 22, 1968, "Castro Reneged on Promise of Nonintervention"; Anderson, *Che Guevara*, pp. 695–96.

10. CIA Intelligence Report, "Cuban Subversive Policy and the Bolivian Guerrilla Episode," May 1968, pp. 29–33; Guevara's diary, Dec. 31, 1966, Jan. 1, 1967.

11. CIA Intelligence Report, "Cuban Subversive Policy and the Bolivian Guerrilla Episode," May 1968, pp. 31–33; Guevara's diary, Jan. and Feb. 1967 summaries and Feb. 14, Mar. 25, 1967, entries.

12. *New York Times*, editorial, Aug. 24, 1967.

13. For a biography of Tania made up largely of collected letters, reports, Guevara's diary entries, and observations by Pombo, see Rojas and Rodríguez, *Tania*. Because this work is hagiographic, however, it must be used with caution, as must almost everything written about Tania for one reason or another. Many others who have written about Guevara in Bolivia mention her, most notably Anderson in *Che Guevara* and James in *Ché Guevara*, esp. pp. 197–205. See also James, "The Girl Who Betrayed Che Guevara."

14. "In Search of the Real Che Guevara," Nov. 16, 1971, BBC-TV.

15. For different versions of Tania's marriage, see Rojas and Rodríguez, *Tania*, pp. 153–54; González and Sánchez Salazar, *The Great Rebel*, p. 83; and James, *Ché Guevara*, p. 202.

16. CIA, Memorandum, Subject: "Briefing of the New York Times on 22 July 1968"; *New York Times,* July 15, 1968, p. 1; author's interviews with former CIA agents, Apr. 11, 15, 1992; Anderson, *Che Guevara,* pp. 549–51.

17. James, *Ché Guevara,* pp. 197–205, 237–41, and "The Girl Who Betrayed Che Guevara."

18. Bustos provides the best account of the trip in testimony after his capture. See Mallin, *"Che" Guevara on Revolution,* pp. 187–90. He also described it in Anderson, *Che Guevara,* pp. 708–9, portraying Tania as dangerously amateurish throughout the trip. Detailed stories of Tania's trip can also be found in González and Sánchez Salazar, *The Great Rebel,* pp. 80–81, and James, *Ché Guevara,* pp. 237–38.

19. Rojas and Rodríguez, *Tania,* pp. 193–94, quoting Pombo.

20. Guevara mentions Tania's visit in diary entries for March 19, 20, 21, and 27, 1967. For Pombo's observations, see Rojas and Rodríguez, *Tania,* pp. 192–96. For the Bolivian press release on the ambush and a summary of remarks by Barrientos, see telegrams, La Paz to State, #026097, Mar. 27, 1967, and #028009, Mar. 28, 1967.

21. For Bustos's description of conditions in the camp, see Mallin, *"Che" Guevara on Revolution,* pp. 203–4, 211–12; for local fear of the guerrillas, see p. 219.

22. For a thumbnail sketch of Debray's life until he went to Bolivia, see Oliver Todd, "Will They Shoot Régis Debray?" *Atlas,* Aug. 1967, trans. from *Le Nouvel Observateur.* It has an extremely leftist bias and continues the pretense that Debray was in Bolivia only as a writer but is useful regarding other phases of his life. For Debray's views regarding Guevara's insurrection and his part in it, see his own *Che's Guerrilla War.* For a discussion within the U.S. government of Debray's influence on revolutionary theory in the 1960s, see CIA Intelligence Report, "Cuban Subversive Policy and the Bolivian Guerrilla Episode," May 1968, pp. 6–10.

23. See Debray, *Che's Guerrilla War,* pp. 94–99, regarding the site selection.

24. Waters, *The Bolivian Diary,* pp. 422–23.

25. Anderson, *Che Guevara,* p. 693.

26. Guevara's diary, Jan. 1967 summary, and Mar. 20, 21, Apr. 14, 1967, entries. See also Bustos's account of talks with Guevara about his mission, Mallin, *"Che" Guevara on Revolution,* pp. 199–203, 223–24. It should be remembered that Bustos was speaking to his captors.

27. Guevara's diary, Mar. 27, 1967.

28. Guevara's diary, Apr. 17, 19, 20, 1967; Debray, *Che's Guerrilla War,* pp. 153–54; Mallin, *"Che" Guevara on Revolution,* pp. 218–23, for Bustos's account.

29. Telegram, La Paz to State, #022786, Apr. 22, 1967.

30. Telegrams, La Paz to State, #020745, Apr. 20, 1967, and #022786, Apr. 22, 1967.

31. Telegrams, State to La Paz, #181245, Apr. 24, 1967; La Paz to State, #026097, Mar. 27, 1967; and #024948, Apr. 25, 1967; airgram, La Paz to State, #A-329, Apr. 26, 1967, "Guerrilla Activity, April 20–24"; Guevara's diary, Apr. 20–27, 1967.

32. Telegrams, State to La Paz, #181245, Apr. 24, 1967; La Paz to State, #026097, Mar. 27, 1967; and #024948, Apr. 25, 1967; airgram, La Paz to State, #A-329, Apr. 26, 1967.

33. Telegram, La Paz to State, #027367, Apr. 27, 1967.

34. Ebon, *Che*, p. 109 (one of the best accounts of the Debray capture and trial), telegram, La Paz to State, #006232, May 6, 1967, about Debray's mother.

35. Telegrams, La Paz to State, #006232, May 6, 1967, and #006276, May 26, 1967; author's interview with Henderson, FAOHP, Sept. 22, 1990, pp. 11–12, 26–27.

36. Telegram, State to Paris, #190427, May 9, 1967.

37. Ebon, *Che*, p. 109.

38. Telegram, La Paz to State, #025843, June 29, 1967.

39. Harris, *The Death of a Revolutionary*, p. 98. See also Bustos's detailed account of the band in his testimony after his capture, Mallin, *"Che" Guevara on Revolution*, chap. 11.

40. Telegram, La Paz to State, #020968, June 24, 1967.

41. Department of Defense Intelligence Information Report, Bolivia, Associated Press Interview with Jules Régis Debray, July 5, 1967.

42. Airgram, La Paz to State, #A-144, Nov. 4, 1967, p. 3.

43. *New York Times*, July 7, 1967, p. 5. (about Roth); Dec. 24, 1970, p. 1 (about Debray and Bustos).

44. Guevara's diary, Apr. 16, 17, 20, 1967; Braulio's diary, July 20, in James, *The Complete Bolivian Diaries*. I am indebted to González and Sánchez Salazar, *The Great Rebel*, for background on some of the guerrilla movements. It is also one of several sources of real names of people with the code names.

45. Guevara's diary, Jan. 11, 1967.

46. Telegrams, La Paz to State, #030728, Mar. 31, 1967; #000576, Apr. 1, 1967; #022667, Apr. 22, 1967; #013250, June 15, 1967; and #003379, July 5, 1967; LBJ Libr., NSF, Country File: Bolivia, vol. 4, box 8, memo, Rostow to Johnson, June 23, 1967; *The Times*, (London), Apr. 12, 1967, repeated in telegram, State to La Paz, #173504, Apr. 12, 1967.

47. LBJ Libr., NSF, Country File: Cuba, INR Reports, doc. 7.

48. Telegram, La Paz to State, #028586, Mar. 29, 1967; memo, Gen. William Tope to CINC, "Trip Report—Visit of Director, J-5, to Bolivia 18–30 April 1967," May 6, 1967, p. 11.

49. LBJ Libr., NSF, Country File: Bolivia, vol. 4, box 8, memo, June 23, 1967, and Intelligence File, "Guerrilla Problem in Latin America," box 2, draft memo, June 24, 1967.

50. Department of Defense Intelligence Information Report, #2 808 0020 67,

Mar. 31, 1967, Bolivia, Counterinsurgency Capabilities, item c. (K) (1), p. 6; Guevara's diary, Apr. 1967 summary.

51. Telegrams, State to American embassy Buenos Aires and five other addressees, #166641, n.d., and La Paz to State, #000587, Apr. 1, 1967; Department of Defense Intelligence Information Report, Bolivia, Counterinsurgency Capabilities, item 1. (A4), p. 2.

CHAPTER FOUR

1. Author's conversation with the officer during the course of this study; name and date must be withheld.

2. Author's conversation with Tope, Nov. 19, 1990, and interviews with Henderson, FAOHP, Sept. 22, 1990, pp. 15, 16, and Jan. 12, 1992.

3. Author's interview with Henderson, FAOHP, Sept. 22, 1990, p. 16.

4. Telegram, La Paz to State, #022736, Apr. 22, 1967 (report by Tope sent through embassy channels).

5. Tope's report to Southern Command, "Meeting with President Rene BARRIENTOS Ortuno, etc.," May 3, 1967, p. 3. Tope submitted a report on his trip to the commander in chief of Southern Command on May 6, 1967. The author is indebted to him for a copy that he sent, which is now deposited with the NSA.

6. LBJ Libr., NSF, Country File: Bolivia, vol. 4, box 8, doc. 113a.

7. *The Times* (London), Apr. 11, 1967, "U.S. Aid for Fight Against Guerrillas," from Murray Sayle, La Paz.

8. Tope's report, "Meeting with President Rene BARRIENTOS Ortuno, etc.," May 3, 1967, p. 2.

9. Waters, *The Bolivian Diary*, pp. 156, n. 21, 305–7. Guevara put out five communiqués between March and June, one specifically for Bolivia's miners. The first, issued on March 27, 1967, appeared in Cochabamba's *La Prensa*, but not until May 1, 1967.

10. Tope's report, "Meeting with President Rene BARRIENTOS Ortuno, etc.," May 3, 1967, p. 2.

11. Guevara's diary, Mar. 31–Apr. 13, 1967; telegram, La Paz to State, #011226, Apr. 12, 1967; airgram, La Paz to State, #A-320, "Second Guerrilla Encounter for Bolivian Armed Forces," Apr. 15, 1967; González and Sánchez Salazar, *The Great Rebel*, pp. 97–110.

12. Bolivia has nine departments, each divided into provinces.

13. Telegrams, La Paz to State, #009594, May 10, 1987, and #001395, June 1, 1967.

14. Guevara's diary, Apr. 1967 summary.

15. Guevara, *Guerilla Warfare*, p. 17.

16. Harris, *The Death of a Revolutionary*, frontispiece map, "Zone of Guer-

rilla Operations"; NARA, RG 287, Y4.F76/1:C73/9, "Communist Activities in Latin America," Hearings before the House Subcommittee on Inter-American Affairs, Henderson testimony, May, 4, 1967, p. 10.

17. Telegram, La Paz to State, #013861, Apr. 14, 1967.

18. Biographic background regarding Shelton comes from author interviews, May 30, 31, 1991.

19. Author's interviews with Shelton, May 30, 31, 1991, Fricke, Apr. 3, 1992, and Lazar, June 14, 1995.

20. The dates and other details of the training come from a slide presentation Shelton showed to the general staff in Panama upon his return from Bolivia, which he has retained.

21. Author's interviews with Henderson, Jan. 12, 1992, Shelton, May 30, 31, 1991, and Fricke, Apr. 3, 1992.

22. Ciro Roberto Bustos's testimony, in Mallin, *"Che" Guevara on Revolution*, p. 219.

23. Tope memo to CINC, May 6, 1967, p. 15.

24. Telegram, La Paz to State, #001469, Apr. 1, 1967.

25. State Department, Memorandum of Conversation, Subj.: Bolivian Guerrilla Situation (Part 1 of 2), June 7, 1967.

26. Information about the intelligence establishment comes largely from author's interviews in April 1992 and June 1995 with a number of American officials who must remain anonymous, plus certain useful printed materials, which give numbers if one knows how to interpret them. Neither their names nor the method of interpretation should be revealed.

27. Author's interviews with Tilton, Apr. 6, 1992, and Rodríguez, June 6, 1995; Gott, "The Ribs of Rosinante," p. 5.

28. Author's interview with Porter, Oct. 22, 1991.

29. Telegram, Buenos Aires to State, #013250, June 15, 1967.

30. LBJ Libr., NSF, Country File: Bolivia, vol. 4, box 8, Memorandum of Conversation by Bowdler, June 29, 1967; Tope's report, "Meeting with President Rene BARRIENTOS Ortuno, etc.," May 3, 1967, p. 3; telegram, La Paz to USCINCSO (State Department copy available, #025035), May 24, 1967.

31. For reports of the May confrontations, see *New York Times*, May 24, p. 1; May 25, pp. 1, 14; May 26, p. 1; for September, see Sept. 23, p. 1; Oct. 10 (supp.), p. 8. For the June episode, see NSA, U.S. Army, IAGS Bolivia Project Monthly Progress Report, RCS SCPIAGS-2 (R-2). The 200 figure comes from Dunkerley, *Rebellion in the Veins*, pp. 124–25. For background on the mining issue in this period, see also Klein, *Bolivia*, pp. 246–49, and Malloy, "Revolutionary Politics," in Malloy and Thorn, *Beyond the Revolution*, pp. 145–50.

32. LBJ Libr., NSF, Country File: Cuba, INR Reports, doc. 7.

33. Dunkerley, *Rebellion in the Veins*, p. 149; CIA, Cuba, Guevara file, JPRS Sum. #45,203, Apr. 29, 1968, Franco Pierini, "The Last Guerrillas of

Guevara," *Bohemia* (Caracas), Apr. 21, 1968 (interview with survivors of Guevara's band).

34. Guevara's diary, June summary, point 8; Waters, *The Bolivian Diary*, p. 156, n. 21, 312, 378 (Inti Paredo's essay, "My Campaign with Che").

35. Telegram, La Paz to State, #024574, June 28, 1967.

36. United States Southern Command Military Assistance Plan, Regional (Latin America), FY 1967–72, vol. 1, Narrative G—Internal Security.

37. United States Southern Command Military Assistance Plan, FY 1967–72, Bolivia, vol. 1, Narrative F—Past Accomplishments, p. 5; see also United States Southern Command Military Assistance Plan, Regional (Latin America), 1 July 1965, Narrative B—Threat and Capabilities Analysis, p. 10.

38. Telegrams, La Paz to State, #010072, July 12, 1967, and #012944, July 14, 1967.

39. LBJ Libr., NSF, Country File: Bolivia, vol. 4, box 8, doc. 28 and attachment.

40. Guevara's diary, July 9, 1967.

41. Guevara's diary, June 30, 1967.

42. CIA, FBIS, DR #133, July 11, 1967, "Argentine Says He Talked with Guevara Twice," La Paz INTERPRESS in Spanish; see also Cuba, Ernesto Guevara file, FBIS 21, July 16, 1967, Rio de Janeiro in Portuguese; FB #159, Aug. 16, 1967, "Preparations for Debray Trial," Lima AFP in Spanish; FB #193, "Debray Declares Innocence in Interview," La Paz INTERPRESS in Spanish; airgram, La Paz to State, #A-10, "Is 'Che' Guevara in Bolivia?" July 12, 1967.

43. Author's interview with Henderson, FAOHP, Sept. 22, 1990, p. 19.

44. LBJ Libr., NSF, Country File: Bolivia, vol. 4, box 8, doc. 112.

45. Ibid., memo, June 23, 1967, and Intelligence File, "Guerrilla Problem in Latin America," box 2, draft memo, June 24, 1967.

46. Airgram, La Paz to State, #A-10, July 12, 1967; author's interview with Grover, FAOHP, Nov. 2, 1990, pp. 12–13.

47. Guevara's diary, July 8–11, 1967.

CHAPTER FIVE

1. Telegram, La Paz to State, #009258, July 11, 1967.

2. The account of the Samaipata raid is based on Guevara's diary, July 6, 1967; telegrams, La Paz to State, #008005, July 10, 1967, and #009258, July 11, 1967; and González and Sánchez Salazar, *The Great Rebel*, pp. 163–66.

3. CIA, Directorate of Intelligence, Weekly Summary, Special Report, "The Che Guevara Diary," Dec. 15, 1967.

4. Author's interviews with Shelton, May 30, 31, 1991.

5. Telegram, La Paz to State, #012944, July 14, 1967.

6. NARA, RG 287, Y4.F76/1:C73/9, "Communist Activities in Latin America," Hearings before the House Subcommittee on Inter-American Affairs, Henderson testimony, May 4, 1967, p. 10; United States Southern Command Military Assistance Plan, Bolivia, vol. 2, MAP Element Description, Nine Separate Infantry Companies.

7. Author's interview with Fricke, Apr. 3, 1992; United States Southern Command Military Assistance Plan (FY 1968–73), Bolivia, vol. 1, Narrative F—Past Accomplishments, p. 6; James, *Ché Guevara*, pp. 266–67.

8. Guevara's diary, April, May, June, July 1967 summaries.

9. Department of Defense Intelligence Information Report, Bolivia, Operation Cynthia, Aug. 11, 1967.

10. For Henderson's testimony, see NARA, RG 287, Y4.F76/1:C73/9, May 4, 1967.

11. *U.S. News & World Report*, June 26, 1967; *New York Times*, June 18, 1967, sec. 4, p. 3.

12. *New York Times*, July 9, 1967, sec. 4, p. 3; telegrams, State to Buenos Aires and La Paz, #000943, July 5, 1967; State to La Paz #003457, July 9, 1967; Buenos Aires to State, #004804, July 6, 1967; #008104, July 10, 1967; #008940, July 11, 1967; and La Paz to State, #00507, Sept. 30, 1967.

13. For Barrientos's remarks and for background on the misunderstanding, see telegrams, La Paz to State, #010432, July 12, 1967; #10517, July 13, 1967; #013022, July 14, 1967; and State to La Paz, #005881, July 13, 1967.

14. CIA, FBIS, DR #148, Aug. 1, 23, 1967, "First LASO Conference."

15. CIA, JPRS Sum. #45,147, Cuba, Aug. 23, 1968, "The Blocking of Fidel Castro in Bolivia" (article by Manuel Castillo, *Est & Ouest*, Paris, Feb. 16–29, 1968).

16. CIA, Directorate of Intelligence, Intelligence Memorandum, "The Bolivian Guerrilla Movement: An Interim Assessment," Aug. 8, 1967.

17. For Helms's remark, see LBJ Libr., NSF, Bolivia, vol. 4, box 8, doc. 108a. Carmichael's comments are reported in *Granma*, English weekly edition, Aug. 13, 1967, and quoted in James, *Ché Guevara*, pp. 325–26.

18. LBJ Libr., NSF, Country File: Bolivia, vol. 4, box 8, docs. 108, 108a, b, c.

19. Guevara's diary, July 1967 summary.

20. Ibid., Aug. 7, 1961.

21. Besides Guevara's testimony throughout his diary to difficult relations with the campesinos, see, for example, Inti Paredo's diary, *Pensamiento Critico* (Havana), no. 52, May 1971, (trans. in CIA, JPRS Sum #54,606, Dec. 2, 1971, p. 66). Paredo describes a peasant spotting fleeing survivors of the band after Guevara's death and running to tell a nearby army unit. See also Pombo's article in *Verde Olivo* (Havana), Oct. 11, 1970 (trans. in CIA, JPRS Sum #51,834, Nov. 20, 1970).

22. Author's interviews with Grover, Nov. 2, 1990, and Horras, Apr. 8, 1992.

23. James puts Guevara's maximum strength at 51, listing the names and nationalities in *The Complete Bolivian Diaries*, p. 323. González and Sánchez Salazar, *The Great Rebel*, list a total of 60 guerrillas in addition to Guevara, but not all served at the same time; see pp. 234–39.

24. U.S. Department of State, Director of Intelligence and Research, Research Memorandum, RAR-18, July 18, 1967.

25. Martinez describes the discovery of the caves and itemizes their contents in detail, including texts of the documents. See *Ñancahuazú*, pp. 201–44. Additional accounts of the cache discovery can be found in the author's interviews with Henderson, FAOHP, Sept. 22, 1990, p. 16, and Morris, FAOHP, Oct. 17, 1990, p. 28, and in the JFK Libr., Henderson oral history, Aug. 30, 1978, p. 132.

26. Martinez includes copies of Bustos's maps in his account of the discovery of the caves, *Ñancahuazú*, p. 206.

27. Telegram, La Paz to State, #00638, Sept. 18, 1967; Martinez, *Ñancahuazú*, p. 209; Guevara's diary, Jan. 1, 1967, about Guzmán's responsibilities.

28. Author's interview with Henderson, FAOHP, Sept. 22, 1990, pp. 17–19.

29. Nance's letter of July 6, 1991, replying to written questions from author.

30. Author's interview with Broderick, FAOHP, Oct. 8, 1990, p. 3.

31. LBJ Libr., NSF, Country File: Latin America, vol. 6, box 3, doc. 7a, and Country File: Bolivia, vol. 4, box 8, doc. 106.

32. CIA, FBIS, FB #186, Sept. 25, 1967, "Bolivian Guerrillas Directed by Ché Guevara," La Paz INTERPRESS in Spanish.

33. Telegram, State to All American Republic Diplomatic Posts, etc., #39522, Sept. 18, 1967.

34. Telegram, State to La Paz, #42310, Sept. 25, 1967. For the slide story, see author's interview with Morris, FAOHP, Oct. 17, 1990, p. 28.

35. Guevara's diary, Feb. 10, Sept. 1, 2, 1967.

36. González Berzejo, "Joaquín and His Guerrillas," trans. in CIA, JPRS Sum. #53,788, Aug. 10, 1971. González interviewed Rojas and José Castillo Chavez (Paco), the only survivor of Joaquín's band.

37. He should not be confused with Pacho (Alberto Fernández Montes de Oca), a Cuban guerrilla who died in battle on October 8, 1967.

38. Various versions of this story place either one or two soldiers at the farmhouse (buying a pig, according to one story) when the guerrillas arrived. As the tale is frequently told, one soldier was at the farmhouse at the time; the farmer's wife told him to strip, hide his uniform, jump into bed, and say nothing, while she told the guerrillas he was her son, sick with malaria. Meanwhile, she sent her real son off to tell the army that guerrillas were at the farmhouse. Other versions speak of two soldiers dressed as peasants who encountered the guerrillas and tricked them. Furthermore, according to some, these were Second Ranger Battalion soldiers whom CIA agent Rodríguez dis-

guised occasionally to sniff out information. Rodríguez himself, however, dismisses this colorful adaptation of the story. No Second Rangers ever left training. The CIA itself forwarded yet another account to Washington in a report, "not finally evaluated," that said simply that the guerrillas asked a peasant to scout out a good crossing point and display a white cloth if it was safe, a red one if it was not. He ran into the infantry patrol, which convinced him to give the wrong signal.

Versions of this story were collected from LBJ Libr., NSF, Country File: Bolivia, vol. 4, box 8, doc. 66a (CIA, Intelligence Information Cable); Martinez, *Ñancahuazú*, pp. 260–68; González and Sánchez Salazar, *The Great Rebel*, pp. 168–76; James, *Ché Guevara*, pp. 263–66; author's interviews with Waghelstein, Jan. 10, 1992, and Rodríguez, June 16, 1995.

39. Many accounts of this event agree that the stream Joaquín wanted to cross was the Vado del Yeso. Paco, however, speaking to González Berzejo, says it was the nearby Rio Grande; see González, "Joaquín and His Guerrillas."

40. For El Negro, see CIA, FBIS, FB #172, Bolivia, Sept. 5, 1967, "Bolivian Guerrilla Tentatively Identified," Paris AFP in Spanish; telegram, La Paz to State, #00530, Sept. 6, 1967; González and Sánchez Salazar, *The Great Rebel*, p. 235; James, *The Complete Bolivian Diaries*, p. 326; for Tania, see telegram, La Paz to State, #00540, Sept. 7, 1967.

41. See Guevara's diary for the appropriate days regarding events related in this and subsequent paragraphs.

42. LBJ Libr., NSF, Country File: Bolivia, vol. 4, box 8, doc. 106.

43. Telegram, State to American embassies, etc., #33044, Sept. 6, 1967.

44. Guevara's diary, Sept. 8, 1967.

45. Telegram, La Paz to State, #00563, Sept. 9, 1967; CIA, FBIS, FB #192, Oct. 3, 1967, "Guerrillas Who Surrender Will Be Spared," Buenos Aires Reuters in English; Anderson, *Che Guevara*, p. 725.

46. Telegrams, La Paz to State, #00581, Sept. 11, 1967, and #00715, Sept. 27, 1967; CIA, FBIS, Bolivia, Sept. 12, 1967, "Reward for Guevara's Capture Offered," Paris AFP in Spanish. Guevara commented on the reward, which he heard about on his radio, in his September 11, 1967, diary entry.

47. Guevara's diary, Aug. 18, 19, 1967, and Aug. 1967 summary.

48. Edwin Chacón in *Presencia*, Oct. 4, 1967; trans. in Department of Defense Intelligence Information Report #2 808 0076 67, Oct. 5, 1967, Bolivia, Alto Seco Incident. González and Sánchez Salazar also rely on the article in their description of the Alto Seco incident, *The Great Rebel*, pp. 178–79.

49. Guevara's diary, Sept. 26, 1967.

50. Telegrams, La Paz to State, #00725 and #00726, both Sept. 27, 1967; CIA, FBIS, FB #190, Sept. 29, 1967, Bolivia, "Army Seeks Guerrilla Band Led by Guevara," Paris AFP in English.

51. Minà, *An Encounter with Fidel*, pp. 232–33. Minà's chapter on Guevara,

"Memories of Che," is reproduced in Castro, *Che,* chap. 6. The remarks quoted here are on pp. 125–26.

52. For Guevara's account of the events from the band's entry into Alto Seco until the battle at La Higuera, see Guevara's diary, Sept. 22–27, 1967.

53. CIA, FB #191, Oct. 2, 1967, "Guevara Reported Ill," Lima AFP in Spanish; FBIS 40, Sept. 30, 1967, "Che Guevara Activity," Santiago INTERPRESS in Spanish; FBIS 67, Sept. 30, 1967, "Che Guevara Illness," Buenos Aires Reuters in English.

54. Guevara's diary, Oct. 3, 1967; author's interview with Rodríguez, June 16, 1995. See also Rodríguez and Weisman, *Shadow Warrior*, pp. 143–56.

55. CIA, FBIS, FB #190, Sept. 29, 1967, Bolivia, "Army Seeks Guerrilla Band Led by Guevara," Paris AFP in English; FB #191, Oct. 2, 1967, "Troops Close in on Guerrillas Led by Guevara," Buenos Aires Reuters in English; FB #195, Oct. 4, 1967, "Guerrillas Report Che's New Alias, Illness," La Paz INTERPRESS in Spanish.

56. CIA, FBIS, FB #195, Oct. 4, 1967, Bolivia, "Debray Declares Innocence in Interview," La Paz INTERPRESS in Spanish.

57. Guevara's diary, Oct. 3, 1967.

58. Author's interviews with Shelton, May 30, 31, 1991, and Fricke, Apr. 3, 1992; González and Sánchez Salazar, *The Great Rebel*, p. 185.

CHAPTER SIX

1. Author's interviews with Moser, Sept. 8, 1994, and Gott, Sept. 6, 1994; Gott, *Guerrilla Movements in Latin America*, pp. 1–5.

2. Martinez, *Ñancahuazú*, p. 283.

3. Leagues vary greatly in South America, but the woman seems to have meant approximately three miles. Other sources indicate that that is how far the guerrillas were from La Higuera, which, incidentally, is often referred to as Higueras, much as Vallegrande is frequently called Valle Grande.

4. Guevara's diary, Oct. 6, 7, 1967.

5. Guevara's diary, Sept. 25–27, 1967.

6. DIA, Department of Defense Intelligence Information Report, Bolivia, "Activities of the 2nd Ranger Battalion and Death of 'Che' Guevara," #2 230 0754 67, Nov. 28, 1967. This report consists of a debriefing of ranger battalion personnel.

7. Franco Pierini, "How I Killed Guevara," *L'Europeo*, Oct. 26, 1967, CIA trans., NSA.

8. Author's interview with Rodríguez, June 16, 1995.

9. DIA, Department of Defense Intelligence Information Report, "Activities of the 2nd Ranger Battalion," Nov. 28, 1967.

10. Moser's film for Britain's Granada TV program, "World in Action," although not aired until December 1967, is a good example.

11. Author's interview with Rodríguez, June 16, 1995; Rodríguez and Weisman, *Shadow Warrior*, pp. 157–59.

12. Nance's letter of July 6, 1991, replying to written questions from author.

13. Author's interviews with Rodríguez, June 16, 1995, and anonymous embassy officials, Apr. 11, 15, 1992.

14. Author's interviews with Nance, July 6, 1991; Rodríguez, June 16, 1995; and an anonymous embassy officer, Apr. 15, 1992.

15. Telegrams, La Paz to State, #00820 and #00832, both Oct. 9, 1967; LBJ Libr., NSF, Country File: Bolivia, vol. 4, box 8, memo, Rostow to President, Oct. 9, 1967, 6:10 P.M.

16. Prado, *The Defeat of Che Guevara*, p. 183.

17. CIA, FBIS, FB #197, Oct. 10, 1967, "Clash in Higueras Leads to Guevara's Death," Buenos Aires, ANSA in Spanish, Oct. 9, 1967, and FB #199, Cuba, Oct. 12, 1967, "Press Agency Dispatches," Havana Domestic Service in Spanish, Oct. 11, 1967; airgram, La Paz to State, #843, "Press Conference on the Death of Che Guevara"; Department of Defense Intelligence Information Report, #1 808 0080 67, Country: Bolivia, "Death of Ernesto (Che) Guevara," Nov. 28, 1967. The debriefings took place from October 29 to 31, 1967.

18. Prado, *The Defeat of Che Guevara*, p. 182.

19. Rodríguez and Weisman, *Shadow Warrior*, chap. 11.

20. Prado, *The Defeat of Che Guevara*, pp. 182–3, 211, 219, 254.

21. Telegram, La Paz to State, #00843, Oct. 11, 1967; CIA, FBIS, FB #200, Oct. 13, 1967, Bolivia, "Barrientos: Che's Body to Remain in Bolivia," Lima AFP in Spanish, Oct. 13, 1967.

22. Author's interviews with Gott, Sept. 6, 1994, and Moser, Sept. 8, 1994; Rodríguez and Weisman, *Shadow Warrior*, pp. 16–18; telegram, La Paz to State, #00833, Oct. 10, 1967.

23. Both Moser and Gott agree on the time, Moser in a letter to the author, May 14, 1996, Gott in *Guerrilla Movements in Latin America*, p. 3. Rodríguez is not precise about the time.

24. Author's interviews with Gott, Sept. 6, 1994, and Moser, Sept. 8, 1994; Rodríguez and Weisman, *Shadow Warrior*, pp. 16–18; *Manchester Guardian*, Oct. 11, 1967; telegram, London to State, #02825, Oct. 11, 1967.

25. Author's interviews with Tilton, Apr. 6, 1992, and anonymous official, Apr. 15, 1992; Gott, *Guerrilla Movements in Latin America*, pp. 1–5.

26. Author's interviews with Gott, Sept. 6, 1994, and Chatten, May 1, 1995. For the story of Gott's relations with the KGB, see especially *Spectator*, Dec. 10, 1994, *Sunday Times*, Dec. 11, 1994, and Gott's version in the *Independent*, Dec. 9, 1994. Roper's words are from a story dated October 12, 1967, quoted by González and Sánchez Salazar, *The Great Rebel*, p. 112. For Gott's remarks

about the *New York Times*'s coverage, see his article in the *Nation*, Nov. 20, 1967.

27. *Ramparts*, Mar. 1967.

28. LBJ Libr., NSF, Country File: Bolivia, vol. 4, box 8, doc. #98.

29. Ibid., doc. 99.

30. Ibid., doc. 15, 92.

31. CIA, Weekly Summary, Western Hemisphere, "Effects of 'Che' Guevara's Death," Oct. 20, 1967, p. 26.

32. Ibid.

33. Telegrams, La Paz to State, #00858, Oct. 12, 1967, and #00874, Oct. 14, 1967; CIA, FBIS, FB #201, Argentina, Oct. 16, 1967, "Roberto Guevara Statement," Buenos Aires ANSA in Spanish, Oct. 14, 1967; FB #200, Bolivia, Oct. 13, 1967, "La Paz Press Confused over Disposal of Body," Lima AFP in Spanish, Oct. 13, 1967; FB #201, Venezuela, Oct. 16, 1967, "Che's Uncle and Father Discredit [word blurred] His Death," Paris AFP in English, Oct. 14, 1967; "Castro Killed Che Years Ago, Venezuelan Says," Buenos Aires Reuters in English, Oct. 13, 1967; Cuba, Guevara file, Paris AFP in English, Oct. 13, 1967, title blurred; FB #231, Bolivia, Nov. 29, 1967, "Che Betrayed by Havana, Ovando Candia Says," Buenos Aires ANSA in Spanish, Nov. 28, 1967.

34. CIA, FBIS, FB #227, Nov. 22, 1967, "Che's Hands," Buenos Aires ANSA in Spanish, Nov. 17, 1967; DR #170 (LA & WE), Bolivia, Aug. 29, 1968, "Guevara's Hands, Death Mask Reported Stolen," Cochabamba, *Los Tiempos*, Aug. 17, 1968; "CIA: Executive Action," July 29, 1992, BBC-TV.

35. *New York Times*, Nov. 21, 1995, p. 3; Reuters, Dec. 1, 1995; Associated Press, Jan. 31, 1996; Gott, "The Ribs of Rosinante," p. 5.

36. *New York Times*, Oct. 16, 1967, p. 4; CIA, FBIS, FB #204, Cuba, Oct. 19, 1967, "Fidel Castro Delivers Eulogy on Che Guevara," Havana Radio and Television Services in Spanish, Oct. 19, 1967 (includes text; FBIS dates the speech October 19 because it uses Greenwich Mean Time, though it was 8:44 P.M., October 18, in Havana); CIA, JPRS Sum. #68,527, Jan. 25, 1977.

37. LBJ Libr., NSF, Country File: Bolivia, vol. 4, box 8, doc. 60a.

38. DIA, Department of Defense Intelligence Information Report, Bolivia, "Activities of the 2nd Ranger Battalion," Nov. 28, 1967; CIA, JPRS Sum. #45,203, Apr. 29, 1968, Cuba, "Interview with Survivors of Guevara's Last Battle" (CIA's title; the item consists of an article by Franco Pierini, "The Last Guerrillas of Guevara," *Bohemia* [Caracas], Apr. 21, 1968).

39. DIA, Department of Defense Intelligence Information Report, Bolivia, "Activities of the 2nd Ranger Battalion," Nov. 28, 1967; LBJ Libr., NSF, Country File: Bolivia, vol. 4, box 8, doc. 21a.

40. Telegram, La Paz to State, #00872, Oct. 13, 1967; LBJ Libr., NSF, Country File: Bolivia, vol. 4, box 8, doc. 21a.

41. CIA, FBIS, FB #39, Chile, Feb. 26, 1968, "Cuban Guerrilla Gives Press

Conference," Buenos Aires ANSA in Spanish, Feb. 24, 1968; telegram, La Paz to State, #00881, Oct. 15, 1967.

42. DIA, Department of Defense Intelligence Information Report, Bolivia, "Activities of the 2nd Ranger Battalion," Nov. 28, 1967.

43. Ibid.

44. Anonymous authoritative CIA source.

45. Author's interview with anonymous U.S. military source.

46. CIA, JPRS Sum. #45,203, Apr. 29, 1968, "Interview with Survivors,"; FBIS, FB #39, Bolivia, Feb. 26, 1968, "Army Leader Denies Clash with Guerrillas," La Paz INTERPRESS in Spanish, Feb. 24, 1968.

47. Author's interview with Rodríguez, June 16, 1995.

48. CIA, JPRS Sum. #45,203, Apr. 29, 1968, "Interview with Survivors."

49. Ibid., CIA FBIS, DR #8, Jan. 13, 1970, "Death of a Guerrilla," Buenos Aires ANSA in Spanish, Jan. 13, 1970; Dunkerley, *Rebellion in the Veins*, p. 151.

50. *New York Times*, Mar. 6, 1968, p. 13; CIA, FBIS, FB #39, Chile, Feb. 26, 1968, "Official Answers Marxists on Guerrilla Issue," Santiago, Emisoras Nuevo Mundo in Spanish, Feb. 23, 1968, and "Cuban Guerrilla Gives Press Conference," Buenos Aires ANSA in Spanish, Feb. 24, 1968.

51. CIA, FBIS, FB #199, Bolivia, Oct. 12, 1967, "Debray Announces Intention to Reverse Plea," Buenos Aires Reuters in English, Oct. 11, 1967; airgram, La Paz to State, #A-144, Nov. 4, 1967, p. 3.

52. CIA, FBIS, FB #221, Bolivia, Nov. 14, 1967, "Guerrilla Disagreements Disclosed," Lima AFP in Spanish, Nov. 14, 1967; airgram, La Paz to State, #A-123, Oct. 13, 1967, p. 3; *New York Times*, Dec. 24, 1970, p. 1.

53. Author's interview with Onis, June 4, 1995.

54. CIA, FBIS, FB #219, Bolivia, Nov. 9, 1967, "Publishing Houses Bid for Guevara Diary," Paris AFP in English, Nov. 7, 1967; FB #221, Bolivia, Nov. 14, 1967, "Che Diary Reveals Havana Guerilla Contacts" (various items dated in mid-November 1967 from AFP, ANSA, and Reuters); FB #131 (LA & WE), Cuba, July 5, 1968, "Castro Says His Copy of Diary Is Authentic," Havana Domestic Radio and TV, July 4, 1968; FB #137 (LA & WE), Cuba, "Granma Publishes Guevara Documents, Messages," n.d.; CIA, JPRS Sum #46,204, Aug. 15, 1968, "Bolivian Peasant Support to Guevara Claimed" (article by Richard Gott in Havana's *Juventud Rebelde*, July 5, 1968); *New York Times*, Dec. 3, 1967, p. 79, Dec. 10, 1967, p. 80.

55. CIA, FBIS, FB #131 (LA & WE), Cuba, July 5, 1967, "Book Institute to Publish Second Edition," Havana Domestic Service, July 3, 1968.

56. *New York Times*, Oct. 16, 1967, p. 4; CIA, FBIS, FB #129, (LA & WE), Bolivia, July 2, 1968, "Regime: Cuba Does Not Have Guevara Diary," La Paz INTERPRESS in Spanish, July 1, 1968; FB #131 (LA & WE), Cuba, July 5, 1968, "Castro Says His Copy of Diary Is Authentic"; FB #134 (LA & WE), Bo-

livia, July 10, 1968, "Barrientos' Views," Lima AFP in Spanish, July 10, 1968; FB #139 (LA & WE), Cuba, July 17, 1968, "Barrientos' Remarks on Che's Diary Attacked," Havana in Spanish to the Americas, July 16, 1968.

57. CIA, FBIS, Bolivia, FB #136 (LA & WE), "CIA Agent González Blamed for Diary Removal," Buenos Aires ANSA in Spanish, July 11, 1968; FB #136 (LA & WE), July 12, 1968, "Newsmen Criticize Military on Guevara Matter," Santiago INTERPRESS in Spanish, July 11, 1968; FB #134 (LA & WE), July 10, 1968, "Siles Admits That Guevara Diary Is Authentic," Lima AFP in Spanish, July 10, 1968; FB #137 (LA & WE), "Officials Speculate on Guevara Diary Issue," Lima AFP in Spanish, July 13, 1968, and "Cuban Agent Posing as Writer Took Photos," Buenos Aires Reuters in English, July 13, 1968; FB #138 (LA & WE), July 16, 1968, "Radio: Regime Official Sent Diary to Cuba," Santiago Radio Balmaceda in Spanish, July 15, 1968; DR #143 (LA & WE), July 23, 1968, "Prensa Latina Interviews Newsmen about Diary," Santiago Prensa Latina in Spanish, July 18, 1968; FB #131 (LA & WE), July 5, 1968, "Opposition Questions Security Provisions," Buenos Aires ANSA in Spanish, July 4, 1968; González and Sánchez Salazar, *The Great Rebel*, p. 213, Rodríguez and Weisman, *Shadow Warrior*, p. 163.

58. Sauvage, *Che Guevara*, p. 214.

59. Rodríguez and Weisman, *Shadow Warrior*, p. 135; Sauvage, *Che Guevara*, p. 215; *New York Times*, Aug. 18, 1968.

60. Sauvage, *Che Guevara*, chap. 9, "The Arguedas Episode."

61. *New York Times*, Aug. 3, 1968, p. 5; Aug. 9, 1968, p. 16; CIA, FBIS, Peru, no no., Aug. 12, 1968, "Antonio Arguedas Explains His Recent Actions," Havana Prensa Latina in Spanish, Aug. 12, 1968.

62. *New York Times*, Aug. 18, 1968, p. 1.

63. Sauvage, *Che Guevara*, p. 235.

64. CIA, JPRS Sum. #50,114, "Arguedas Denounces CIA in Che Guevara Affair," Luis Suarez, *Siempre*, Mexico City, Feb. 4, 1970; FBIS, FB #210, Chile, Oct. 27, 1967, "CIA Falsifies Che's Diary to Pressure Chile," Santiago Prensa Latina in Spanish, Oct. 26, 1967.

65. Author's interviews with anonymous CIA agents, Apr. 11, 15, 1992, June 10, 1995.

66. Author's interview with Rodríguez, June 16, 1995.

67. LBJ Libr., NSF, Country File: Bolivia, vol. 4, box 8, doc. 83.

68. Ibid., doc. 80.

69. *New York Times*, July 27, 1968, p. 23; July 28, 1968, p. 2; Aug. 5, 1968, p. 2; Aug. 17, 1968, p. 6; Sauvage, *Che Guevara*, pp. 219–24; CIA, FBIS, Mexico, no no., Apr. 27, 1970, "Former Bolivian Minister Arguedas Given Asylum," Mexico City Reuters in English, Apr. 24, 1970.

70. Rodríguez and Weisman, *Shadow Warrior*, p. 166.

71. DIA, Department of Defense Intelligence Information Report, Bolivia,

"Activities of the 2nd Ranger Battalion," Nov. 28, 1967. Anderson, in *Che Guevara*, p. 739, quotes Guevara as saying, "Shoot, coward, you are only killing a man," based on an interview with Terán in the 1990s. I prefer the DIA report because it was written soon after the event. It was compiled by U.S. officers based upon interviews with combatants. To my knowledge there is no written Spanish original of any of the reported remarks.

CHAPTER SEVEN

1. The number of Cuban guerrillas comes from Mallin, *"Che" Guevara on Revolution*, pp. 229–31.

2. Guevara, *Guerrilla Warfare*, pp. 49–50.

3. Ibid., pp. 4, 5.

4. Author's interview with Henderson, June 18, 1995. Moser's film was aired on a weekly program, "World in Action," Dec. 7, 1967, Granada TV (U.K.)

5. LBJ Libr., NSF, Country File: Cuba, Meetings, doc. 35b (excerpt from President Kennedy's speech to Inter-American Press Association).

6. Author's interview with Helms, June 16, 1995.

7. Criticism of the CIA is fairly constant, but it intensified in 1991 with President Bush's controversial nomination of Robert M. Gates as director. See *New York Times*, July 14, 1991, p. 1, Oct. 2, 1991, p. 16. Former CIA employee Melvin Goodman made a strong call for reform, including relinquishing covert operations, in *New York Times*, Jan. 7, 1993, and former ambassador Robert E. White called for reforms in *Washington Post*, Feb. 7, 1991.

8. For Moynihan's discussion of this issue, see *New York Times*, May 19, 1991.

9. For background on the photograph, see *Independent*, June 12, 1994, Sunday Review, p. 40.

10. The March on the Pentagon received massive publicity. I have relied especially on *New York Times*, Oct. 22, 1967, p. 1, and personal accounts of eyewitnesses. The description of the Moscow observances comes largely from Wayne S. Smith, who was then serving at the U.S. embassy there.

11. CIA, Directorate of Intelligence, Intelligence Report, "Cuban Subversive Policy and the Bolivian Guerrilla Episode," May 1968, pp. 45–46.

12. CIA, JPRS Sum. #45,147, Apr. 23, 1968, Cuba, "The Blocking of Fidel Castro in Bolivia" (Castillo article).

13. Author's interview with Helms, June 16, 1995.

Bibliography

U.S. GOVERNMENT DOCUMENTS

The following documents were released through the Freedom of Information Act and are now housed at the National Security Archive, Washington, D.C.

U.S. Army, Southern Command
Documents regarding command operations in Latin America

U.S. Central Intelligence Agency
Documents on Fidel Castro
Documents on Ernesto "Che" Guevara

U.S. Defense Intelligence Agency
Documents relating to Guevara's insurgency in Bolivia

U.S. Department of State
Documents on Guevara's insurrection in Bolivia and the U.S. government response

ARCHIVES

Agency for International Development, Washington D.C.
"Bolivia Country Program Digest, 1965"
"Bolivia Country Program Digest, 1967"
"Pre-Feasibility Rail and Highway Study, Santa Cruz-Yacuiba Corridor, Bolivia," Jan. 1967

201

"Republic of Bolivia Police; Communications Survey," Apr. 1964
"Study and Report of Police Organization and Operations in Bolivia,"
 June 1967

John Fitzgerald Kennedy Library, Boston, Mass.
 National Security File
 Oral History Collection
 Personal Papers of Douglas Henderson
 President's Office File

Lyndon Baines Johnson Library, Austin, Tex.
 National Security File
 Oral History Collection

National Archives and Records Administration, Washington, D.C.
 Record Group 43, Records of International Conferences, Commissions,
  and Expositions
 Record Group 46, Records of the U.S. Senate
 Record Group 59, Records of the Department of State
 Record Group 287, Publications of the Federal Government
 Record Group 353, Records of Inter- and Intra-departmental Committees
 Record Group 490, Records of the Peace Corps
 Record Group 111, Photographic Records of the Army Signal Corps
 Record Group 306-PSB, Photographic Records of the U.S. Information
  Agency
 Record Group 59-0, Photographic Records of the Department of State

U.S. Senate Library, Washington, D.C.
 Congressional Hearings Supplement (microfiche)
 House of Representatives Committee Hearings
 Senate Committee Hearings

PUBLISHED DOCUMENTS AND STATISTICS

Aguilar, Luis, ed., *Operation Zapata: The "Ultrasensitive" Report and Testimony of the Board of Inquiry on the Bay of Pigs*, Frederick, Md., 1981
 (text of the Taylor report and transcripts of the meetings that produced it).
U.S. Department of State, *Foreign Relations of the United States*, Washington,
 D.C. 1942, vol. 5; 1943, vol. 5; 1944, vol. 7; 1945, vol. 9; 1946, vol. 11;
 1947, vol. 8; 1948, vol. 9; 1949, vol. 2; 1950, vol. 7; 1951, vol. 2;
 1952–54, vol. 4; 1955–57, vols. 6, 7; 1958–60, vols. 5, 6.
———, *Intervention of International Communism in Guatemala*, Washington,
 D.C., 1954.

U.S. National Archives and Records Administration Library, U.S. Congressional Serial Set, House and Senate Reports and Documents, Washington, D.C., 1953–69, vols. 11659–12928.

INTERVIEWS

Positions listed here are those held by the interviewees at the time of this study. The dates indicate when the interviews took place.

Anonymous friend of Guevara's during his youth, Nov. 5, 1991.

Anonymous U.S. government officials regarding Guevara's insurgency in Bolivia, Nov. 3, 1990, Apr. 11, 15, Nov. 2, 1992, June 10, 1995.

Anonymous U.S. government official regarding Guevara's mission in the Congo in 1965–66, Dec. 5, 1991.

Beruff, Jorge, director, Cuban National Bank for Economy and Social Development, Mar. 4, 1992.

Betancourt, Ernesto, director, Cuban National Bank, Dec. 16, 1991.

Bonachea, Ramón, teenage activist with students' Revolutionary Directorate during the Cuban Revolution, Apr. 10, 1992.

Broderick, William D., assistant director of the State Department's Office of Bolivian-Chilean Affairs, Oct. 8, 1990.

Chatten, Robert, information officer, U.S. embassy in Bolivia, May 1, 1995.

Fox, Edward, air attaché and senior military attaché to the U.S. embassy in Bolivia, June 23, 1991.

Fricke, Edmond L., executive officer and second in command of the Green Beret detachment sent to Bolivia in 1967, Apr. 3, 1992.

Garcia, Enrique, employee, Ministry of Industries, Cuba, Apr. 12, 1992.

Gott, Richard, *Manchester Guardian*, Sept. 6, 1994.

Grover, Charles, chief of the political section, U.S. embassy in Bolivia, Nov. 2, 19, 1990, Feb. and Mar., various dates, 1996.

Helms, Richard, director, Central Intelligence Agency June 16, 1995.

Henderson, Douglas, U.S. ambassador to Bolivia, Sept. 22, 1990, Jan. 12, 1992, June 18, 1995.

Horras, Lawrence, chief of the U.S. Military Advisory Group in Bolivia, April 8, 1992.

Lazar, David, deputy director, U.S. AID mission in Bolivia, June 14, 1995.

Maidanik, Kiva, professor, Institute of International Relations, Ministry of Foreign Relations, USSR, Dec. 4, 1990.

Matos, Huber, Cuban guerrilla leader, government official, political prisoner, Apr. 14, 1992.

Mikoyan, Sergo, secretary to his father, Soviet deputy premier Anastas Mikoyan and editor, *Latinskaya Amerika*, Dec. 13, 1990.

Morris, Patrick, director of the State Department's Office of Bolivian-Chilean Affairs, 1965–67, Oct. 17, Nov. 12, 1990.

Moser, Brian, Granada TV, Great Britain, Sept. 3, 1994.

Moyano Martin, Dolores, friend of Guevara during his childhood and youth, Oct. 17, 1991, Mar. 17, 1992.

Nance, Ernest, air attaché and senior military attaché to the U.S. embassy in Bolivia, July 6, 1991, May 12, 1995.

Nasário, Andres, Cuban guerrilla leader, Apr. 10, 1992.

Nuñez, Rafael, Cuban foreign-affairs official, Apr. 10, 1992.

Oliver, Covey, U.S. assistant secretary of state for inter-American affairs, July 7, 1991.

Onis, Juan de, *New York Times* correspondent, June 4, 1995.

Pino, Rafael del, guerrilla in Pinar del Rio and later Cuban Air Force officer, Aug. 22, 1992.

Porter, Robert W., Jr., commander in chief, U.S. Southern Command, Oct. 22, 1991.

Rodríguez, Félix I., CIA agent, June 16, 1995.

Rostow, Walt, national security adviser to President Johnson, July 11, 1991.

Shelton, Ralph "Pappy," commander of the Green Beret detachment sent to Bolivia in 1967, May 30, 31, 1991.

Smith, Wayne S., third secretary, U.S. embassy, Havana; Cuban desk official, State Department; second secretary, U.S. embassy, Moscow, Nov. 27, 1990, Mar. 5, 1992.

Stevenson, Robert A., State Department chief, Middle American Branch, INR; Cuba desk officer; deputy director, Office of Mexican, Caribbean, and Central American Affairs; coordinator, Cuban Affairs, May 15, 1995.

Tilton, John, CIA station chief in La Paz, Apr. 6, 1992.

Tope, William, chief of operations, U.S. Southern Command, Nov. 19, 1990.

Tuthill, John, U.S. ambassador to Brazil, Mar. 11, 1992.

Waghelstein, John D., U.S. Military Advisory Group representative in Cochabamba, Jan. 10, 1992.

ORAL HISTORIES

The names of interviewers are enclosed in parentheses.

Acheson, Dean, Apr. 27, 1964 (Lucius D. Battle), JFK Libr.

Bailey, John M., Apr. 10, 1964 (Charles T. Morrisey), JFK Libr.

Bell, David E., July 11, 1964 (Robert C. Turner), and Jan. 2, 1965 (William T. Dentzer), JFK Libr.

Bosch, Juan, Spring 1964 (Lloyd N. Cutler), JFK Libr.

Bowles, Chester, Feb. 2, 1965 (Robert R. R. Brooks), and July 1, 1970 (Dennis J. O'Brien), JFK Libr.

Broderick, William D., Oct. 8, 1990 (Henry Butterfield Ryan), FAOHP.

Coffin, Frank, Mar. 2–3, 1964 (Elizabeth Donahue), JFK Libr.

Cooper, Chester, May 6, 1966 (Joseph E. O'Connor), JFK Libr.

Crimmins, John H., May 23, 1964 (John N. Plank), JFK Libr.

Cull, Richard, Mario Noto, Richard Ffrench, and Robert Schoenberger, Dec. 17, 1970 (James A. Oesterle), JFK Libr. (about release of Bay of Pigs prisoners).

Cutler, Lloyd N., June 22, 1964 (Francis J. Hunt DeRosa), JFK Libr.

Dantas, Santiago, Dec. 1, 1963 (translated statement from *Journal do Brasil*).

Dutton, Frederick G., May 3, 1965 (Charles Morrisey), JFK Libr.

Ellender, Allen, Aug. 29, 1967 (Larry Hackman), JFK Libr.

Gaud, William, Feb. 16, 1966 (Joseph E. O'Connor), JFK Libr.

Gilpatric, Roswell L., May 5, 27, June 30, Aug. 12, 1970 (Dennis J. O'Brien), JFK Libr.

Gordon, Lincoln, May 30, 1964 (John E. Rielly), JFK Libr.

Gordon, Lincoln, July 10, 1969, Dec. 3, 1978 (Paige Mulhollan), LBJ Libr.

Gordon, Lincoln, Sept. 8, 1980 (Craig VanGrasstek), JFK Libr.

Gordon, Lincoln, Sept. 30, 1987 (Charles Stuart Kennedy), FAOHP.

Grover, Charles, Nov. 2, 1990 (Henry Butterfield Ryan), FAOHP.

Hamilton, Fowler, Aug. 18, 1964 (Edwin R. Bayley), JFK Libr.

Harriman, W. Averell, Apr. 13, 1964 (Michael V. Forrestal), and Jan. 17, June 6, 1965 (Arthur M. Schlesinger, Jr.), JFK Libr.

Heinz, Luther, July 20, 27, 1970 (William W. Moss), JFK Libr.

Helms, Richard, Apr. 4, 1969 (Paige Mulhollan), and Sept. 16, 1981 (Ted Gittinger), LBJ Libr.

Henderson, Douglas, Aug. 30, 1978 (Sheldon Stern), JFK Libr.

Henderson, Douglas, Apr. 29, 1988 (Richard Nethercut), FAOHP.

Henderson, Douglas, Sept. 22, 1990 (Henry Butterfield Ryan), FAOHP.

Hickenlooper, Bourke B., July 30, 1964 (Pat Holt), JFK Libr.

Hilsman, Roger, Jan. 26, 1970 (David Nunnerley), JFK Libr.

Holt, Pat M., Sept. 9–Dec. 12, 1980 (Donald A. Ritchie), Senate Historical Office.

Johnson, Douglas V., July 13, 1970 (William W. Moss), JFK Libr.

Johnson, U. Alexis, 2 interviews, n.d., monologue, Nov. 7 1964 (William Brubeck), JFK Libr.

Kennedy, Robert F., Feb. 29–May 14, 1964 (John Bartlow Martin); with Burke Marshall, Dec. 4–22, 1964 (Anthony Lewis); Feb. 27, 1965 (Arthur Schlesinger, Jr.); July 20–Aug. 1, 1967 (John Stewart), JFK Libr.

McGhee, George, Aug. 13, 1964 (Martin J. Hillenbrand), JFK Libr.

McNamara, Robert S., Feb. 26, 1970 (interviewer not identified), JFK Libr.

Mann, Thomas C., Mar. 13, 1968 (Larry J. Hackman), JFK Libr.
Marcy, Carl M., Sept. 14–Nov. 16, 1983 (Donald A. Ritchie), Senate Historical Office.
Martin, Edwin M., Apr. 7–May 3, 1988 (Melbourne L. Spector), FAOHP.
Merchant, Livingston, Spring 1965 (Philander P. Claxton, Jr.), JFK Libr.
Morris, Patrick F., Oct. 17, Nov. 12, 1990 (Henry Butterfield Ryan), FAOHP.
Oberdorfer, Louis F., John B. Jones, and Mitchell Rogovin, June 2, 1964 (Francis J. Hunt DeRosa), JFK Libr., (about release of Bay of Pigs prisoners).
Oliver, Covey T., Dec. 2, 12, 1968 (Paige Mulhollan), LBJ Libr.
Palmer, Williston B., Aug. 5, 1970 (William W. Moss), JFK Libr.
Plimpton, Francis, Oct. 21, 1969 (Dennis J. O'Brien), JFK Libr.
Proxmire, William, Mar. 25, 1966 (Charles T. Morrissey), JFK Libr.
Read, Benjamin H., Feb. 22, 1966, Oct. 17, 1969, Jan. 13, 1970 (Joseph E. O'Connor), JFK Libr.
Rostow, Walt W., Apr. 11, 1964 (Richard Neustadt), JFK Libr.
Rusk, Dean (Dec. 2, 1969–Aug. 21, 1970 (Dennis J. O'Brien), JFK Libr. (eight interviews).
Sorensen, Theodore, Mar. 26–May 20, 1964 (Carl Kaysen), JFK Libr.
Stevenson, Robert A., Sept. 19, 1989 (Charles Stuart Kennedy), FAOHP.
Taylor, Maxwell, Apr. 12, 26, June 21, 1964 (Elspeth Rostow), JFK Libr.
Wheeler, Earle, 1964 (Chester Clinton), JFK Libr.
Yarmolinsky, Adam, Nov. 11, 28, 1964 (Daniel Ellsberg), JFK Libr.
Zuckert, Eugene M., Apr. 18–July 25, 1964 (Lawrence E. McQuade), JFK Libr.

BROADCASTS

"Che Guevara," Aug. 22, 1996, Discovery Channel.
"CIA: Executive Action," July 29, 1992, BBC-TV.
"In Search of the Real Che Guevara," Nov. 16, 1971, BBC-TV.
"Secret Lives: Che Guevara," Dec. 21, 1995, Channel 4 (U.K.).
"World in Action," Dec. 7, 1967, Granada TV (U.K.).

NEWSPAPERS, NEWS SERVICES, AND PERIODICALS

Associated Press
Baltimore Sun
British Broadcasting Company (BBC)
Chicago Tribune
Diario (La Paz)

Granada TV
Granma
Manchester Guardian
Nación (La Paz)
Nation
Newsweek
New Yorker
New York Times
Philadelphia Inquirer
Ramparts
Reuters
The Times (London)
Time
United Press International (UPI)
U.S. News & World Report
Washington Post

ARTICLES AND THESES

Arguedas, Antonio, "Antonio Arguedas Relates Che Guevara's Last Days," *Punto Final* (Santiago, Chile), June 9, 1970 (FBIS translation).
"The Americas," *Newsweek*, Nov. 14, 1966.
Castillo, Manuel, "The Blocking of Fidel Castro in Bolivia," *Est & Ouest* (Paris), Feb. 16–29, 1968 (FBIS Trans.).
"Castro's Brain," *Time*, Aug. 8, 1960.
"Cuba, 1962," Cold War International History Project *Bulletin*, Woodrow Wilson International Center for Scholars, Washington, D.C., Spring 1995.
Davis, Jason, "Che: A Symbol of Rebellion and Struggle," *Bolivian Times*, Jan. 13–20, 1995.
Durch, William J., "The Cuban Military in Africa and the Middle East: From Algeria to Angola," *Studies in Comparative Communism* 11, nos. 1 & 2 (Spring/Summer 1978).
Gall, Norman, "The Legacy of Che Guevara," *Commentary* 44 (Dec. 1967).
Gatti, Claudio, "Así fueron las últimas horas del Che Guevara," *Cambio 16*, Dec. 18, 1989 (interview with CIA agent Félix I. Rodríguez).
Geyer, Georgie Anne, "Why Guevara Failed: An Interview with Régis Debray," *Saturday Review*, Aug. 24, 1968.
González Berzejo, Ernesto, "Joaquín and His Guerrillas: The Ford of Betrayal," *Verde Olivo* (Havana), July 4, 1971 (FBIS trans.).
Goodwin, Richard, "Annals of Politics: A Footnote," *New Yorker*, May 25, 1968.

Gott, Richard, "Guevara, Debray, and the CIA," *Nation*, Nov. 20, 1967.

———, "The Ribs of Rosinante," *London Review of Books*, Aug. 21, 1997.

Guevara, Ernesto Che, "The Cuban Economy: Its Past and Its Present Importance," *International Affairs* 40, no. 4 (Oct. 1964).

James, Daniel, "The Girl Who Betrayed Ché Guevara," *Chicago Tribune Sunday Magazine*, Sept. 21, 1969.

Meers, Sharon I., "U.S. Tracks in the 1954 Coup in Guatemala," *Diplomatic
History* 6, no. 3 (Summer 1992).

Moreno, José A., "Che Guevara on Guerrilla Warfare: Doctrine, Practice, and
Evaluation," *Comparative Studies in Society and History* 12 (Apr. 1970).

Moyano Martin, Dolores, "A Memoir of the Young Guevara," *New York Times
Magazine*, Aug. 18, 1968.

———, "From El Cid to El Che: The Hero and the Mystique of Liberation in
Latin America," *The World & I*, Feb. 1988.

Paredo, Inti, "My Campaign with Che," *Pensamiento Critico* (Havana), no. 52,
May 1971 (part of Paredo's diary) (FBIS trans.).

Pueblo ha triumfado, Difusion S.R.L., Santa Cruz, Bolivia, 1964.

Rand, Christopher, "Letter from La Paz," *New Yorker*, Dec. 31, 1966.

Ray, Michèle, "The Execution of Che by the CIA," *Ramparts* 6 (Mar. 1968).

St. George, Andrew, "How the U.S. Got Che," *True*, April 1969.

Shelton, Ralph W., "Advice for Advisers," *Infantry Magazine* 54 (July/Aug.
1964).

Suarez, Luis, "Arguedas Denounces CIA in the Che Guevara Affair," *Siempre*
(Mexico City), Feb. 4, 1970 (FBIS trans.).

———, "Arguedas Recounts Death of Tania the Guerrilla," *Siempre*, July 8,
1970 (FBIS trans.).

Tuthill, John W., "Operation Topsy," *Foreign Policy*, no. 8 (Fall 1972).

———, "U.S. Foreign Policy, the State Department, and U.S. Missions Abroad,"
Atlantic Community Quarterly 26 (Spring 1988).

Valenta, Jiri, "The Soviet-Cuban Intervention in Angola, 1975," *Studies in
Comparative Communism* 11, nos. 1 & 2 (Spring/Summer 1978).

Vandenbroucke, Lucien S., "Confessions of Allen Dulles," *Diplomatic History*
8, no. 4 (Fall 1984).

Villegas, Harry (Pombo), "Che's Activities in Bolivia," *Verde Olivo* (Havana),
Oct. 11, 1970 (trans. in CIA, JPRS Sum. #51,834, Nov. 20, 1970).

Waghelstein, John D., " 'Che's' Bolivian Adventure," *Military Review* 59 (Aug.
1979).

———, "A Theory of Revolutionary Warfare and Its Application to the Bolivian
Adventure of Che Guevara," master's thesis, Cornell University, 1973.

"The Woman Who Betrayed Che," *Ambre* (Paris), May 1971 (FBIS trans.).

Zahniser, Marvin R., and Michael W. Weis, "A Diplomatic Pearl Harbor?:
Richard Nixon's Goodwill Mission to Latin America in 1958," *Diplomatic
History* 13, no. 2 (Spring 1989).

Zéndegui, Guilerme de, "Bolivia, View from the Altiplano," *Américas* 21, no. 2 (Feb. 1969).

BOOKS

Aguero, Luis, *Che Commandante*, Mexico City, 1969.

Alexander, Robert J., *The Bolivian National Revolution*, New Brunswick, N.J., 1958.

———, *Bolivia: Past, Present, and Future*, New York, 1982.

Alexandre, Marianne, *!Viva Che!: Contributions in Tribute to Ernesto "Che" Guevara*, London, 1968.

Allen, Charles, *The Savage Wars of Peace: Soldiers Voices, 1945–1989*, London, 1990.

Allyn, Bruce J., James G. Blight, and David A. Welch, eds., *Back to the Brink: Proceedings of the Moscow Conference on the Cuban Missile Crisis, January 27–28, 1989*, Lanham, M.D., 1992.

Alvarez Garcia, John, *Che Guevara*, Medellin, 1968.

Ambrose, Stephen E., and Richard H. Immerman, *Milton S. Eisenhower, Educational Statesman*, Baltimore, 1983.

Anderson, Jon Lee, *Che Guevara: A Revolutionary Life*, New York, 1997.

Atkinson, James D., *The Politics of Struggle: The Communist Front and Political Warfare*, Chicago, 1966.

Barton, Robert, *A Short History of the Republic of Bolivia*, La Paz, 1968.

Batista, Fulgencio, *The Growth and Decline of the Cuban Republic*, New York, 1964.

Beckett, Ian F. W., *The Roots of Counter-Insurgency: Armies and Guerrilla Warfare, 1900–1945*, London, 1988.

Beckett, Ian, F. W., and John Pimlott, eds., *Armed Forces and Modern Counterinsurgency*, New York, 1985.

Beckovic, Matija, and Dusan Radovic, *Che: A Permanent Tragedy*, New York, 1970.

Bell, J. Boyer, *The Myth of the Guerrilla*, New York, 1971.

Benemelis, Juan F., *Castro, subversion y terrorismo en Africa*, Madrid, 1988.

Benjamin, Jules R., *The United States and the Origins of the Cuban Revolution: An Empire of Liberty in an Age of National Liberation*, Princeton, 1990.

Betancourt, Ernesto, *A Revolutionary Strategy: A Handbook for Practitioners*, New Brunswick, N.J. 1991.

Bethel, Paul D., *The Losers: The Definitive Report, by an Eyewitness of the Communist Conquest of Cuba and the Soviet Penetration in Latin America*, New Rochelle, N.Y., 1969.

Blanksten, George I., *Peron's Argentina*, Chicago, 1953.

Blasier, Cole, *The Hovering Giant*, Pittsburgh, 1985.

Blaufarb, Douglas S., *The Counterinsurgency Era: U.S. Doctrine and Performance, 1950 to the Present*, New York, 1977.

Blaufarb, Douglas S., and George K. Tanham, *Who Will Win? A Key to the Puzzle of Revolutionary War*, New York, 1989.

Blight, James G., Bruce J. Allyn, and David A. Welch, eds., *Cuba on the Brink: Castro, the Missile Crisis, and the Soviet Collapse*, New York, 1993.

Blight, James G., and David A. Welch, eds., *On the Brink: Americans and the Soviets Reexamine the Cuban Missile Crisis*, 2d ed., New York, 1990.

Bonachea, Rolando E., and Nelson Valdés, eds., *Cuba in Revolution*, New York, 1972.

Bonsal, Philip W., *Cuba, Castro, and the United States*, Pittsburgh, 1971.

Bourne, Peter G., *Fidel: A Biography of Fidel Castro*, New York, 1986.

Brill, William H., *Military Intervention in Bolivia: The Overthrow of Paz Estenssoro and the MNR*, Washington, 1967.

Buckley, William, Jr., *See You Later Alligator*, Garden City, N.Y., 1985.

Buhle, Paul, *History and the New Left: Madison, Wisconsin, 1950–1970*, Philadelphia, 1990.

Bundy, McGeorge, *Danger and Survival*, New York, 1988.

Cabrera Alvarez, Guillermo, ed., *Memories of Che*, Secaucus, N.J., 1987.

Calvert, Peter, *Guatemala: A Nation in Turmoil*, Boulder, Colo., 1985.

Cantor, Jay, *The Death of Che Guevara*, New York, 1983.

Castro, Fidel, *Che: A Memoir*, New York, 1994.

———, *Fidel Castro Speaks*, ed. Martin Kenner and James Petras, New York, 1969.

———, *History Will Absolve Me: The Moncado Trial Defense Speech, Santiago de Cuba, October 16, 1953*, London, 1969.

———, *To Speak the Truth: Why Washington's "Cold War" against Cuba Doesn't End*, with Che Guevara (public statements), New York, 1992.

Caws, Ian, *The View from Two Murders: Ernesto Che Guevara, Martin Luther King*, Leicester, 1972.

Cline, Ray S., *Secrets, Spies, and Scholars*, Washington, D.C., 1978.

Cook, Blanche, *The Declassified Eisenhower*, New York, 1981.

Crawley, Eduardo, *A House Divided: Argentina, 1880–1980*, London, 1984.

Cross, James Eliot, *Conflict in the Shadows: The Nature and Politics of Guerrilla War*, Garden City, N.Y., 1963.

Debray, Régis, *Che's Guerrilla's War*, Baltimore, 1975.

———, *Revolution in the Revolution? Armed Struggle and Political Struggle in Latin America*, Westport, Conn., 1967.

Deutschmann, David, ed., *Che Guevara and the Cuban Revolution: Writing and Speeches of Ernesto Che Guevara*, Sydney, 1987.

Diendorfer, G. Robert, ed., *The Spies*, Greenwich, Conn., 1969.

Diez de Medina, Fernando, *El general del pueblo: René Barrientos Ortuño, Caudillo Mayor de la Revolucion Boliviana*, La Paz, 1972.

Draper, Theodore, *Castroism: Theory and Practice*, New York, 1965.

———, *Castro's Revolution: Myths and Realities*, New York, 1962.

Dubois, Jules, *Fidel Castro: Rebel, Liberator, or Dictator*, Indianapolis, 1959.

Dulles, Allen W., *The Craft of Intelligence*, New York, 1963.

Dunkerley, James, *Rebellion in the Veins: Political Struggle in Bolivia, 1952–82*, London, 1984.

Ebon, Martin, *Che: The Making of a Legend*, New York, 1969.

Eisenhower, Dwight D., *The White House Years*, vol. 1, *Mandate for Change, 1953–1956*; vol. 2, *Waging Peace, 1956–1961*, New York, 1963, 1965.

Eisenhower, Milton S., *The President Is Calling*, Garden City, N.Y., 1974.

———, *The Wine Is Bitter*, Garden City, N.Y., 1963.

Escobar, Froylán, and Félix Guerra, eds., *El Che en la Sierra Maestra*, Mexico City, 1973.

Fauriol, Georges, ed., *Latin American Insurgencies*, Washington, D.C., 1985.

Ferns, H.S., *Argentina*, London, 1969.

Ferrell, Robert H., ed., *The Eisenhower Diaries*, New York, 1981.

Franqui, Carlos, *Family Portrait with Fidel*, New York, 1984.

———, ed., *Diary of the Cuban Revolution*, New York, 1980.

Freemantle, Brian, *CIA*, New York, 1984.

Fried, Jonathan L., Marvin E. Gettleman, Deborah T. Levenson, and Nancy Peckenham, eds., *Guatemala in Rebellion: Unfinished History*, New York, 1983.

Gadea, Hilda, *Ernesto: A Memoir of Che Guevara*, Garden City, N.Y., 1972.

Garcés, María, *Materiales sobre la guerrilla de Ñancahuazú: La campaña del Che en Bolivia (1967) a través de la prensa*, La Paz, 1987.

Gerassi, John, ed., *Venceremos! The Speeches and Writings of Ernesto Che Guevara*, New York, 1968.

Geyer, Georgie Anne, *Guerrilla Prince: The Untold Story of Fidel Castro*, Boston, 1991.

Giap, Vo Nguyên, *People's War, People's Army: The Viet Công's Insurrection Manual for Underdeveloped Countries*, New York, 1962.

Gleijeses, Piero, *Shattered Hope: The Guatemalan Revolution and the United States*, Princeton, 1991.

Goldston, James, *Shattered Hope: Guatamalan Workers and the Promise of Democracy*, Boulder, Colo., 1989.

Goldvert, Marvin, *Democracy, Militarism, and Nationalism in Argentina, 1930–1966*, Austin, Tex., 1972.

González, Luis J., and Gustavo A. Sánchez Salazar, *The Great Rebel: Che Guevara in Bolivia*, New York, 1969.

Gott, Richard, *Guerrilla Movements in Latin America*, London, 1970.

Granado, Alberto, *Con El Che por Sudamérica*, Havana, 1986.

Greene, Thomas Nicholls, ed., *The Guerrilla and How to Fight Him: Selections from the Marine Corps Gazette*, New York, 1962.

Gribkov, Anatoli I., and William Y. Smith, eds., *Operation ANADYR*, Chicago, 1994.

Guevara, Ernesto "Che," *Che: Selected Works of Ernesto Guevara*, Cambridge, Mass., 1969.

———, *The Diary of Che Guevara*, New York, 1968 (Bilingual Ramparts/Bantam edition).

———, *Episodes of the Revolutionary War*, Havana, 1967.

———, *Guerrilla Warfare*, New York, 1961.

———, *Man and Socialism in Cuba*, Havana, 1967.

———, *The Motorcycle Diaries: A Journey around South America*, New York, 1995.

———, *Reminiscences of the Cuban Revolutionary War*, New York, 1968.

Guevara Lynch, Ernesto, *Aquí va un soldado de América*, Buenos Aires, 1987.

———, *Mi hijo El Che*, Barcelona, 1981.

Halperin, Maurice, *The Rise and Decline of Fidel Castro: An Essay in Contemporary History*, Berkeley, 1972.

———, *The Taming of Fidel Castro*, Berkeley, 1981.

Hansen, Carlos P., and Andrew Sinclair, *The Bolivian Diary of Ernesto "Che" Guevara*, London, 1968.

Harris, Richard, *The Death of a Revolutionary: Che Guevara's Last Mission*, New York, 1970.

Hatcher, Patrick Lloyd, *The Suicide of an Elite: American Internationalists and Vietnam*, Stanford, 1990.

Higgins, Trumbull, *The Perfect Failure: Kennedy, Eisenhower, and the C.I.A. at the Bay of Pigs*, New York, 1987.

Hoare, Mike, *Congo Mercenary*, London, 1978.

Hodges, Donald C., *Argentina, 1943–1976*, Albuquerque, 1976.

———, *The Legacy of Che Guevara: A Documentary Study*, London, 1977.

Horowitz, David, *Empire of the Revolution: A Radical Interpretation of Contemporary History*, New York, 1969.

Hunt, E. Howard, *Give Us This Day*, New Rochelle, N.Y., 1973.

Hyde, Douglas, *The Peaceful Assault: The Pattern of Subversion*, London, 1963.

Immerman, Richard H., *The CIA in Guatemala: The Foreign Policy of Intervention*, Austin, Tex., 1982.

Instituto Geográfico Militar, *Atlas de Bolivia*, Barcelona, 1985.

Jahadhmy, Ali Ahmed, ed., *Learners Swahili-English, English-Swahili Dictionary*, London, 1981.

James, Daniel, *Ché Guevara, a Biography*, New York, 1969.

———, *Red Design for the Americas*, John Day, 1954.

———, ed., *The Complete Bolivian Diaries of Che Guevara and Other Captured Documents*, New York, 1968.

Jeffreys-Jones, Rhodri, *The CIA and American Democracy*, New Haven, 1989.

Johnson, Haynes, *The Bay of Pigs*, New York, 1964.

Jones, Howard, *The Course of American Diplomacy: From the Revolution to the Present*, New York, 1985.

Karol, K.S., *Guerrillas in Power: The Course of the Cuban Revolution*, New York, 1970.

Kelley, Jonathan, and Herbert S. Klein, *Revolution and the Rebirth of Inequality*, Berkeley, 1981.

Kellner, Douglas, *Ernesto "Che" Guevara*, New York, 1989.

Kinter, William Roscoe, *The New Frontier of War: Political Warfare, Present and Future*, Chicago, 1962.

Klein, Herbert S., *Bolivia: The Evolution of a Multi-ethnic Society*, 2d ed., New York, 1992.

———, *Parties and Political Change in Bolivia*, 1880–1952, Cambridge, 1969.

Konigsberg, Hans, *The Future of Che Guevara*, Garden City, N.Y., 1971.

Larteguy, Jean, *The Guerrillas*, New York, 1970.

Lavretsky, I., *Ernesto Che Guevara*, Moscow, 1976.

Leacock, Ruth, *Requiem for Revolution: The United States and Brazil, 1961–1969*, Kent, Ohio, 1990.

Leighton, Richard M., and Ralph Sanders, eds., *Insurgency and Counterinsurgency: An Anthology*, Washington, D.C., 1962.

Llosa M., José A., *René Barrientos Ortuño: Paladin de la Bolivianidad,* La Paz, 1966.

Llovio-Menéndez, José Luis, *Insider*, New York, 1988.

Loveman, Brian, and Thomas M. Davis, Jr., eds. *Guerrilla Warfare by Che Guevara plus Case Studies*, Lincoln, Nebr., 1985.

Lowy, Michael, *The Marxism of Che Guevara: Philosophy, Economics, and Revolutionary Warfare*, New York, 1973.

McAuliffe, Mary S., ed., *CIA Documents on the Cuban Missile Crisis, 1962*, Washington, D.C., 1992.

McManus, Jane, ed., *From the Palm Tree: Voices of the Cuban Revolution*, Secaucus, N.J., 1983.

Mallin, Jay, *Ernesto "Che" Guevara: Modern Revolutionary, Guerrilla Theorist*, Charlotteville, N.Y., 1973.

———, *Strategy for Conquest: Communist Documents on Guerilla Warfare*, Coral Gables, Fla., 1970.

———, ed., *"Che" Guevara on Revolution*, Coral Gables, Fla., 1969.

Malloy, James M., and Eduardo Gamarra, *Bolivia: The Uncompleted Revolution*, Pittsburgh, 1970.

———, *Revolution and Reaction: Bolivia, 1964–1985*, New Brunswick, N.J., 1988.

Malloy, James M., and Richard S. Thorn, eds., *Beyond the Revolution: Bolivia since 1952*, Pittsburgh, 1971.

Mao Tse-Tung, *On Guerrilla Warfare*, New York, 1961.

Marchetti, Victor, and John Marks, *The CIA and the Cult of Intelligence*, New York, 1974.

Martinez Estevez, Diego, *Ñancahuazú: apuntes para la historia militar de Bolivia*, La Paz, 1989.

Matthews, Herbert L., *Castro: A Political Biography*, London, 1969.

———, *Fidel Castro*, New York, 1969.

———, *Revolution in Cuba*, New York, 1975.

Merwin, W. S., trans., *Poema del Cid/Poem of the Cid* (bilingual version), New York, 1959.

Meyer, Karl E., and Tad Szulc, *The Cuban Invasion: The Chronicle of a Disaster*, New York, 1962.

Minà, Gianni, *An Encounter with Fidel*, Melbourne, 1991.

Mitchell, Christopher, *The Legacy of Populism in Bolivia: From the MNR to Military Rule*, New York, 1977.

Mockaitis, Thomas R., *British Counterinsurgency in the Post-Imperial Era*, Manchester, 1995.

Moore, Carlos, *Castro, the Blacks, and Africa*, Los Angeles, 1988.

Morrison, DeLesseps S., *Latin American Mission*, New York, 1965.

Myers, David R., ed., *Toward a History of the New Left: Essays from within the Movement*, Brooklyn, 1989.

Nash, June, *We Eat the Mines and the Mines Eat Us*, New York, 1993.

Nathan, James A., ed., *The Cuban Missile Crisis Revisited*, New York, 1992.

Neimark, Anne E., *Che: Latin America's Legendary Guerrilla Leader*, New York, 1989.

Ney, Virgil, *Notes on Guerrilla War: Principles and Practices*, Washington, D.C., 1961.

Nieto Quesada, Julio, *El affaire Che Guevara*, Miami, 1982.

———, *La conspiración Guevara en Bolivia*, Miami, 1984.

Nixon, Richard, *The Memoirs of Richard Nixon*, New York, 1978.

———, *Six Crises*, New York, 1962.

Osanka, Franklin Mark, ed., *Modern Guerrilla Warfare: Fighting Communist Guerrilla Movements, 1941–1961*, New York, 1962.

Pach, Chester J., Jr., *Arming the Free World: The Origins of the United States Military Assistance Program, 1945–1950*, Chapel Hill, N.C., 1991.

Palmer, Bruce, Jr., *Intervention in the Caribbean: The Dominican Crisis of 1965*, Lexington, Ky., 1989.

Paret, Peter, and John W. Shy, *Guerrillas in the 1960s*, New York, 1962.

Paterson, Thomas G., *Contesting Castro: The United States and the Triumph of the Cuban Revolution*, New York, 1994.

———, ed., *Kennedy's Quest for Victory: American Foreign Policy, 1961–1963*, New York, 1989.

Pena Bravo, Raul, *Hechos y dichos del General Barrientos*, La Paz, 1982.

Pendle, George, *Argentina*, London, 1963.

Persons, Albert C., *Bay of Pigs: A Firsthand Account of the Mission by a U.S. Pilot in Support of the Cuban Invasion Force in 1961*, Jefferson, N.C., 1990.

Phillips, R. Hart, *Cuba, Island of Paradox*, New York, 1959.

———, *The Cuban Dilemma*, New York, 1962.

Pike, Frederick B., *The United States and the Andean Republics: Peru, Bolivia, and Ecuador*, Cambridge, Mass., 1977.

Porter, Melinda Chamber, *Through Parisian Eyes: Reflections on Contemporary French Arts and Culture*, New York, 1993.

Pozzi, Pablo A., *The University of Buenos Aires: Social Crisis and Democratization*, Amherst, Mass., 1987.

Prado Salmón, Gary, *The Defeat of Che Guevara: Military Response to Guerrilla Challenge*, New York, 1990.

Pratt, Julius W., Vincent P. DeSantis, and Joseph M. Siracusa, *A History of United States Foreign Policy*, 4th ed., Englewood Cliffs, N.J., 1980.

Quirk, Robert E., *Fidel Castro*, New York, 1993.

Ramm, Hartmut, *The Marxism of Régis Debray: Between Lenin and Guevara*, Lawrence, Kans., 1978.

Reeves, Richard, *President Kennedy: Profile of Power*, New York, 1993.

Resnick, Marion D., *The Black Beret*, New York, 1970.

Reynolds, Steve, and Gene Carver, *The Murder of Che Guevara*, Soddy-Daisy, Tenn., 1983.

Rock, David, *Argentina, 1516–1987: From Spanish Colonization to Alfonsin*, Berkeley, 1987.

Rodó, José Enrique, *Ariel*, Austin, Tex., 1988.

Rodríguez, Félix I., and John Weisman, *Shadow Warrior*, New York, 1989.

Rodríguez Herrera, Mariano, *Ellos lucharon con El Che*, Havana, 1982.

Rojas, Marta, and Mirta Rodríguez Calderon, *Tania: The Unforgettable Guerrilla*, New York, 1971.

Rojo, Ricardo, *My Friend Che*, New York, 1968.

Saucedo Parada, Arnaldo, *No disparen . . . soy El Che*, Santa Cruz, Bolivia, n.d.

Sauvage, Leo, *Che Guevara: The Failure of a Revolutionary*, Englewood Cliffs, N.J., 1973.

Schlesinger, Stephen C., and Stephen Kinzer, *Bitter Fruit*, Garden City, N.Y., 1983.

Sinclair, Andrew, *Guevara*, London, 1970.

Smith, Earl E. T., *The Fourth Floor*, New York, 1962.

Smith, Wayne S., *Castro's Cuba: Soviet Partner or Non-Aligned?*, Washington, D.C., 1984.

——, *The Closest of Enemies*, New York, 1987.

——, *Portrait of Cuba*, Atlanta, 1991.

Smith, Wayne S., and Esteban Morales Dominguez, *Subject to Solution: Problems in Cuban-U.S. Relations*, Boulder, Colo., 1988.

Spurling, John, *MacRune's Guevara*, London, 1969.

Sturgill, Claude C., *Low-Intensity Conflict in American History*, Westport, Conn., 1993.

Szulc, Tad, *Fidel: A Critical Portrait*, New York, 1986.

Tablada Perez, Carlos, *Che Guevara: Economics and Politics in the Transition to Socialism*, Sydney, 1989.

Taylor, Maxwell D., *Responsibility and Response*, New York, 1967.

——, *The Uncertain Trumpet*, New York, 1959.

Tetlow, Edwin, *Eye on Cuba*, New York, 1966.

Thayer, Charles W., *Guerrilla*, New York, 1963.

Thomas, Hugh, *Cuba: The Pursuit of Freedom*, New York, 1971.

Thompson, Robert Grainger Ker, *Defeating Communist Insurgency: The Lessons of Malaya and Vietnam*, New York, 1966.

——, *Revolutionary War in World Strategy, 1945–1969*, London, 1970.

Thompson, Robert Grainger Ker, and John Keegan, eds., *War in Peace: Conventional and Guerrilla Warfare since 1945*, London, 1981.

Thompson, Robert Smith, *The Missiles of October*, New York, 1992.

Tindall, George Brown, *America: A Narrative History*, New York, 1984.

U.S. Naval Institute, *Studies in Guerrilla Warfare*, Annapolis, Md., 1963.

Vandenbroucke, Lucien S., *Perilous Options: Special Operations as an Instrument of U.S. Foreign Policy*, New York, 1993.

Valeriano, Napoleon D., and Charles T. R. Bohannan, *Counter-Guerrilla Options: The Philippine Experience*, New York, 1962.

Vazquez-Viana, Humberto, *Antecedentes de la guerrilla de Che en Bolivia*, Stockholm, 1986.

Waters, Mary-Alice, ed., *The Bolivian Diary of Ernesto Che Guevara*, New York, 1994.

——, *Episodes of the Cuban Revolutionary War, 1956–58*, New York, 1996.

Watson, Bruce W., Susan M. Watson, and Gerald W. Hopple, eds., *United States Intelligence: An Encyclopedia*, New York, 1990.

Wilkie, James W., *The Bolivian Revolution and U.S. Aid since 1952*, Los Angeles, 1969.

Wyden, Peter H., *Bay of Pigs: The Untold Story*, New York, 1979.

Ydígoras Fuentes, Miguel, *My War with Communism*, Englewood Cliffs, N.J., 1963.

Index

Adriázola, David (Darío), 145
Acuña Núñez, Juan Vitalio (Joaquín),
    77, 78, 88, 108, 112, 122, 123,
    125
  column liquidated, 118–21
Africa, 5, 26–30
Afro-Asian Solidarity Organization, 27
Agency for International Develop-
    ment (AID), 24, 25, 92
AID. *See* Agency for International
    Development
Alegría de Pío firefight, 15, 156
Algeria, 26, 28, 39
Allende, Salvador, 146
Alliance for Progress, 91, 142
Althusser, Louis, 71
Altiplano (Bolivia), 40, 42, 114
Alto Seco raid, 122, 123, 124
Anderson, Jon Lee, 72
Arana Campero, Jaime (Chapaco),
    122
Arbenz regime, 14, 18
Argentina, 20, 36, 47, 53, 54, 64, 65,
    72, 78–79, 109, 164
Arguedas, Antonio, 149–53, 161
Associated Press, 108

Bantam Books, 148
Barrientos, President, 42, 43, 60, 64,
    80, 87, 97, 113, 114, 117, 135,
    160
  appeals to Americans, 46–49,
    55–56, 85
  and Arguedas, 150
  and captured guerrillas, 73, 74, 75,
    76
  disposition toward United States,
    131–32
  and early reports of Guevara, 44, 45
  on Guevara's death, 133, 140, 141
  and Guevara's diary, 148, 149, 150
  offer of clemency to guerrillas,
    121, 123
  policy on guerrillas, 121–22
  and political crisis, 152, 153
  press reports on, 109–10
  and rebellion in mines, 98, 99, 100,
    106
Batista, Fulgencio, 15, 16, 17, 155
Bay of Pigs, 6, 12, 21–23, 25, 156,
    161
BBC. *See* British Broadcasting Cor-
    poration

Belmonte Ardiles, Jorge, 131
Benemelis, Juan, 30
Bohemia (magazine), 38, 148
Bolivia, 3, 4, 18, 20
    armed forces, 40–41, 55, 56,
        79–80, 81, 106, 107–8, 112,
        113–14, 135. *See also* Bo-
        livia: Eighth Division, Fourth
        Division, Second Ranger Bat-
        talion
    CIA report on insurgency in,
        111–15
    Cuban involvement in, 5–6, 64–66
    Cuban miscalculations in, 156–57
    Eighth Division, 91, 105, 121, 125,
        126, 130
    Fourth Division, 107, 108, 121,
        127
    Guevara in, 6, 8, 10–13, 40–46,
        61–63, 76, 77–78, 101–2,
        115–16
    rebellion in, 5–6, 12–13, 40–57,
        64–66, 156–58
    Second Ranger Battalion, 10, 89,
        97, 106, 115
        and Bolivian High Command,
            85, 105
        and CIA's report, 114
        in active service, 125, 127
        and reports to President Johnson,
            121
        still unformed, 41
        training, 81, 86, 91, 92
    U.S. involvement in, 12–13, 41,
        46–57, 61, 73, 75, 79–97,
        100, 106–7, 108–10, 129–32,
        156
Bolivian Socialist Falange, 114, 152
Bowdler, William G., 85, 97, 138,
    139, 152–53
Braulio. *See* Reyes Zayas, Israel
Brazil, 36, 37, 53, 64

Brezhnev, Leonid, 62, 164
British Broadcasting Corporation
    (BBC), 4, 35
Broderick, William, 55
Bunke, Haidee Tamara. *See* Tania
Bureau of Intelligence and Research
    (INR; U.S. State Department),
    18, 79, 80, 142, 162
Bustos, Ciro Roberto, 68, 69, 73, 76,
    77, 78, 81, 101, 102, 114, 116,
    120, 146

Camba. *See* Jiménez Bazán, Orlando
Camiri (Bolivia), 43, 52, 55, 69, 74,
    75, 76, 77, 107
campesinos, 40, 77, 78, 113–14
Carmichael, Stokely, 111
Castillo Chávez, José (Paco), 119,
    120, 124
Castro, Fidel, 123
    and Cuban insurgency in Latin
        America, 63–64, 110–11,
        155–56
    exporting of revolution, 20–21, 26
    and Guevara, 4–5, 14–15, 19, 29,
        33–36
    on Guevara's death, 141–42
    and Guevara's diary, 148–49, 151,
        152
    and Guevara's "disappearance,"
        31–33, 38
    revolutionary efforts in Cuba,
        15–16
Castro, Raúl, 18, 20, 26, 38
Catavi (Bolivia), 145
Central Intelligence Agency (CIA), 3,
    23, 30, 96, 116
    and Arguedas, 149, 150, 161
    and base camp cache, 117–18
    and Guevara's death, 10–11, 132,
        135–38, 161
    and Guevara's diary, 151, 152, 153

and Guevara's presumed death, 37,
101–2
and news of Guevara's capture,
130–31
"operations," 161–62
report on Bolivian insurgency,
111–15
reports on Guevara, 19
Chang Navarro, Juan Pablo (El
Chino), 72, 77, 104, 142
Channel 4 (UK), 4
Chapaco. *See* Arana Campero, Jaime
Chile, 64, 125, 146
China, 25, 26, 27, 28, 34, 63, 164,
165
Churo creek and ravine, 127, 128,
145
CIA. *See* Central Intelligence Agency
Cienfuegos, Camilo, 16, 35
Cienfuegos, Osmany, 38
Cochabamba (Bolivia), 42, 43, 114
Cold War, 12
Colombia, 20, 36, 63, 113
communists and communism, 8, 17,
29, 59–60, 61, 62–63, 72, 79,
88, 110, 125, 157, 158, 160,
164
Congo, 5, 13, 18, 26, 28, 30, 35, 36,
39, 155, 156, 162
Cordova, Juan Orta, 20
counterinsurgency, 7, 9, 13, 23, 24, 92
Cuba, 159–60, 165
and Africa, 5, 28–29
and Bolivian rebellion, 5–6, 64–66,
156–57
characteristics of revolution, 16–18
exporting of revolution, 20–21, 26
insurgency in Latin America,
63–64, 155–56
mourning of Guevara's death,
141–42
need for military victory, 62–63

principle of revolution, 157–58
See also Bay of Pigs
Cuba, Simón (Willy), 128, 129
Cuban Book Institute, 148

Darío. *See* Adriázola, David
Debray, Régis, 64, 112, 114, 117, 129,
159
arrest, 73–74
background, 70–71
and the guerrilla band, 70–72
Guevara on, 78, 125
and Guevara's diary, 139, 146–47
as prisoner, 75–77
statements on Guevara, 81, 101, 102
and Tania, 68, 69
testimony against, 124
U.S. intervention for, 3–4, 11–12,
74, 75–76
Defense Intelligence Agency (DIA),
102, 117, 131, 143
de Gaulle, Charles, 75
de Onis, Juan, 138, 147
developing countries. *See* Third
World; *specific countries*
DIA. *See* Defense Intelligence Agency
Diaz Gutierra, Alberto (Korda), 163
Discovery Channel, 4
Domínguez Flores, Antonio (León),
123
Dominican Republic, 20, 91, 94, 101,
160
Dorticós, Osvaldo, 33

economics, 25–26, 27, 34
Egypt, 28
Eisenhower, Dwight D., 9, 23
Elbrick, C. Burke, 37
El Cajon, 143
El Chino. *See* Chang Navarro, Juan
Pablo
El Filo, 102

El Negro (guerrilla), 120
El Rubio. *See* Suárez Gayol, Jésus
El Siglo (newspaper), 151
Escambray Mountains, 16

Feltrinelli, Giangiacomo, 163
field intelligence, 95–97
Fisher, John W., 49
Fitzgerald, Desmond, 37, 101
Flores, Aldo, 111, 113
Flores Torrico, Walter, 76
Foreign Broadcast Service, 112
Fort Bragg, 24
Fort Gulick, 107
Fox, Edward, 150
France, 164
Fricke, Edmond L., 91, 93, 94

Gadea, Hilda, 14
García García, Gabriel, 149
Gbenye, Christopher, 28
Ghioldi, Rodolfo, 164
Giap, Vo Nguyên, 18
Glassboro, 62
González, Eduardo. *See* Villoldo Gustavo
González, Luis J., 103
González, Marco. *See* García García, Gabriel
Gott, Richard, 53, 126, 135–36, 137
Green Berets, 10, 54, 94, 95
    and Bolivian government, 55, 82, 85, 86, 97
    and counterinsurgency emphasis, 24
    and Guevara, 78, 89
    and Horras, 50, 51
    training Bolivian Rangers, 81, 91, 92
Grosset and Dunlap, 148
Grove Press, 147
Grover, Charles, 42, 43, 53, 113

Guantánamo naval base, 18
Guatemala, 14, 18, 19, 20, 63, 113, 172n. 7
guerrillas, 17–18, 22–23, 88, 111, 115
    flight of survivors, 142–46
Guerrilla Warfare (Guevara), 18, 23, 24, 71, 156, 158
Guevara, Ernesto "Che"
    and Africa, 5, 26–30
    antipathy toward United States, 14
    in Bolivia, 5–6, 8, 10–12, 40–46, 61–63, 76, 77–78, 103–8, 122–25
    and Castro, 4–5, 14–15, 29, 33–36
    chronology, 39, 167–70
    CIA report on, 112–15
    communist reaction to death of, 164–65
    as Cuban operative, 6
    Cuban war memoirs, 173n. 11
    death, 10–12, 133–34, 138–39, 154, 161
    on Debray, 72, 78
    desire to alleviate suffering, 8
    diary, 146–53, 182n. 1
    as diplomat, 5, 25–29
    "disappearance," 30–33
    dossier on, 18–20
    downfall, 122–25
    early years, 14–16
    exporting of revolution, 20–21, 26
    ideological commitment, 7
    on LASO, 111
    last days, 126–32, 134, 153–54
    media reaction to death, 135–38
    memory, 162–64
    and Monje, 65–66, 157
    need for armed confrontation, 8
    need to reassess life, 4–6
    presence or not in Bolivia, 101–2, 115–16

remains, 140–41
Rojas's betrayal, 118–20
Samaipata raid, 104, 105, 106, 112, 115
"sightings," 36–38
and Tania, 67–70
views on revolution, 13, 14
Guevara, Martin, 36
Guevara, Moisés, 44, 72, 77, 98, 108, 145
Guevara, Roberto, 140–41
Guevara, Walter, 118
Guzmán, Arturo, 31
Guzmán, Loyola, 116, 149

Harriman, Averell, 59
Havana, 29, 146, 153, 156
effort to spread revolution, 7, 155
and Guevara, 35, 78
and Guevara's diary, 148, 151
relations with Africa, 5, 28, 30
relations with Soviet Union, 13, 61, 62
Helms, Richard, 34, 37, 111, 138, 139, 159, 161, 165
Henderson, Douglas, 8, 50–51, 87, 88, 116, 117, 140, 158
background, 57–60
and Barrientos government, 153
Barrientos on, 109–10
Barrientos's appeals to, 46–49, 56
calming influence, 9
and Debray affair, 12, 73–74, 75, 129
Guevara's capture and death, 11, 132
Guevara's presumed death, 101
on incipient guerrilla uprising, 44
lack of credit for, 158–60
and Shelton, 93
testimony to House subcommittee, 108
and Tope, 83

Horras, Lawrence E., 50–51, 93, 113
Hughes, Thomas L., 115
Hungary, 27

ideology, 7
Indians, 42
INR. *See* Bureau of Intelligence and Research
intelligence gathering, 95–97, 161–62

James, Daniel, viii, 68, 69, 147
Jiménez Bazán, Orlando (Camba), 122, 123, 128
Joaquín. *See* Acuña Núñez, Juan Vitalio
Johnson, Lyndon B., 9, 62, 80, 93, 100, 101, 102, 111, 117, 121, 133, 152, 153, 159
Joint Chiefs of Staff, 24
July 26 Movement, 15, 16

Kennedy, Andrés, 76
Kennedy, John F., 9, 12, 22, 23, 24, 93, 159
Kennedy, Robert, 24, 59, 159
KGB, 62, 68, 137
Kolle, Jorge, 66, 164
Kolle Cueto, Leon, 78
Korda. *See* Diaz Gutierra, Alberto
Kosygin, Alexei, 62
Kremlin. *See* Soviet Union

La Esperanza (Bolivia), 91–92, 93, 94, 95
La guerra de guerrillas, 17
La Higuera (Bolivia), 123, 124, 126, 129, 142
La Paz (Bolivia), 62, 68, 74, 78, 95, 96, 98
LASO. *See* Latin American Solidarity Organization

Latin America, 7, 8, 20, 29, 36, 87, 155, 157, 165
Latin American Solidarity Organization (LASO), 110–11, 112, 113, 114
León. *See* Domínguez Flores, Antonio
Les Temps Modernes, 71
"limited warfare" concepts, 12
López Muñoz, Gonzálo, 67
Lora, César, 98

Magnum Photos, 147
Maloney, Arthur, 95–96
Manchester Guardian, 136, 137
Männel, Günther, 68
Mao Tse-Tung, 18
March, Aleida, 32
Marcos (guerrilla), 44
Martin, Edwin, 54
Marxism, 8, 13, 164, 165
Masetti, Jorge, 54
Matos, Huber, 16
McGraw-Hill, 147
media. *See* press reports
Mexico, 14, 15, 36
MILGP. *See* U.S. Military Advisory Group
Minas Gerais (Brazil), 37
miners, 43, 97–101, 157, 162
Moncada Barracks attack, 15, 35
Monje, Mario, 62, 64–66, 69, 72, 157, 158
Monteagudo (Bolivia), 43
Morris, Patrick, 51, 53, 118
Moscow. *See* Soviet Union
Moser, Brian, 126, 135, 136, 159
Moynihan, Daniel, 162
Muyupampa (Bolivia), 43, 72, 73, 77

Ñancahuazú base, 44, 71–72, 102, 104, 107, 108, 112, 125, 157
incriminating cache at, 115–18

Nance, Ernest, 116, 117, 130–31, 132
napalm, 97
Nasser, Gamal Abdel, 28
nationalism, 157
National Security Council, 23, 85, 139
New York Times, 4, 37, 66, 68, 98, 109, 136, 138, 147, 148
Nicaragua, 20

OAS. *See* Organization of American States
Ongania, President, 112
Operation Cynthia, 121
Operation Parabanó, 121
Organization of American States (OAS), 21, 159
Ovando Candia, Alfredo, 43, 55, 74, 85, 101, 117, 123, 124, 130, 131, 133, 139, 140, 141, 144, 147, 149, 160

Paco. *See* Castillo Chávez, José
País, Frank, 105
Paraguay, 47, 53, 54, 64
Paredo, Coco, 69, 122, 123
Paredo, Inti, 123, 142, 143, 144, 145
Pauvert, Jean-Jacques, 137
Paz Estenssoro, Victor, 55, 58, 59, 160
peasants. *See* campesinos
Pentagon, 24, 50, 159
Peru, 36, 64, 72
Pinar del Rio, 39
Pizaro, Molina, 97
Pombo. *See* Villegas Tamayo, Harry
Porter, Robert W., Jr., 50, 53, 82, 83, 92, 93
Prado Salmón, Gary, 128, 129, 133–34, 142
Prague, 39
Prensa Latina, 151

Presencia, 135
press reports, 108–9, 127, 135–38

Ramos, Félix. *See* Rodríguez, Félix
Ramparts (magazine), 137–38, 147, 148
Ray, Michèle, 137–38, 147
Reuters, 136, 137
revolution, 13, 14, 71, 155–58
  characteristics of Cuban, 16–18
  Cuba's exporting of, 20–21, 26, 72
Revolutionary Workers Party, 88
Revolution in the Revolution? (Debray), 71
Reyes Rodríguez, Eliseo (Rolando), 88
Reyes Zayas, Israel (Braulio), 119–20
Rice, Joseph P., 92–93
Rodríguez, Félix (Félix Ramos), 10–12, 96, 124, 129, 130, 131, 134, 135, 136, 144, 145, 152, 154
Rojas, Honorato, 118–21
Rolando. *See* Reyes Rodríguez, Eliseo
Roper, Christopher, 126, 136
Ross, Irving, 119
Rostow, Walt, 62, 80, 81, 85, 100, 101, 102, 117, 121, 133, 138, 139–40
Roth, George Andrew, 73, 77
Rusk, Dean, 50, 95, 115

Sabaya, 145
Samaipata raid, 104, 105, 112, 114, 115, 162
Sánchez Salazar, Gustavo A., 103
Sanjines, Ambassador, 56, 74, 97
Santa Clara, 35, 141
Santa Cruz (Bolivia), 91, 94, 95, 96, 105, 119, 127

Santa Cruz Province, 41
São Paulo, 39
Sartre, Jean-Paul, 71
Sauvage, Leo, viii, 150, 151
Sayre, Robert M., 50, 51
Shadow Warrior (Rodríguez), 96
Shelton, Ralph "Pappy," 8, 57, 82, 85, 86, 92–95
Siempre, 38
Sierra Maestra campaign, 16, 42, 71, 156, 157, 158
Siglo XX mine, 99, 100
Siles Salinas, Luiz Adolfo, 54, 95, 152, 160
Singh, Harry, 92
Skaer, William K., 95, 96
Smith, Wayne S., 35
socialism, 27–28
Southern Command (U.S.), 41, 50, 52, 53, 82, 96, 97
Soviet bloc, 25
Soviet Union, 6, 13, 17, 27, 28, 34–35, 63, 159
  and Guevara's memory, 164
  and Guevara's mission to Bolivia, 61–62, 157
Special Forces, 38. *See also* Green Berets
Special Group for Counterinsurgency, 24, 59
State Department (U.S.), 29, 30, 51, 59, 79, 118, 121, 158, 159. *See also* Bureau of Intelligence and Research
Stein and Day, 147
Sternfield, Larry, 150
Stroessner, President, 112
Suárez Gayol, Jésus (El Rubio), 88
Sucesos, 71
Sulzberger, Cyrus L., 37

Tani (Indian guide), 145
Tania (Haidee Tamara Bunke), 67–70, 77, 112, 120, 185n. 13
Tanzania, 39
Taylor, Maxwell D., 23–24
Terán, Mario, 154
Third World, 25, 26, 27, 28, 56, 155
Thomas, Charles, 59
Tilton, John, 132, 136
Time-Life, 147
Tope, William A., 83–87, 88, 89, 95, 97, 111
Tricontinental (magazine), 38
Tri-Continental Conference (1966), 64
TV Globo, 135

Ugarteche, Horacio, 87
Uncertain Trumpet, The (Taylor), 23
United Nations General Assembly, 26
United Press International (UPI), 54
United States
    as ally of Guevara's enemies, 18
    Bay of Pigs, 6, 12, 21–23, 25, 161
    dossier on Guevara, 18–20
    foreign relations, 6–7
    involvement in Bolivia, 12–13, 41, 46–57, 61, 73, 75, 79–87, 91–97, 100, 106–7, 108–10, 129–32, 156, 158–60
    involvement in Western Hemisphere, 8–9
    restraint, 158–60
    Tope's fact–finding mission, 83–87
    See also Central Intelligence Agency; State Department
Uruguay, 36
U.S. embassy (La Paz), 44
    and Debray, 74, 147
    and guerrillas, 52, 105–6, 116–17
        and Guevara's capture and death, 130, 131, 133
    and Guevara's diary, 151
    relations with Bolivian government, 40, 56, 82, 100, 110, 121
    staff members held hostage, 58
U.S. Military Advisory Group (MILGP), 41, 47, 117
    and Green Berets, 85, 92
    and observers in guerrilla zone, 49, 50, 52
    relations with Bolivians, 86
U.S. News & World Report, 109

Vado del Yeso incident, 119–21
Vallegrande (Bolivia), 119, 121, 123, 126, 127, 129, 130, 135
Vallegrande Province, 107
Vargas Salinas, Mario, 119, 141
Vasquez Sempertegui, Marcos, 133
Venezuela, 20, 21, 63, 113
Verde Olivo (magazine), 31, 148
Vietnam, 9, 12, 36, 38, 89, 111
Villegas Tamayo, Harry (Pombo), 45, 70, 71, 142, 143, 144, 146
Villoldo, Gustavo (Eduardo González), 96, 136, 137, 144

Washington, 110, 152, 159
    versus Guevara, 3, 4, 22
    and Guevara's capture and death, 4, 131, 139
Washington Post, 136
weapons, 27
Welles, Benjamin, 68
White House, 12, 105, 112, 161
Willy. *See* Cuba, Simón

Zenteno Anaya, Joaquín, 91, 127, 133, 134, 135